D0231196

DAD'S ARMY

Graham McCann writes regularly on politics and culture for a wide range of publications. His previous books include *Cary Grant: A Class Apart* and *Morecambe & Wise*, also published by Fourth Estate.

For more information on Graham McCann visit www.4thestate.com/grahammccann

Also by Graham McCann

CARY GRANT: A CLASS APART
MORECAMBE & WISE

Dad's Army

The Story of a Classic Television Show

Graham McCann

FOURTH ESTATE · *London*

This paperback edition first published in 2002
First published in Great Britain in 2001 by
Fourth Estate
A Division of HarperCollins*Publishers*
77–85 Fulham Palace Road
London W6 8JB
www.4thestate.com

Copyright © Graham McCann 2001

3 5 7 9 10 8 6 4 2

The right of Graham McCann to be identified as the author of
this work has been asserted by him in accordance with the
Copyright, Designs and Patents Act 1988.

A catalogue record for this book is available from
the British Library.

ISBN 1-84115-309-5

All rights reserved. No part of this publication may be reproduced,
transmitted, or stored in a retrieval system, in any form or by any
means, without permission in writing from Fourth Estate.

Typeset by Rowland Phototypesetting Ltd,
Bury St Edmunds, Suffolk
Printed in Great Britain by
Clays Ltd, St Ives plc

For Vera,
Giles and Freddie

Contents

Contents

List of Photographs

Love and celebration
are matchless foundations
for programme-making,
given there is skill as well.
HUW WHELDON

Acknowledgements

I am happy to express my heartfelt thanks to David Croft and Jimmy Perry for their support, advice and memories. I am also extremely grateful to Ian Lavender, Bill Pertwee, Harold Snoad and Frank Williams for their personal recollections of *Dad's Army*, and to Sir Bill Cotton, Sir Paul Fox and Barry Took for their insights into the BBC. My sincere appreciation extends to Brad Ashton, Colin Bean, Julius Cain, Lynsay Carruthers-Jones, Fiona Cushley, John Davis, David Jason, Bobbie Mitchell, Laura Palmer and Sir Tom Stoppard for their invaluable help with particular queries.

I would also like to thank the staff from the following organisations, libraries and archives for their assistance: the BBC Photographic Library; BBC Worldwide; the BBC Written Archives Centre; Birmingham University Library; the Bodleian Library, Oxford; the British Film Institute; the British Library; the Gloucestershire Record Office; the Imperial War Museum; the Liddell Hart Centre, King's College, London; the Public Record Office, Kew; and the University Library, Cambridge.

I am indebted to my agent, Mic Cheetham, and to everyone at Fourth Estate – especially Christopher Potter and Catherine Blyth – for having faith in me, and for being patient. Finally, my profound thanks go to my parents and Silvana Dean, without whose unstinting support and encouragement this book would not have been completed.

PROLOGUE

This is my country
These are my people
This is the world I understand
This is my country
These are my people
And I know 'em like the back of my own hand.

RANDY NEWMAN[1]

Whistle while you work.
Hitler is a twerp.
He's half barmy,
So's his army.
Whistle while you –

'*Your* name will *also* go on the list!' exclaims the German. 'What is it?' 'Don't tell him, Pike!' orders the Englishman.

'Don't tell him, Pike!' What a beautiful comic line, patently apt yet palpably absurd, so funny for being so true. It encapsulates not only the kind of qualities – brightness, decisiveness and bravery – we tend to associate with our best self, but also those – foolishness, fearfulness and frailty – that we tend to associate with our worst. It makes us laugh so much because we laugh most unaffectedly at what we know most about, and what we know most about is ourselves: each of us, at some point or other in our life, has said or done something equally as apt and equally as absurd as 'Don't tell him, Pike!'

It is really no wonder then that this scene has been hailed by some as the funniest moment in the history of British television,[4] nor that the show in which it featured has come to be recognised as one of this medium's most treasurable achievements.[5] We do not warm to just any old thing that the small screen serves up to us; for all of the hours, days, months and even years of television that we watch in the course of a lifetime, we actually remember very little, and cherish even less. We tend to recall and respect only those few programmes which try neither to be momentous nor mundane, but which simply try, right here, right now, to engage our minds and our moods.

Dad's Army was just such a programme. It ran for nine years – from the summer of 1968 to the winter of 1977, stretching out over nine series and eighty episodes – and has continued to be a frequently repeated favourite ever since. Its extraordinary appeal, in terms both of breadth and of depth, has remained remarkably solid over the years. For example, the episode entitled 'The Deadly Attachment' (which featured that 'Don't tell him, Pike!' line) attracted an estimated audience of 12,928,000 when it was first broadcast on BBC1 back in 1973; when, the following year, it received its initial repeat, 10,908,000 people tuned in to see it, as did 9,082,800 for the second repeat in 1978 and 10,600,000 for the third in 1989.[6] Such rare and special constancy has little to do with any clinging need for nostalgia:[7] among the programme's most devoted admirers are some of those who would prefer to forget the war, as well as some of those who are not able to recall it. *Dad's Army*'s lasting appeal has a great deal to do with an unquenchable craving for quality.

Dad's Army, as a television programme, was something special. It stood out back then, when television's aim was to entertain a nation, and it stands out even more prominently now, when the intention is merely to indulge a niche. It was – it is – an exceptional piece of programme-making. Every element epitomised the unshakeable commitment to excellence: the gloriously apposite theme song, a flawless recreation of the sound of wartime defiance; the well-chosen setting, animated by the meticulously assembled authenticating detail; the quietly effective style of direction, focusing our attention on the action rather than the art; and, at the very heart of it all, the consistently fine acting and writing which combined to cultivate a set of characterisations that audiences came not only to laugh at but also to live with and love.

The comedy that comes from character, observed J. B. Priestley, is 'the richest and wisest kind of humour, sweetening and mellowing life for us'.[8] Context can supply the catalyst for the comedy, but only characters can supply the *raison d'être*. 'The humour of incident and situation that does not proceed from character, however artfully it may be contrived,' argued Priestley, 'only an elaborate play, making a glitter and commotion on the surface of things. But the humour of character goes down and touches, surely but tenderly, the very roots of our common human nature.'[9]

Not everyone who has watched *Dad's Army* will have known much, if anything, about the last world war, or the history of the Home Guard, or life in early 1940s England, but everyone, surely, will have known someone like the portly, pushy, pompous little provincial bank manager and platoon commander, George Mainwaring ('Oh, they'll know by the tone of my voice that I'm in charge . . .'), or his sleepily urbane and vaguely insouciant chief clerk and sergeant, Arthur Wilson ('Would you all mind falling into three ranks, please? Just as quickly as you can, in three nice, neat lines. That would be absolutely *lovely*, thank you so much'). Most, if not all of us, will have known someone very much like the indomitably doughty but somewhat over-excitable local butcher and lance corporal, Jack Jones ('Get help? Right ho, sir! Don't panic! *Don't panic!*'), or the sly and saturnine Scot, undertaker and part-time private, James Frazer ('I knew it: we're doomed. *Doomed*, I tell ye!'), or the frail, permanently fatigued former gentleman's outfitter and conscientious dispenser of bicarbonate of soda, Charles Godfrey ('Do you think I could possibly be excused, sir?'), or the sharp, street-smart spiv Joe Walker (''Old on a minute – I said they were *difficult* to get, I didn't say *impossible!*'), or the mollycoddled, maladroit and callow clerk and combatant, Frank Pike ('Uncle Arthur, if you don't let me up on that bunk I'll tell Mum!'), or the vulgar and obstreperous greengrocer and chief air raid warden, Bill Hodges ('Ruddy 'ooligans!'), or the camply effete Anglican vicar, Timothy Farthing ('I must say, you're a much braver man than I am') and his fawning, flat-capped verger, Maurice Yeatman ('Ah, well, there's all sorts of courage, your Reverence – *I* don't know how *you* have the nerve to get up and give those sermons every Sunday'). *Dad's Army*, deep down, was not really about the war. It was about England. It was about us.

It was about our amateurism ('I think we can quite happily say that Jerry's parachutists will be as dead as mutton from Stead & Simpson's to Timothy White's. We'd get a clear run down to the Pier Pavilion if that blasted woman would get out of the telephone box!'), our faith in good form ('*Break the glass?* Have you lost your senses? We're not *savages*, you know! We're a well-trained British army of *sportsmen!*'), our willingness to help out ('I'd be delighted to oblige in any capacity that doesn't involve too much running about'), our reluctance to be regimented ('I'm afraid I'm just not awfully good at strutting and swaggering'), our cosy eccentricities ('I'm so sorry my sister Dolly couldn't come tonight – she's got a touch of rheumatism – but she sent you some of her upside-down cakes'), our irrepressible playfulness ('We'll do "Underneath The Spreading Chestnut Tree"! Sergeant Wilson will do the cheerful actions, and we'll follow'), our loyalty ('I'd go through fire, and brimstone, and, and, treacle for you, sir!'), our caution ('Do you really think that's *wise*?'), our courage ('They could put *twenty* bombs down my trousers and they will not make me crack!'), our deep-rooted distrust of outsiders ('Damned foreigners! They come over here and then have the cheek to *fire* at us!'), and, most of all, it was about our chronic consciousness of class.[10]

Class provided the grit that made this pearl. As Dennis Potter put it:

> *Dad's Army* is made possible by the extended joke which allows the British, or more specifically the English, to turn every possible encounter into a subtle joust about status. There is as much drama swilling about in our casual 'good mornings' as in the whole of *Il Trovatore*, and more armour-plating on a foot of suburban privet than in the latest Nato tanks . . . [*Dad's Army*] is a conspiracy of manners between the loving caricatures in crumpled khaki and the complicit delight of an audience which likes pips as well as chips on its shoulders.[11]

There, on one side of the desk, sits the middle-class, grammar school-educated George Mainwaring, an overachiever desperate to seize the day, and there, on the other side, sits the upper-class, public school-educated Arthur Wilson, an underachiever content to cast a lazily discerning eye over each approaching day and remark on how perfectly lovely it looks before allowing it to amble idly by. There, between them, sparks and fizzes every kind of subtle slight, scornful sniff and furtive little dig that one class can direct at another without risking the ignition of outright civil war:

MAINWARING No question about it at all. It's the families that make the trouble. I had to contend with all sorts of snobbish rubbish when I married Elizabeth.

WILSON (*smiling mischievously*) Did you, er, did you, as it were, 'marry beneath you'?

MAINWARING Oh, no, no! The family rather thought that *she* did. She was very well-connected, you know, Elizabeth. Her father was the suffragan Bishop of Clagthorpe.

WILSON (*in mock awe*) Was he really!

MAINWARING Led a very sheltered life, you know, Elizabeth. (*chuckles to himself*) Do you know, she hadn't

	even tried tomato sauce before she met me? Ah, I soon put that right!
WILSON	(*sarcastically*) You know, marrying *you* must have opened up a whole new *world* to her.
MAINWARING	Oh, yes, I think it did. But I never felt at ease with her parents, you know. Always got the impression they were looking down their noses at me. This was even after I'd become Assistant Manager.
WILSON	Weren't they impressed by *that*?
MAINWARING	Oh, not a bit. It was quite a big branch, too, you know. I had my own partitioned cubicle.
WILSON	Ooh! *Did* you?[12]

George Orwell, who was an active member of the real-life Home Guard, likened England to 'a family with the wrong members in control'.[13] In wartime Walmington-on-Sea, the wrong members are recruited from Wilson's side of the family, but Mainwaring continues to harbour the hope that one day the wrong members will arise from *his* side. There is, in the meantime, an uneasy truce, with both sides trapped in the same small, neat and nosy seaside town, the same tiny tumbledown church hall, the same ageing bodies, the same sobering predicament. 'Still,' as Orwell added, 'it is a family. It has its private language and its common memories, and at the approach of an enemy it closes its ranks.'[14]

Any vision of England is bound to be partial. The vision of England projected by *Dad's Army* is England at its kindest, gentlest and most decent. This is the England that George Santayana hailed as 'the paradise of individuality, eccentricity, heresy, anomalies, hobbies, and humors',[15] the England that Emerson respected for its ability to 'see a little better on a cloudy day',[16] the England that Arnold Bennett cherished for its 'powerful simplicity',[17] the England that Orwell loved for the fact that the most stirring battle-poem in its history 'is about a brigade of cavalry which charged in the wrong direction'.[18] This is the England in which one can find oneself saying, with the very best of intentions, something as silly as 'Don't tell him, Pike!' Few partial visions seem quite as familiar as this, and fewer still seem quite as appealing.

Dad's Army encouraged the nation to laugh at itself, and that, as services go, is one of the most precious that any nation can receive. It does not deserve to be remembered merely as an extremely popular situation-comedy, nor as an admirable piece of light entertainment, nor as an ever-reliable ratings winner. It deserves to be treated with a little more respect, a little more *care*, than that. It deserves to be remembered as a truly great television programme, a fine example of what Huw Wheldon once described so well as 'good programmes made for good purposes by good people doing their best and doing it well'.[19]

THE SITUATION

The day war broke out, my missus looked at me and she said:
'What good are yer?' I said: 'How d'you mean, what good
am I?' 'Well,' she said, 'you're too old for the Army,
you couldn't get into the Navy and they wouldn't have you in
the Air Force, so . . . what good are yer?' I said: 'I'll do
something.' She said: 'What?' I said: 'How do I know? I'll
have to think.' She said: 'I don't see how THAT's going to
help you – you've never done it before . . . So, what good are
yer?' I said: 'Don't keep saying what good am I!'

ROBB WILTON[1]

CHAPTER I

A Peculiar Race

I think it's true to say that at the present time this country of ours, because of its courage and its proud defiance, its determination to put an end to this international brigandage and racketeering of the Hitlers and Mussolinis and their riff-raff is the hope of all that is best in the world, which watches us with admiration.

J. B. PRIESTLEY[1]

MAINWARING   *You can't win this war! See the sort of men that this country breeds?*

U-BOAT CAPTAIN   *Rather stupid ones.*

DAD'S ARMY[2]

It all began, in a way, one day back in the summer of 1940. Shortly after nine o'clock on the evening of Tuesday, 14 May, Anthony Eden, Great Britain's newly-appointed Secretary of State for War, began his broadcast to the nation on the BBC's Home Service:

I want to speak to you tonight about the form of warfare which the Germans have been employing so extensively against Holland and Belgium – namely the dropping of troops by parachute behind the main defensive lines . . . [I]n order to leave nothing to chance, and to supplement from sources as yet untapped the means of defence already arranged, we are going to ask you to help us in a manner in which I know will be welcome to thousands of you. Since the war began the government have received countless inquiries from all over the Kingdom from men of all ages who are for one reason or another not at present engaged in military service, and who wish to do something for the defence of their country. Well, now is your opportunity.

We want large numbers of such men in Great Britain, who are British subjects, between the ages of seventeen and sixty-five, to come forward now and offer their services in order to make assurance [that an invasion will be repelled] doubly sure. The name of the new Force which is now to be raised will be 'The Local Defence Volunteers'. This name describes its duties in three words . . . This is . . . a spare-time job, so there will be no need for any volunteer to abandon his present occupation . . . When on duty you will form part of the armed forces . . . You will not be paid, but you will receive uniform and will be armed . . . In order to volunteer, what you have to do is to give in your name at your local police station and then, as and when we want you, we will let you know . . . Here, then, is the opportunity for which so many of you have been waiting. Your loyal help, added to the arrangements which already exist, will make and keep our country safe.[3]

Now there could be no turning back: eight months into the war, and four days after the commencement of Germany's offensive in the West, Britain was set to launch the largest, most quixotic and, in a way, least militaristic volunteer army in its history.[4]

The government, in truth, had never been keen on its formation, believing, to begin with, that such a force would find itself with far too little to do, and then later fearing that it might find itself trying to do far too much. There was one prominent political figure, however, who had supported the idea right from the start: Winston Churchill. On 8 October 1939, Churchill – then newly installed as First Lord of the Admiralty – had written to Sir Samuel Hoare, the Lord Privy Seal, with a proposal:

Why do we not form a Home Guard of half-a-million men over forty (if they like to volunteer) and put all our elder stars at the head and in the structure of these new formations? Let these five hundred thousand men come along and push the young and active out of all their home billets. If uniforms are lacking, a brassard would suffice, and I am assured there are plenty of rifles at any rate.[5]

Nothing came of the suggestion, however, as the military's chiefs of staff were of the opinion that any danger of invasion or raids was slight so long as sufficient naval and air forces were guarding the sea approaches to Britain, and, as all of the belligerents settled into the six-month stalemate that came to be known as the 'Phoney War',[6] it seemed as if Churchill's notion of an army of ageing amateurs had been left to die a quiet death. Then, quite suddenly, things changed: on 9 April 1940, the Allies were startled by the first in a series of sudden and strikingly effective enemy thrusts when German units moved in to occupy Denmark and Norway; barely a month later, as the Allies were still struggling to come up with a suitable response to the events in Scandinavia, the main offensive began in earnest when Germany took control of both The Netherlands and Belgium. These developments transformed the public mood; now that it appeared possible that most, if not all, of the Channel coastline might soon be under German occupation, the prospect of England being invaded suddenly seemed startlingly real.

Anxiety swiftly took the place of apathy. There were fears of a fifth column, and fears of airborne landings. Facts may have been scarce but there was an abundance of rumours, and soon newspapers were full of speculation regarding the possibility that enemy agents were already operating inside the nation. The intelligence division of the Ministry of Information, which had been set up to monitor civilian opinion and morale, noted that such talk of espionage and sabotage was causing widespread unease, and 'the situation in a few places has become slightly hysterical'.[7] The prospect of parachute landings was, if anything, the source of even greater anxiety. The Home Office distributed a distinctly unsettling circular to the public informing them that 'German parachutists may land disguised as British policemen and Air Raid Wardens',[8] and *The Times* ran a sobering editorial warning its readers that these enemy paratroopers 'might speak English quite well. Some might be sent over in civilian dress to act as spies. The general public must be alert.'[9]

Something, clearly, had to be done, and, whatever it was, it had to be done quickly. The government had initially been reluctant to contemplate any policy which involved ordinary citizens being allowed to take matters into their own hands instead of relying on the orthodox forces of security and public order – namely, the Army and the police – but it soon found itself placed under mounting pressure from both Parliament and press to do precisely that.[10] When reports started to reach the War Office concerning the appearance up and down the country of 'bands of civilians . . . arming themselves with shotguns',[11] the time had arrived for a serious rethink. Without pausing to determine whether its ultimate goal was to sustain or suppress this burgeoning grass-roots activism, the War Office proceeded to improvise some plans and, as one observer put it, evoked 'a new army out of nothingness'.[12]

On Sunday, 12 May, at a hastily arranged meeting, a way forward was agreed. A breathless succession of *ad hoc* decisions followed throughout the next day until, at 8 p.m., all of the essential details had been assembled and readied for dispatch. It was originally intended that the first news of the novel force would be broadcast on the wireless by the man most responsible for the shape it was set to take – namely, General Sir Walter Kirke, Commander-in-Chief of the Home Forces – but Anthony Eden, recognising an early opportunity to impose his presence upon the public's consciousness, decided that he should be the one to address the nation on this subject. As he sat down on that Tuesday evening and faced the microphone, he had two aims in mind: the first was to demonstrate that the government was responsive to popular opinion, and the second was to promote a policy which he hoped would curb any public propensity for spontaneity. He succeeded in doing the former, but the latter would prove far harder to accomplish.[13]

Before Eden's broadcast had concluded, police stations up and down the country found themselves deluged with eager volunteers. On the Kent coast, the most threatened area, men were still queuing at midnight. Early the following morning the lines once again began to form, and throughout the rest of the day they grew longer and longer. Over the country as a whole 250,000 men – equal in number to the peacetime Regular Army – registered their names within the first twenty-four hours. One of those responsible for enrolling the applicants in Birmingham recalled his experience:

The weather was sweltering and we were allotted the small decontamination room in the police station yard . . . Applicants seemed to form a never-ending stream. They started to queue up as soon as they could leave their work and by 11 p.m. there were still scores of them waiting to enrol. Every night we worked until the small hours of the morning, trying to get some sort of shape into the organisation in preparation for the next day's rush. Within a few days the platoon was three or four hundred strong and it seemed that if every police station [in the city] were experiencing the same influx, all the male population of Birmingham would be enrolled within a week or two.[14]

Form lagged behind content. The Local Defence Volunteers was launched without any staff, or funds, or premises of its own. An air of edgy amateurism accompanied its inception. No registration forms had been printed, so the police were simply instructed to ask each prospective new recruit four basic questions:

(a) Are you familiar with firearms?
(b) Occupation?
(c) What military experience have you?
(d) Are you prepared to serve away from your home?[15]

The applicants, noted the novelist Ernest Raymond, received a less than fulsome welcome:

The uniformed policeman behind his desk sighed as he said, 'We can take your name and address. That's all.' A detective-inspector in mufti, whom I knew, explained this absence of fervour. 'You're about the hundred-and-fiftieth who's come in so far, Mr Raymond, and it's not yet half past nine. Ten per cent of 'em may be some use to Mr Eden but, lor' luv-a-duck, we've had 'em stumping in more or less on crutches. We've taken their names but this is going to be Alexander's rag-time army.'
    As I passed out through the sandbags I met three more volunteers about to file in through the crack. I knew them all. One was an elderly gentleman-farmer who'd brought his sporting

gun . . . Another had his hunting dog with him . . . All explained that they were 'joining up' . . . so I prepared them for the worst, I said, 'Well, don't expect any welcome in there. They don't love us. And get it over quickly. I rather suspected that if I stayed around too long, I'd be arrested for loitering.'[16]

What momentum the fledgling LDV was able to gather originated from its untended but irrepressible new members. Eden's initial message had asked merely for men to sign up and then wait ('we will let you know'), but the first wave of volunteers, desperate to help frustrate the enemy's knavish tricks, were in no mood to sit idly by. Like actors who had passed an audition for a play that had yet to be written, they gathered together and improvised. No later than a day after the call had come, the new men of the LDV had armed themselves with everything from antique shotguns and sabres to stout sticks and packets of pepper and, without waiting for official instructions, had started going out on patrol.

Membership continued to grow at a remarkably rapid rate: by the end of May the total number of volunteers had risen to between 300,000 and 400,000, and by the end of the following month it would exceed 1,400,000 – around 1,200,000 more than any of the War Office mandarins had anticipated.[17] Order did not need to be restored: it had yet to be created. A rough-and-ready administrative structure was duly scrambled into place,[18] and Sir Edward Grigg (the joint Under-Secretary of State for War and the man to whom Eden had handed responsibility for the day-to-day running of the LDV) spelled out 'the three main purposes for which the Local Defence Volunteers are wanted':

First, observation and information. We want the earliest possible information, either from observation posts or from patrols as to landings. The second purpose is to help, in the very earliest stages, in preventing movement by these enemy parties landed from the air, by blocking roads, by denying them access to means of movement, motors and so on, and by seeing that they are hemmed in as completely as possible from the moment they land. Their third purpose is to assist in patrolling and protecting vulnerable spots, of which there is a great number everywhere, particularly in certain parts of the country where the demands for local guard duties are really greater than the present forces can meet.[19]

Grigg then proceeded to cloud his clarification by adding that, 'I do not want to suggest that it is the duty of the War Office to issue instructions in detail as to how these Local Defence Volunteers should be used ... If we started giving instructions in detail the whole organisation would be at once tied up in voluminous red tape. Their general function is far better left at the discretion of the local commands.'[20] Such cautious guidance, though welcomed as better than nothing, did little, in itself, to lift morale. Deeds were needed, not words. The two tangible things most keenly anticipated by the Volunteers were still not forthcoming: uniforms and weapons.

Eden had stated quite clearly on 14 May that the LDV would 'receive uniform and will be armed'. The following day, however, the War Office intervened to point out that for the time being only armbands bearing the stencilled initials 'LDV' would be available until a sufficient number of khaki denim two-piece overalls and extra field service caps could be manufactured (and no mention at all was made of any imminent issuing of weapons).[21] A few enterprising individuals took matters into their own hands and fashioned their own versions of the LDV uniform: Sir Montague Burton, Leeds's famous 'popular' tailor, promptly turned out 1,500 sets of well-cut battledress made from officers' quality barathea cloth. The vast majority, however, were left to soldier on in civilian clothes amid fears that, with only a humble armband to identify them, they might end up being shot by invading Germans as *francs tireurs*.[22] Eventually, after weeks of waiting,[23] official uniforms began arriving, but in some places the denims came without the caps while in other places the caps came without the denims. One commanding officer reflected on the sartorial chaos:

The issue of denim clothing forms a memorable epoch in [the history of the LDV]. If a prize had been offered for the designer of garments that would caricature the human form and present it in its sloppiest and most slovenly aspect, the artist who conceived the ... denim was in a class apart. Though marked with different size numbers, it was always a toss-up whether a man resembled an expectant mother or an attenuated scarecrow.[24]

The despised denims would be replaced during the autumn by ordinary Army battledress, yet the distribution of the new outfits proved almost as shambolic as that of the old. Whereas the denims had seemingly been designed for exceptionally well-upholstered figures, the battledress appeared to have been intended for 'men of lamp-post silhouettes', and it was not long before local tailors were busy carrying out covert conversions of two 'thin' suits into one to fit the somewhat fuller figure.[25]

The wait for weapons was almost as long and, if anything, even more frustrating. While the War Office dithered, the new recruits, determined to equip themselves with something that resembled a firearm, again proceeded to improvise: an Essex unit, for example, made use of some old fowling-pieces, blunderbusses and cutlasses. One Lancashire battalion raided Manchester's Belle Vue Zoo in order to take possession of some antique Snyder rifles, while another commandeered fifty Martini-Henry carbines from a Lancaster Boys' Brigade unit (much to the latter's annoyance), and a third acquired an impressive supply of six-foot spears. In Shropshire, a cache of rusty Crimean War cavalry carbines were returned to active service; and in London, fifty ancient Lee-Enfield rifles (used most recently by chorus boys in a patriotic tableaux) were liberated from the Theatre Royal, Drury Lane.[26] By the end of May the War Office had managed to purchase 75,000 First World War-vintage Ross rifles from Canada and 500,000 well-worn. 300 Springfield and Remington P14 and P17 rifles from the United States, but neither of these orders would arrive before late June or early July, so, in the meantime, recruits were advised to make do with 'this thing they developed in Finland, called the "Molotov cocktail"', which, they were assured, would prove most useful in the event of an invasion by enemy tanks.[27]

The LDV seemed destined during the sterner days of that first summer to remain dogged by such delays and diversions. The rank and file grew resentful, the public sceptical and the press scornful.[28] It was high time, argued the critics, that these amateur soldiers were taken seriously by professional strategists. Finally, in the middle of June, the beleaguered War Office deemed it prudent – in the light of plans for more than one hundred MPs to make a formal protest about its conduct[29] – to appoint Lieutenant-General Sir Henry Pownall as Inspector-General of the LDV ('a nice thing to take over,' he grumbled as he contemplated this 'rare dog's dinner').[30] Pownall's mission – and he had no choice but to accept it – was to turn the LDV into a well-organised, well-trained and effective fighting force. During the next two months, he duly attempted to rationalise the administration, speed up the supply of uniforms and guns, oversee the establishment of more appropriate methods of training and generally see to it that the force fitted as neatly as possible within the overall strategy for the conduct of the war.

If Pownall was prepared to do everything that seemed necessary to make the members of the LDV *look* like proper soldiers, then it soon became evident that Winston Churchill was equally determined to ensure that they *felt* like proper soldiers. Ever since he had replaced the broken-spirited Neville Chamberlain as Prime Minister on 10 May, Churchill's energy and attention had, understandably, been diverted into other areas, but by the middle of June he had begun to involve himself more directly in the affairs of the LDV. There was something inevitable about the way in which he proceeded to impose his formidable personality on this fledgling force: it was, for him, a tailor-made enterprise – a proud, worthy, One Nation, volunteer army of ordinary Britons united in their determination to defend their homes and defeat the invader. It was, to a romantic such as Churchill, an irresistible enterprise. He had to make it his.

On 22 June he asked the War Office to prepare for him a concise summary of the current LDV position.[31] After considering its contents for a number of days, he came to the conclusion that one of the main problems with the force was its name. On 26 June he wrote a note to Eden, informing the Secretary of State for War that he did not 'think much of the name Local Defence Volunteers for your very large new force' – the word 'local', he explained, was 'uninspiring' – and he made it clear that he believed that it should be changed.[32] Ever the shrewd populist, Churchill was right: the official title had signally failed to strike the right chord, and from the moment of its inception the force had been saddled with a number of nicknames – 'Parashots', 'Parashooters', 'Parapotters', 'Fencibles' – by the press,[33] and a variety of unflattering epithets – 'the Look,

Duck and Vanish Brigade', 'the Long Dentured Veterans', 'the Last Desperate Venture' – by the more sardonic sections of the public.[34] Herbert Morrison, the Home Secretary, argued that a better name would be 'Town Guard' or 'Civic Guard', but Churchill bridled at the suggestion, exclaiming that such names struck him as sounding 'too similar to the wild men of the French Revolution'. No, he declared, he had another, a better, name in mind for the LDV: *his* name, 'Home Guard'.[35]

Eden was far from keen, protesting that the term LDV 'has now passed into current military jargon', and that a million armbands bearing these initials had already been manufactured. 'On the whole,' he concluded, 'I should prefer to hold by our existing name.'[36] Duff Cooper, the Minister of Information, agreed with Eden, complaining that not only would a name change prove too costly, but also that the adoption of a new name whose initials were HG 'would suggest association with the Horse Guards or Mr Wells'.[37] Churchill was angered by such insolence: he was, after all, Prime Minister, and an astonishingly popular prime minister at that (the latest polls had revealed that, in spite of various setbacks, a remarkable 88 per cent of respondents continued to express confidence in his leadership),[38] and he had grown accustomed to getting his own way.[39] On 6 July he sent a curt note to Cooper, informing him in no uncertain terms that 'I am going to have the name "Home Guard" adopted, and I hope you will, when notified, get the Press to put it across.'[40] The War Office, however, continued to resist, and General Pownall, while acknowledging, grudgingly, that ' "Home Guard" rolls better off the tongue and makes a better headline', was similarly obstructive, regarding the proposal as a 'pure Winstonian' publicity manoeuvre which would end up costing, by his estimation, around £40,000. He confided to his diary that the Prime Minister 'could well have left things alone!'[41]

Churchill chose simply to ignore the objections, making a point of mentioning his preferred new name whenever and wherever he had occasion either to meet or to speak about the LDV. On 14 July, for example, he seized on the opportunity to broadcast the name to the nation, referring in passing to the existence 'behind the Regular Army' of 'more than a million of the LDV, or, as they are much better called, the Home Guard'.[42] Further resistance was futile. Churchill, as one of his colleagues freely conceded, possessed 'a quite extraordinary capacity . . . for expressing in Elizabethan English the sentiments of the public',[43] and there could only be one winner in this, or any other, war of words. On 22 July, Eden, after another awkward meeting with Churchill, wrote despairingly in his diary: 'We discussed LDV. He was still determined to change the name to Home Guard. I told him that neither officers nor men wanted the change, but he insisted.'[44]

Churchill had won. On 23 July 1940, the Local Defence Volunteers officially became the Home Guard.[45] From this moment on, the force would bear an unmistakable Churchillian signature. Sturdy, patriotic, loyal and dependable, the Home Guard, just like its spiritual leader, had 'nothing to offer but blood, toil, tears and sweat', but was determined to achieve victory 'however long and hard the road may be'.[46] The LDV appealed to the head, the Home Guard to the heart. Writers, drawn in by its rich composition, found it an easy force to eulogise and, in some cases, romanticise. C. Day Lewis, for example, wrote a lyrical account of how he had helped 'to guard the star–lit village',[47] while J. B. Priestley, in one of his regular BBC broadcasts, likened the first night that he shared on guard with 'a parson, a bailiff, a builder, farmers and farm labourers' to 'one of those rich chapters of Thomas Hardy's fiction in which his rustics meet in the gathering darkness of some Wessex hillside':

I think the countryman knows, without being told, that we hold our lives here, as we hold our farms, upon certain terms. One of those terms is that while wars still continue, while one nation is ready to hurl its armed men at another, you must if necessary stand up and fight for your own. And this decision comes from the natural piety of simple but sane men. Such men, you will notice, are happier now than the men who have lost that natural piety.

Well, as we talked on our post on the hilltop, we watched the dusk deepen in the valleys below, when our women-folk listened to the news as they knitted by the hearth, and we remembered that these were our homes and that now at any time they might be blazing ruins, and that half-crazy German youths, in whose empty eyes the idea of honour and glory seems to include every form of beastliness, might soon be let loose down there.[48]

There was nothing but society in the Home Guard. For the more retiring or aloof of individuals, moving straight from a pinched and hidebound privacy to a bold and busy community, the first rush of novelty proved acute. The poet John Lehmann set off to his local headquarters cradling 'a volume of poems or a novel by Conrad', but it was not long before he found himself listening intently instead 'to dramatic detail of the more intimate side of village life that had been shrewdly and silently absorbed by the carpenter or builder in the course of their work. Gradually, the quiet, humdrum, respectable façade of the neighbourhood dropped away, and I had glimpses of violent passions . . . appalling vices . . . reckless ambitions . . . and innumerable fantastic evasions of the law.'[49] The age range (especially during that first year, when the official upper limit of sixty-five was not rigidly enforced) was remarkable, with raw adolescents mixing with seasoned veterans. One unit contained an elderly storyteller who claimed to have been nursed by Florence Nightingale in the Crimea, but, as this would have made him at least 104 years old by the time of the current war, the detail seems dubious. The real doyen is generally accepted to have been the sprightly octogenarian Alexander Taylor, an ex-company sergeant major in the Black Watch, who had first seen action in the Sudan during 1884–5, and had gone on to serve in South Africa and Flanders before finally answering Eden's call, deliberately misremembering his date of birth, picking up a pitchfork and marching proudly off to help guard his local gasworks.[50]

Old soldiers such as Taylor were simply grateful for the chance, once again, to take part, but there were other veterans who were impatient not only to take part but also to take over. 'The Home Guard,' wrote George Orwell (then of the Primrose Hill platoon), 'is the most anti-Fascist body existing in England at this moment, and at the same time is an astonishing phenomenon, a sort of People's Army officered by Blimps.'[51] The character of Colonel Blimp – the round-eyed, ruddy-faced, reactionary old windbag with the walrus moustache who regularly lectured the nation ('Gad, sir . . .') from the confines of David Low's satirical cartoons[52] – had long been laughed at; now, in the flesh, he had to be lived with. It made sense for the Home Guard to make full use of the most experienced military men in its midst, and it was therefore no surprise that its earliest administrative appointments were weighted towards retired middle- and senior-ranking officers. Not all of the old grandees could serve in higher appointments – an East Sussex company had to accommodate no fewer than six retired generals, while one squad in Kensington-Belgravia consisted of eight former field-rank officers and one token civilian.[53] The War Office privately acknowledged that it was inevitable that problems would be caused by 'the masses of retired officers who have joined up, who are all registering hard and say they know much better than anyone else how everything should be done'.[54] The urgent need for class to cohabit with class had led to a quelling of old conflicts. The presence of these haughty, hoary ex-officers, however, ensured that they would never be cancelled entirely. In one Devon village unit, for example, a fight broke out between a retired Army captain who, it was alleged, had 'roped in his pals of like kind', and a young man who had 'asked why *he* hadn't been invited to join' and had been informed that he did not measure up to the required social standards.[55] The novelist A. G. Street noted how the most snobbish of old soldiers would turn up for training 'clad in their old regimentals, pleading that the issue uniform did not fit', and would make men 'almost mutinous' by regularly flaunting the full regalia of a distinguished military past:

> [I]n some cases it would seem that winning the war was a trivial thing compared with the really important one of always establishing rank and position. So they disobeyed orders and wore their old uniforms, just to prove to everybody that once they had been colonels. In fact, some of them, if given a choice between a heaven minus all class distinctions and a hell that insisted on them, would definitely prefer the latter.[56]

The War Office, straining to strike the right diplomatic note, took steps to settle things down. 'Though this is a deeply united country,' said Sir Edward Grigg, 'it is immensely various; and the Home Guard reflects its almost infinite variety of habit and type. The home-bred quality must not be impaired in order to secure the uniformity and organisation which are necessary for armed forces of other sorts. We want the Home Guard to have a military status as unimpeachable as that of any Corps or Regiment . . . But we do not want it to be trained or strained beyond its powers as a voluntary spare-time Force.'[57] On 6 November 1940, it was announced in the House of Commons that the Home Guard, 'which has hitherto been largely provisional in character', was to be given 'a firmer and more permanent shape'; it was now, like the Regular Army, to have commissioned officers and NCOs, a fixed organisation, systematic training and better uniforms (battledress, trench-capes, soft service caps and steel helmets) and weapons (automatic rifles, machine guns and grenades).[58] On 19 November, Grigg announced that, as 'there had been criticism' of some of the early appointments, all existing and future officers would now have to go before an independent selection board, which would ignore each man's 'political, business [and] social affiliations' and consider only his ability 'to command the confidence of all ranks under the special circumstances and conditions of the locality concerned'. Likening the force to 'a lusty infant . . . strong of constitution, powerful of lung and avid, like all healthy infants, for supplies', he promised to remain attentive to its needs. 'It is Britain incarnate,' he declared, 'an epitome of British character in its gift for comradeship in trouble, its resourcefulness at need, its deep love of its own land, and its surging anger at the thought that any invader should set foot on our soil.' No one, Grigg insisted, wanted the Home Guard to lose the 'free and easy, home-spun, moorland, village-green, workshop or pithead character [that was] essential to its strength and happiness', but it had grown so fast – 'like a mustard tree' – that it now required 'sympathetic attention to its needs and difficulties' in order for it to become truly 'efficient in its own way as a voluntary, auxiliary, part-time Force'.[59]

Now that the Home Guard had won the War Office's attention it was determined never to lose it. 'They are a troublesome and querulous party,' moaned General Pownall to his diary. 'There is mighty little pleasing them, and the minority is always noisy.'[60] This constant carping was in fact their one reliable weapon. 'The Home Guard always groused,' acknowledged one former member. 'Grousing is a useful vent for what otherwise might become a disruptive pressure of opinion. And in the Home Guard it was almost always directed to a justifiable purpose – the attainment of higher efficiency.

"Give us more and better arms, equipment, instruction, practice, drill, field exercises, range-firing, anything and everything which will make us better soldiers": that formed the burden of most Home Guard grousing.'[61] Whenever prominent volunteers did not trust the War Office to act upon some particular request, they would simply go straight to the top and appeal directly to the ever-sympathetic Churchill. Pownall was well aware of which way the wind was blowing: 'The H.G. are voters first and soldiers afterwards,' he observed. 'What they think they need, if they say so loudly enough, they will get.'[62]

Pownall had never been happy in his onerous role as the Home Guard's Inspector-General. In October, Lieutenant-General Sir Ralph Eastwood[63] – a younger man championed by Churchill – took over the Home Guard and the changes continued to come. In November, Eastwood was 'upgraded' to the new position of Director-General and handed a more powerful directorate within the War Office.[64] The first half of 1941 saw a marked tightening-up of Home Guard organisation, as well as far more active involvement by regulars in administration and training. The first anniversary of the force was marked in May with a morale-boosting message of congratulation from King George VI, who also invited volunteers from various London units to stand on sentry duty at Buckingham Palace.[65] In November, it was announced that conscription would be introduced in order to keep the Home Guard up to strength. Under the National Service (No. 2) Act, all male civilians aged between eighteen and fifty-one could, from January 1942, be ordered to join the Home Guard, and, once enrolled, would be liable to prosecution in a civil court if they failed to attend up to forty-eight hours of training or guard duties each month. Once recruited, they could not leave before reaching the age of sixty-five (although existing volunteers had the right to resign before the new law took effect on 17 February 1942).[66] This influx of 'directed men'[67] – the opprobrious term 'conscript' was avoided – changed the character of the organisation still further, erasing the last traces of the old LDV, moving beyond the original Corinthian *esprit de corps* and accelerating the transformation of an awkward political after-thought into an integral and well-regarded part of active Home Defence.

Some problems, however, proved more obdurate than others. One of these, as far as the men at the War Office were concerned, was women. Back in June 1940, the government – concerned, it was suggested, that other key voluntary organisations, such as the Women's Voluntary Service, might in future be deprived of personnel due to increased 'competition for a dwindling source of supply'[68] – had ruled that 'women cannot be enrolled in the L.D.V.'.[69] The decision did nothing to deter the more determined of campaigners, such as the redoubtable Labour MP Edith Summerskill, who proceeded to form her own lobby group, Women's Home Defence, and argued her case so persuasively and passionately that some of Whitehall's frailest males branded her an 'Amazonian'.[70] In spite of the fact that Churchill agreed with Summerskill, and in spite of the fact that thousands of women had been contributing to the force from the very beginning as clerks, typists, telephonists, cooks and messengers, the War Office would hold out until April 1943, when, having exhausted all excuses, it finally agreed to relent and permit women to serve, in a limited capacity, as 'Women's Home Guard Auxiliaries'.[71] 'It was generally felt,' recalled one Home Guard officer, 'that these conditions should have been more generous and that women should have been treated with more consideration. To mention one grievance, they were not issued with uniforms and this, according to rumour, was for some political reason. They were without steel helmets and service respirators, although at "Action Stations" they worked alongside with, and [were] exposed to the same risks as, the men.'[72]

Weapons, or rather the scarcity of them, represented another persistent problem. Ever since the massive loss of weapons and equipment at Dunkirk, the production of standard military munitions had been fully taken up by the urgent needs of the regulars and nothing could be spared for the part-time force. Spirits did rise in 1941 when the Thompson (or 'tommy') sub-machine gun, a formidable weapon familiar to every film-goer from endless gangster movies, was issued, but soon fell again when it was promptly withdrawn and redistributed to the Commandos. Aside from a limited supply of outdated rifles, the Home Guard had to make do with bayonets, a variety of hazardous home-made grenades – such as the Woolworth or Thermos bomb (described by one disenchanted veteran as 'just a lump of gelignite in a biscuit tin')[73] and the Sticky bomb (a glass flask filled with nitroglycerine and squeezed inside an adhesive-coated sock – 'when throwing it, it was wise not to brush it against your clothes, for there it was liable to stick firmly, and blow up the thrower instead of the enemy objective').[74] Then there was the Sten gun, a cheaply-made but relatively effective weapon which was only made available at a gun-to-man ratio of one to four. It was summed up by one distinctly underwhelmed recruit as 'a spout, a handle, and a tin box'.[75] There were also such strange and cumbersome contraptions as the Northover projector, which cost under £10 to produce, fired grenades with the aid of a toy pistol cap and a black powder charge, and was likened by one volunteer to 'a large drainpipe mounted on twin legs'.[76] The most despised of all these weapons was, without any doubt, the pike. Although cheeky youths were known to cry out 'Gadzooks!' whenever pike-bearing Home Guards marched by, the 1940s version – consisting of a long metal gas-pipe with a spare bayonet spot-welded in one end – bore scant resemblance to its ancient forebears. Journalists dismissed them immediately as 'worse than useless' and 'demoralising',[77] politicians criticised them as 'an insult',[78] and incredulous quartermasters put them swiftly into storage. The frustration never faded: too many men, for too long a time, found themselves still unfamiliar with firearms.

A third abiding problem was red tape. In spite of the countless War Office assurances to the contrary, the Home Guard grew increasingly bureaucratic. '[T]oo much instructional paper – printed, cyclostyled, or typewritten – was produced and circulated,' recalled one volunteer. 'There seemed to be a paragraph and subparagraph to cover every tiniest event which could possibly happen, not only to every man, but to every buckle and bootlace. In consequence, the administration of Home Guard units tended to follow the placid, careful, and elaborate course of civil service routine, and many a man felt encouraged to take shelter behind an appropriate regulation rather than think and act for himself.'[79] The more that the living reality of war seemed obscured by its paper description, the more enraged the most recalcitrant souls, such as George Orwell, became. 'After two years,' he wrote, 'no real training has been done, no specialised tactics worked out, no battle positions fixed upon, no fortifications built – all this owing to endless changes of plan and complete vagueness as to what we are supposed to be aiming at . . . Nothing ever happens except continuous dithering, resulting in progressive disillusionment all round. The best one can hope is that it is much the same on the other side.'[80]

In spite of its myriad imperfections, however, the Home Guard went on to make a genuine difference. Ever since the start of the Blitz in September 1940, it had come to be valued not just, nor perhaps even primarily, as an anti-invasion force but also, and increasingly, as a vital contributor to civil defence – locating and extinguishing incendiary bombs, clearing rubble, guarding damaged banks, pubs and shops, directing traffic, assisting in rescue work, first aid and fire-fighting, and generally making itself useful in crisis situations. Tales of incompetence – often comic, occasionally tragic – would, inevitably, be told and retold (such as the time a bemused platoon from the 1st Berkshire Battalion mistook a distant cow's swishing tail for some kind of inscrutable 'dot-dash movement of a flag', or the occasion when a Liverpool unit's bid to train on a patch of waste land was thwarted by a gang of small boys who protested that 'we was playing 'ere first'),[81] but the stories of compassion and courage were legion.[82] One Buckinghamshire platoon, it was reported, 'accommodated, fed and slept in their guardroom approximately 250 mothers and children turned out of their homes through time bombs. Half a dozen tired men of the night guard received and fed the refugees out of their rations, and then with umbrella and bowler hat went to town to do a "day's work".'[83] Communities were comforted, spirits were lifted, and lives were saved.

For all its invaluable versatility, however, the self-image of the Home Guard remained resolutely that of a fighting force, so as the fears of invasion started to fade, the feelings of redundancy started to form, and it became increasingly necessary for the government to find ways of reassuring the Home Guard that it still meant something, and still mattered. In May 1942, for example, its second anniversary was marked by a host of measures intended to bolster its self-esteem: a day of parades and field-craft demonstrations – 'Home Guard Sunday' – was held. Lieutenant-General Sir Bernard Paget, the Commander of the British Home Forces, paid public tribute both to the progress that the Home Guard had made, and to the 'spirit of service and self-sacrifice' shown by its members;[84] the Prime Minister reminded the force that it continued to be 'engaged in work of national importance during all hours of the day', and remained 'an invaluable addition to our armed forces and an essential part of the effective defence of the island';[85] and King George VI announced that, as a sign of his 'appreciation of the services given by the Home Guard with such devotion and perseverence', he had agreed to become its Colonel-in-Chief.[86] Early the following year, Churchill – fearing that a forthcoming satirical film by Michael Powell and Emeric Pressburger, *The Life and Death of Colonel Blimp*, would encourage people to regard the Home Guard as little more than a comical anachronism[87] – urged the War Office to find further ways to make the force 'feel that the nation realises all it owes to these devoted men', adding that they needed 'to be nursed and encouraged at this stage in their life'.[88] That May, following Churchill's prompting, the third anniversary celebrations were greater and grander than ever: there was another 'Home Guard Sunday' – Churchill had wanted a 'Home Guard Week'[89] – with ceremonial parades throughout the country and a march of 5,000 Home Guards through central London. The King, who took the salute, praised the force for attaining such a 'high standard of proficiency', and assured it that, as the Army directed its attention elsewhere, 'the importance of your role will . . . inevitably continue to increase'.[90] Churchill was in Washington during the time of these celebrations, but he still managed to make the most memorable contribution with a lengthy radio broadcast designed specifically to restore a sense of pride and self-importance within the force: 'People who note and mark our growing mastery of the air, not only over our islands but penetrating into ever-widening zones on the Continent, ask whether the danger of invasion has not passed away,' he observed. 'Let me assure you of this: That until Hitler and Hitlerism are beaten into unconditional surrender the danger of invasion will never pass away.' Noting that any prospect of invasion hinged on the strength of the forces deployed to meet it, he reaffirmed his faith in the Home Guard:

[I]f the Nazi villains drop down upon us from the skies, any night . . . you will make it clear to them that they have not alighted in the poultry run, or in the rabbit-farm, or even in the sheep-fold, but that they have come down in the lion's den at the Zoo! Here is the reality of your work; here is that

31

sense of imminent emergency which cheers and inspires the
long routine of drills and musters after the hard day's work
is done.

The Allies, he added, were now moving overseas, leaving the Home
Guard with greater responsibility than ever: 'It is this reason which,
above all others, prompted me to make you and all Britain realise
afresh . . . the magnitude and lively importance of your duties and
of the part you have to play in the supreme cause now gathering
momentum as it rolls forward to its goal.'[91]

The celebrations and speeches seemed to work, but not for long,
and before any more bouquets could be brandished the realities of
the strategic situation had started to sink in. During the first half of
1943, it had still been possible to contemplate the possibility of some
sudden reversal in Allied fortunes; by the end of the year it had
become clear that the Germans, now without their Axis partner Italy,
were well on their way to defeat. The Home Guard, as a consequence, gradually lost its sense of purpose. All except the keenest
Home Guards came to resent the obligation to surrender their
evening hours in order to train for a non-existent battle, and absentee-
ism grew increasingly common.[92]

The Home Guard's long, slow, inexorable decline dragged on into
1944. The fourth anniversary of its formation was duly marked in
May with the usual array of strenuously celebratory events; on this
occasion, however, the applause failed to distract the men from their
misgivings. After D-Day, in June, it was evident to all that what the
future held in store was not battle honours but redundancy. On 6
September, it was announced that Home Guard operational duties
were being suspended and all parades would from now on be voluntary.[93] At the end of the following month came confirmation of the
inevitable: the Home Guard was to stand down on 14 November.
Although few volunteers were entirely surprised by the decision to
disband, many were taken aback by the speed at which it was set to
be executed. 'We learned that, like the grin on Alice's Chesire Cat',
wrote one embittered volunteer, 'we were to fade out, leaving no
trace of our existence.'[94] It seemed for a time that the men would
be ordered to give back their uniforms, but Churchill, anticipating
the probable public reaction to such a patently mean-spirited act,

intervened to cancel the plan, insisting that 'there can be no question of the Home Guard returning their boots or uniforms'.[95]

The end, when it came, was met with dignity. On Sunday, 3 December 1944, more than 7,000 Home Guards, drawn from units all over Britain, marched in the rain through the West End of London, and concluded with a parade in Hyde Park before their Colonel-in-Chief, King George VI. 'History,' he told them, 'will say that your share in the greatest of all our struggles for freedom was a vitally important one.'[96] That evening, shortly after nine o'clock, the Home Guard, which had begun with one radio broadcast, ended with another – this one delivered by the King:

Over four years ago, in May 1940, our country was in mortal danger. The most powerful army the world had ever seen had forced its way to within a few miles of our coast. From day to day we were threatened with invasion.

For most of you – and, I must add, for your wives too – your service in the Home Guard has not been easy. Some of you have stood for many hours on the gun sites, in desolate fields, or wind-swept beaches. Many of you, after a long and hard day's work, scarcely had time for food before you changed into uniform for the evening parade. Some of you had to bicycle for long distances to the drill or the rifle range . . .

But you have gained something for yourselves. You have discovered in yourselves new capabilities. You have found how men from all kinds of homes and many different occupations can work together in a great cause, and how happy they can be with each other. I am very proud of what the Home Guard has done and I give my heartfelt thanks to you all . . . I know that your country will not forget that service.[97]

'The Home Guard,' sighed General Pownall back in the early days of its existence, 'are indeed a peculiar race.'[98] If, by 'peculiar', he not only meant 'odd' but also 'special', he had a point, because in spite of the lingering imprecision of its status and the nagging inadequacy of its instruction, this unlikely alliance of the wide and rheumy eyed won real respect for its readiness to stand, and wait, and serve. 'When bad men combine,' wrote Burke, 'the good must associate,'[99] and

CHAPTER II

A Cunning Plan

*Comedy on television is a lot like comedy in Burlesque. It's not
how funny are you; it's how many weeks can you be funny?*[1]

PHIL SILVERS

War is hell. So is TV.[2]

LARRY GELBART

It all began, in another way, one day back in the summer of 1967.
Shortly before 11.30 in the morning, at the end of May, Jimmy Perry,
a 42-year-old actor, was strolling through St James's Park when, in
the distance, he heard the sound of the band playing for the Changing
of the Guards. As he drew nearer, he could make out the rows of
marching men, smart and sharp in their striking scarlet tunics and
their towering bearskin hats. He stopped and watched. The longer
he looked, however, the more vivid, in his mind's eye, seemed a
scene from twenty-six years before, when, as a youth, he had stood in
much the same place at much the same time and surveyed the rows
of oddly shaped, drably dressed men marching rather less neatly but
rather more proudly outside Buckingham Palace on behalf of Britain's
Home Guard. It made for quite a contrast. It gave him an idea.

Jimmy Perry had been searching for an idea, the right idea, for
some time. His career, so far, had been pleasantly varied. There had
been concert parties and Gang Shows during wartime, followed by
RADA, Butlins, repertory companies, and nine absorbing years (in
partnership with his wife, Gilda) as actor-manager of the Palace
Theatre, Watford. His current activity, as a member of Joan
Littlewood's left-wing Theatre Workshop in the east London surburb
of Stratford, was providing him with plenty of challenges (such as

portraying Bobby Kennedy in Barbara Garson's US political satire
MacBird, and then moving straight on to a role in Vanbrugh's Restoration comedy *The Provok'd Wife*), but, nonetheless, he still felt unfulfilled. 'I was doing all right,' he recalled, 'I was earning a living, but,
you know, I didn't seem to be getting anywhere. So let's say I was
looking at that point to really establish myself.'[3]

Although the stage remained, in many ways, his natural habitat –
he cherished its traditions and relished its immediacy – he recognised
that television, with its massive audience and prodigious output, now
represented his best chance to advance. Finding a foothold in the
medium was, however, far from easy: in spite of the fact that Perry
had already made several small-screen appearances over the course
of the previous two years, he was no nearer than ever to making his
mark. 'I needed to get noticed,' he recalled. 'I'd been in situation-
comedies and bits and pieces, but I was still waiting for the role that
would let me show people what I could do. Then one day I thought
to myself: "I *must* have a decent part. I know what – I'll write my
own sit-com, and I'll write a really good part in it for me!"'[4] Writing,
at that stage, was regarded purely as a means, not an end. 'I had no
ambition to be a writer. None at all. Writing is hard – acting is
blooming easy! I just wanted to establish myself as a performer, an
actor, and the only way I thought I could do that was by pushing
myself from the writing side.'[5]

It needed a sharp idea, however, to spark the strategy into life.
'Nothing came to begin with,' Perry admitted. 'I'd written bits of
stuff before, but not really much, and I didn't know *what* I was going
to write about. I just knew I wanted to write a sit-com with a nice
part for myself! So I looked, I thought, I looked, I thought.'[6] Then
came that summer stroll through St James's Park, and the sight of
the soldiers, and the memory of the Home Guard. Perry had been
in the Home Guard himself, in the 19th Hertfordshire Battalion, at
the age of fifteen. 'My mother was always fearful of me being out
at night and catching cold, but I loved it.'[7] Suddenly, all of the old
incidents and images came tumbling back into consciousness: the
late arrival of the ill-fitting uniform, the odd weapons (wire cheese-
cutters, sharpened bicycle chains), the commanding officer who concluded each parade by waving his revolver in the air and shouting,
'Kill Germans!', the elderly lance corporal who continually remin-

isced about fighting for General Kitchener against the 'Fuzzy Wuzz-ies', the long, rambling lectures on how to tackle tanks with burning blankets, the Blimps, the booze-ups, the banter and the bravery. 'To be alive at that time,' he reflected, 'was to experience the British people at their best and at perhaps the greatest moment in their history.'[8]

Then the idea struck him: 'The Home Guard! What an idea for a situation-comedy!'[9] As he made his way back to his flat in Morpeth Terrace, he started to assess the idea in his mind:

> I broke it down. I thought to myself: well, it was important that I wrote about something I'd experienced and understood; and service things are always funny, always popular; and there was that thing about reluctant heroes, you know, people who were civilians in the daytime and part-time soldiers at night; and there was that whole background to it, and the attitude of the British people at that time; and no one had done the Home Guard before, no one had tackled the subject; and I was to be in it. That's how it started.[10]

Later that day, during his regular train journey from Victoria to Stratford East, he took out his notebook and scribbled down some ideas. Research began in earnest the following morning:

> I thought I'd better brush up on my facts, so I went to the Westminster public library and looked through all of the shelves: nothing, not a single book on the subject. Then I asked a young librarian if she could help me: 'The Home Guard?' she said. 'Never heard of it.' Astonishing. So I moved on to the Imperial War Museum, and they did have some Home Guard training pamphlets, a couple of memoirs, that sort of thing. But apart from that there was nothing – no reference to it anywhere. The public had forgotten about the Home Guard, and I thought it was time they were reminded of it.[11]

Devising a basic storyline did not pose the novice scriptwriter too great a problem. 'Don't forget I'd run Watford Rep with my wife for nine years, and we did over six hundred plays. I regarded that as my apprenticeship. If you do a fresh play every week, year after year, boy oh boy, do you know how to move actors about. That's how I learnt my craft. Probably few other writers have had that opportunity, and I like to think that it helped me considerably.'[12] His own wartime memories had enabled him to sketch out the situation, but the focus for the comedy was suggested by a 1937 English movie:

> I'd been asking myself: 'Now, what am I going to *do* with this? What sort of comedy set-up?' And that Sunday afternoon, showing on television, was *Oh! Mr Porter*, with Will Hay, Moore Marriott and Graham Moffatt – the pompous man, the old man and the boy. And the movie's great strength was the wonderful balance of these three characters. So I thought, 'That's it: pompous man, old man, young boy!'[13]

It took him just three days, from start to finish, to write the script. It was called *The Fighting Tigers*. He put it in the drawer of his desk and went back to work: 'I just didn't know who to show it to.'[14]

Early in July, during a break in the Theatre Workshop's run, came a stroke of good fortune. Perry's agent, Ann Callender, called with news of a small but eye-catching role in an episode of a popular prime-time BBC TV situation-comedy. As the situation-comedy was *Beggar My Neighbour*,[15] whose producer-director happened to be David Croft, whose wife happened to be Ann Callender, Perry realised that he had not only found a good part, but also a great contact. David Croft was one of several top producers at the BBC, along with Duncan Wood (*Hancock's Half-Hour*, *Steptoe and Son*), James Gilbert (*It's a Square World*, *The Frost Report*), Dennis Main Wilson (*The Rag Trade*, *Till Death Us Do Part*) and John Ammonds (*Here's Harry*, *The Val Doonican Show*, later *The Morecambe & Wise Show*).[16] He had cut his teeth on a wide range of shows, including one technically inventive series of *The Benny Hill Show* (1961) and thirteen editions of *This Is Your Life* (1962) at its most Reithian, before carving out a niche for himself, starting with *Hugh and I* (1962–8), as the creator of well-crafted, character-driven situation-comedies. He was fortunate to be at the BBC during the era of Hugh Carleton Greene, a cultured and courageous Director-General who reminded his programme-makers that they were there to serve the public rather than the politicians or the press, and the BBC, in turn, was fortunate to be able to call on programme-makers of the calibre of Croft in order to fulfil this obligation. 'It was a wonderful atmosphere in which to work,' Croft recalled. 'There were some very brilliant people there in those days and they were all devoted to the BBC. When commercial television started they could all have gone and earned much more money elsewhere, but they'd stayed with the BBC because they knew you could do good work there. It's always important, you know, in the end, to get good programmes.'[17]

Croft had worked with Jimmy Perry, briefly, once before. At the suggestion of his wife, he had gone down to Watford to see her client appear on stage, and had subsequently cast him in a minor role in one episode of *Hugh and I* at the end of January 1966. Neither man, it seems, emerged from the encounter sensing that the seeds of a lasting friendship had been sown. Croft had been happy enough with Perry's efforts – the lines had been learnt, the marks had been hit – but he was immersed in the production of fourteen half-hour episodes of a high-profile show, and there was no time to dwell on such transient contributions. Perry, on the other hand, had been somewhat intimidated by Croft's briskly efficient style of direction: 'I didn't know if he was having an off day, or I was giving a bad performance, but I do remember thinking to myself: "He looks a bit grim. I'd better watch my step here, better mind my Ps and Qs – I think he could turn nasty."'[18]

The second occasion when Croft met Perry, some eighteen months later, proved a far more memorable affair. Croft had recently started work on the second series of *Beggar My Neighbour* (starring Reg Varney, Pat Coombs, Desmond Walter-Ellis and June Whitfield). 'We had an episode coming up,' Croft remembered, 'in which I wanted someone to play the rather noisy, uncouth brother of Reg Varney's character, Harry Butt. So my wife took me to the theatre again to see Jimmy, and I could tell he was obviously very good for the part. He was a good actor, was Jimmy. And so I cast him in it.'[19] Perry packed two scripts in his briefcase – one of *Beggar My Neighbour*, the other of *The Fighting Tigers* – and set off for his first day of rehearsal feeling, as he put it, 'a bit apprehensive'.[20] Eager to impress, anxious to please, he did what he was told, tried his best to do it well, and waited, patiently, nervously, for the right moment to make his move. It never came. Back in his flat, Perry rang his agent for advice. Croft recalled: 'He said to my wife, "I've got this idea about the Home Guard – do you think I dare show it to David?" She said, "Yes, go ahead." '[21] Eventually, he did. 'It was a hot summer's day, a Friday, and we'd been rehearsing at this boys' club. I'd been waiting, waiting, waiting. Finally, outside, I saw David was on his own, fiddling with this wonderful white sports car that he had, so I thought to myself, "*Now!*" So I went over to him and told him about my script. And he agreed to read it over the weekend.'[22]

The following Monday, the cast and crew congregated at Television Centre to record the next episode. Perry arrived a little earlier than necessary, hoping that, one way or another, Croft would put him out of his misery as promptly as possible, but the anxious actor soon realised that his busy producer-director was not going to have a spare moment for some time, and there was no option but to wait, and watch, and hope. Finally, after several long, agonising hours, Croft came over to Perry and delivered his verdict: 'What a terrific idea!'[23] *The Fighting Tigers* had a future.

Croft's judgement carried some weight within the BBC's Light Entertainment department. Although he had not been directly responsible for the scripts of either *Hugh and I* or *Beggar My Neighbour*, he had, in the past, collaborated on several musicals (including the Cicely Courtneidge vehicle *Starmaker*); contributed to various pantomimes and West End shows; spent eighteen months as a script editor at Associated-Rediffusion and two years as an extraordinarily industrious young producer, director and writer of around two hundred and fifty shows at Tyne Tees Television before moving to the BBC at the start of the 1960s. Consequently, his opinions – and ambitions – were taken very seriously indeed. 'I had it in my contract that I could still write for the Palladium,' he recalled. 'And that was very unusual for the BBC in those days – to allow you to work for somebody else. I was always very busy. I think the BBC were rather pleased that somebody who actually had some sort of *involvement* in showbusiness would work for them.'[24] Another thing that ensured that Croft, as a producer-director, was accorded an encouraging degree of autonomy was the fact that, once he had settled on a project, he could be relied on to pursue it in an exceptionally professional manner. Bill Cotton Jnr, Head of Variety at the time, remarked:

There were no frills with David. He always got in on time every morning. He always left at 5.30. And he'd always done his work. You'd see in other offices people tearing their hair out at seven or eight o'clock at night: 'Oh, God! We've got to do this, we've got to do that!' Dennis Main Wilson, for example, he'd *always* be working late. David never worked late. He'd planned it, he knew how to produce it, he knew how to direct it, he knew who to talk to, he'd delegated a whole lot of work and then he went home and wrote it up. He was remarkable. I'm not denigrating Dennis Main Wilson, who had got tremendous creative abilities, but he was all over the bloody shop! David was remarkably well organised and efficient. And, of course, he was terribly talented.[25]

When, therefore, David Croft decided that his next project should be a situation-comedy about the Home Guard – even though it was 1967, twenty-two years after the end of the Second World War, eleven years after Suez, seven years after the end of conscription, three years after America began bombing Vietnam, and right in the middle of a long, hazy summer of love, peace and pot – no one, said Cotton, felt any strong inclination to object:

There's no percentage in interfering. You trusted people like David, like Jimmy Gilbert, like Johnny Ammonds, to get on with it. And anyway, with most decisions in Entertainment in those days at the BBC, there were always two ways of doing it, so if you agreed one way early enough, and then it became obvious that it wasn't working, there was still time to change it to the other way. So when someone like David came up with an idea you'd just let him go with it. I do admit that, when he first came into my office and told me that he was planning to do a situation-comedy about the Home Guard, I laughed and said, 'You're out of your mind!' And I wasn't the only one. But I knew he was going to make a really professional job of it, and, anyway, it wasn't my decision.[26]

The man whose decision it was, in the first instance, was the BBC's Head of Comedy, Michael Mills. Known affectionately to

his friends as 'dark, satanic Mills'[27] (an epithet inspired by his Mephis-
tophelean beard and deep-set eyes), this worldly, wordy, witty man
had been involved in programme-making since 1947, when he
became the Corporation's – and therefore British television's – first
recognised producer in the field of light entertainment ('a case,' he
liked to joke, 'of the blind leading the short-sighted').[28] Mills was
widely regarded as being one of the most bold and authoritative
arbiters of comic potential in the business. His tastes were catholic
– he adored the work of P. G. Wodehouse, and adapted several of
his stories for the small screen, but he also relished broader styles,
such as bawdy farce. His instincts were sound – he would be the
one, prompted by the plays of Plautus, to come up with the idea of
Up Pompeii! for Frankie Howerd. 'Michael was great,' remembered
Bill Cotton. 'Very, very, well-read, a good judge of a script and a
good judge of actors, too. He was a brilliant producer, with enormous
taste and flair, and he knew how to put a show together, but he
could also be quite impetuous and take some pretty big risks. If he
had faith in something he would just push on with it regardless.'[29]
David Croft agreed:

Michael was a marvellous Head of Comedy. Very enthusiastic.
Everything was possible once you'd decided that you could do
something. He didn't ever really discuss budget. He was quite
flamboyant like that. I remember, for example, taking over a
production of *The Mikado* from him – it was called *Titti-Pu* –
and finding that he'd already ordered elephants, lions, tigers –
the lot. I spent the first few days cancelling all the things we
couldn't afford! So he was wonderfully ambitious, and he had
a very broad picture of what you should be doing and what he
could do for you, and he did it. He was, I suppose, a genius,
and he could do everything in a television studio: if, for example,
he wasn't happy about the way a cameraman was shooting
something, he'd go down there, take the camera from him and
do the shot himself – 'From *there*, understand? *That's* what I
want you to do, so *do* it!' Of course, the result was that the
crews were inclined to hate him! But he knew exactly what he
was doing. No doubt about it. And as soon as I'd read Jimmy's
script I didn't hesitate before taking it to Michael.[30]

Mills duly read the script and agreed immediately with Croft: this was an idea that, if it was handled in the right way, had the potential to run and run.

There was one more obstacle that needed to be overcome, however, before the official programme-making process could really begin. Tom Sloan, the BBC's Head of Light Entertainment and the mercurial Mills' immediate superior, needed to rubber-stamp the decision. In stark contrast to Mills, Sloan was a man who preferred to err on the side of caution, and there was always a chance that he would react warily – or worse – to the prospect of a comedy set in wartime. The son of a Scottish Free Church minister, he was certainly no great admirer of the new strains of humour that seemed intent on mocking all of the old traditional values, and had once insisted upon removing a sketch from a Peter Sellers show on the grounds that 'to refer to someone who was obviously Dorothy Macmillan as "a great steaming nit" was not in good taste'.[31] The brilliant but increasingly embittered programme-maker and executive Donald Baverstock dismissed Sloan as someone who 'didn't have an idea in his head',[32] but, as Paul Fox, the newly-appointed Controller of BBC1 in 1967, recalled, the truth was considerably more complex:

> Tom had ideas. Good, solid ideas. He *did* have old-fashioned BBC standards; I think that is absolutely true. But he wasn't a reactionary. I mean, yes, he spoke out against *That Was The Week That Was*, and that was mainly for territorial reasons – it was made by the Talks Department rather than his own Light Entertainment – but he defended *Till Death Us Do Part* solidly and sincerely through thick and thin. And he was an exceptionally good organiser, a good commander of a difficult group of people in Light Entertainment who needed a little bit of binding together. He wasn't the *inspiration* behind the success of Light Entertainment at that time; but he *was* the man who made sure that all of that success became possible, because he allowed Bill [Cotton] and Duncan [Wood] and Michael [Mills] their heads and let them get on with it.[33]

Barry Took, whom Sloan recruited as a comedy adviser, agreed:

Tom was a decent man. He had a very stiff, military view of the world, but he meant well. He just didn't like *messiness*. He didn't like people who got things wrong, or things that went wrong. And in comedy, of course, people fail most of the time, and many things fail all of the time, so poor old Tom was always a bit anxious, a bit edgy, about it all. But I admired and respected him because his only real concern was to make sure that what ended up on the screen was something to be proud of.[34]

What is beyond doubt is the fact that Sloan was driven by the passionate conviction that the BBC's Reithian fundamentals should be reordered from 'information, education and entertainment' to 'entertainment, information and education'.[35] He was, in his own sober-suited way, a committed populist. When he took over as Head of Light Entertainment in 1963, the department's output, he said, was still regarded by the management as 'something that had to be done rather than something that should be done'.[36] Later on in the decade, after the department had played a pivotal role in the Corporation's successful campaign to win back mass audiences from its commercial competitor (winning every prestigious prize available in the process), the attitude of the powers that be had 'improved', he said, to the point where it reminded him of the Pope's view of the nuns who sold religious relics in St Peter's Square: 'They may not be quite of the true faith, but they do bring a great deal of happiness to millions of people.'[37]

The most promising thing about Sloan, as far as Mills and Croft were concerned, was the fact that he was a great believer in the value of well-made, audience-pleasing situation-comedies. Satire, in his view, was a 'pretentious label' that on countless occasions in the past had been used to legitimise material that was 'quite often unfunny' and sometimes 'needlessly shocking [or] just plain silly'.[38] Many of the new youth-oriented comedy shows that were emerging struck him as reminiscent of 'one large cocktail party – or should one say nowadays, one large wine and cheese party – where everybody is sounding off and no one hears the wit for the noise',[39] and the continuing success of the Variety format, he acknowledged, relied on the availability of peripatetic talent, which was increasingly expensive. The more coherent genre of situation-comedy, he believed, formed the spine of his department's body of work, the one, true, sure thing that drew viewers to the screen on a regular basis and settled them down comfortably within a routine. This was a subject about which he held, and expressed, strong opinions:

> In situation comedy, our aim is to involve you in something you recognise, for thirty minutes, and make you laugh and feel happy. It sounds easy but it is not. There are three key factors in any success: the writers, the performers, and the producer.
>
> The writers . . . are craftsmen who speak from experience and who try and be funny with it. They are the key and without them the door cannot be unlocked . . .
>
> [The performer] is really your guest, and if you don't happen to like him, you ask him to leave by the simple act of switching him off. It is a cruel fact that on television an artist can have mastered every technique of his craft, but if his face or even his voice doesn't fit, he will never be a star on the box . . .
>
> The third and equal element in this complicated business is the producer. It is not enough to have a funny script and acceptable artists to perform it, it has to be presented in television terms in an acceptable way. We must assume that the producer is technically competent. He knows what his cameras can do and he knows how to use them. But the good producer brings something else, he brings flair. What is flair? I wish I could define it . . . Flair is production that brings the qualities of the script and the abilities of the artist face to face with the limitations of the medium, and then adds that magic ingredient, *x*, which makes the whole a memorable experience for those who watch. It is style, it is pace, it is polish, it is technique: it is all these things controlled in harmony, without a discord, and when you see it, you know it. And when any *one* element is missing, you know that too.[40]

Sloan's ideal situation-comedy was the one that seemed most true to life: 'We must be able to identify ourselves with the characters or the situation. We must be able to cry, "He's behaving just like Uncle Fred" or "Do you remember when exactly that happened to us?" '[41]

The Fighting Tigers looked, on paper, as if it would fit fairly neatly

within Sloan's chosen framework, and neither David Croft nor
Michael Mills anticipated a negative response ('Tom's great advantage,' said Croft, 'was that he knew what he didn't know, and therefore he hired people to do the things that he didn't know about and
then he let them get on with it'),[42] but Sloan, as an executive, did
have one or two reasons to be fearful. Mary Whitehouse's private
army of middle-class, middle-brow, middle-Englanders – the self-
appointed National Viewers' and Listeners' Association – had
declared war on Hugh Carleton Greene for having the temerity to,
in his words, 'open the windows and let the fresh air in',[43] or, in
hers, contribute to 'the moral collapse in this country'.[44] Harold
Wilson, the Prime Minister, in response to Whitehouse, had just
switched Charles Hill straight from the chairmanship of the commercial ITA to that of the BBC in order, as Richard Crossman remarked,
'to discipline it and bring it to book, and above all to deal with
Hugh Greene'.[45] The knives were out for the BBC. It was, in short,
the wrong time, politically, to risk causing – or being accused of
causing – unnecessary offence. There had, Sloan appreciated, been
situation-comedies before with military themes: the BBC had
imported *The Phil Silvers Show* (featuring the scheming US Army
sergeant Ernest G. Bilko and his motor-pool platoon of gambling
addicts)[46] in April 1957, and ITV had started screening *The Army
Game* (featuring a group of work-shy Army conscripts in Hut 29 at
the Surplus Ordinance Depot at Nether Hopping in deepest Stafford-
shire)[47] two months later, and both programmes had proved hugely
popular. Neither of these shows, however, had actually been set
during wartime. One current show that was – ITV's *Hogan's Heroes*,
a spectacularly tasteless US-made series set inside a German prisoner-
of-war camp – had either been shunned or condemned by the majority of British critics, and some ITV regions had simply chosen not
to show it.[48] *The Fighting Tigers*, therefore, was – at least as far as
home-grown situation-comedies were concerned – something different, something new, and Sloan had to be satisfied in his own mind
that its humour would not inadvertently aggravate painful memories
or reopen relatively recently-healed wounds.

As soon as he received a copy of the script he proceeded to read,
and reread, it with uncommon care, second-guessing the most likely
objections: 'Were we,' he asked himself, 'making mock of Britain's

Finest Hour?' Once he had finished, he felt absolutely sure of his conclusion: no. 'Of course it was funny,' he reflected, 'but it was *true*. [Such characters] *did* exist in those marvellous days, pepper *was* issued to throw in the face of invading German parachutists, sugar *was* recommended for dropping in the petrol tanks of German tanks, and the possibility of defeat did *not* enter our minds!'[49] Sloan was satisfied. *The Fighting Tigers* would go ahead with his full support.

The pre-production discussions began in earnest. Michael Mills gave Croft his typically incisive critique of Perry's original script: it was, he agreed, a fine first attempt, full of vivid, accurate period details and promising comic characters, but, of course, it still needed a considerable amount of work. The title, he said, would have to go: instead of *The Fighting Tigers*, he suggested, it should be called *Dad's Army*. He liked the south-east coastal town setting, but disliked the choice of 'Brightsea-on-Sea' as its name, so David Croft came up with 'Walmington-on-Sea' as an alternative. Some of the characters' names, too, Mills argued, did not sound quite right: 'Mainwaring' suited the pompous man, as did 'Godfrey' the old man and 'Pike' the young boy. He did not care at all, however, for 'Private Jim Duck', instead he suggested 'Frazer'; for 'Joe Fish' he proposed 'Joe Walker' and for 'Jim Jones' he preferred 'Jack Jones'. Mills also felt that the platoon would benefit from being made somewhat more variegated in terms of background: one character, for example, might be made an ex-colonel or perhaps a retired admiral, another the ex-officer's old gardener, and maybe young Pike would be more interesting if he became the local rapscallion. A little more regional diversity would not go amiss, while one was at it, with a Scot, perhaps, tossed in to the mix. There was one more recommendation that Mills wanted to make: Perry, as an inexperienced television scriptwriter, was in need of a well-qualified collaborator, and the obvious in-house choice, reasoned Mills, was David Croft.[50] Perry happily acceded to the proposal, and the two men set to work on a second script.

Croft visited Perry in his flat in Westminster, Perry visited Croft in his house in Notting Hill; ideas were exchanged, possible plots roughed out, a few comic lines devised, and then each man withdrew to work on the script alone. The collaboration seemed to work, their methods seemed to mesh: Croft was cool, calm and clear-headed,

Perry was warm, lively and enthusiastic; Croft could sit back and visualise entire scenes, Perry could leap up and perform particular routines; Croft was a master of ensemble comedy, Perry a connoisseur of comic turns; Croft had a sharp eye for the telling detail, Perry had a keen ear for the serviceable phrase; neither man was too proud to learn from the other, both men were determined to succeed. They had, they soon realised, much more in common than at first they had thought. Both men had fallen in love with the world of entertainment at a very early age (Croft's parents, Reginald Sharland and Ann Croft, had been stars of the British theatre during the 1920s and 1930s, and the baby David had slept in a prop basket backstage; Perry, thanks to his mother, had visited most of the cinemas, theatres and music-halls in and around London before his childhood was complete). Both had attended a distinguished public school (Croft Rugby, Perry St Paul's), and both had departed prematurely (Croft because the money ran out, Perry because he 'was tired of being thrashed').[51] Both had seen the Home Guard in action at first-hand (Croft as an air-raid warden, Perry as an enthusiastic volunteer) and had gone on to join the Royal Artillery (Croft served in North Africa, India and Singapore, becoming a major at twenty-three, and was on the verge of being made a lieutenant-colonel when he ended the war on General Montgomery's staff in the War Office; Perry served in the Far East, where he rose to the rank of sergeant and became the life and soul of the concert party). Both had been singers (Croft a tenor, Perry a baritone) and actors (Croft starting out as the butcher's boy in the 1938 movie *Goodbye, Mr Chips*, Perry in the 1952 Anna Neagle vehicle *The Glorious Days*); both had worked in holiday camps (Croft as a producer, Perry as a Redcoat); and both had married women from within showbusiness. Both enjoyed fine wines, classic movies and great comedy, and both had the same motto: 'Never take no for an answer.'[52]

They wrote quickly but carefully. A good pilot script, they appreciated, was an introduction, not an imposition; it needed to appear familiar without appearing false, to intrigue without seeming to intrude, to inform without straining to educate. In the space of half an hour, the pilot episode would have to set the right tone, establish the essential situation, adumbrate the key characters, touch on some special central tension, nod at its probable causes, wink at its possible consequences, and, last but by no means least, entertain a curious but uncommitted audience sufficiently to make it want to come back for more. It was not a task for either the faint-hearted or the foolhardy, and countless talented writers before Croft and Perry had tried to come to terms with it and failed. Nevertheless, through a combination of courage and prudence, the two men came up with a creation that seemed as if it might, with a little luck, serve each of their multiple needs.

The first episode of *Dad's Army*, they had decided, would mirror the real-life sequence of events that began on Tuesday, 14 May 1940, with Anthony Eden's announcement of plans for the formation of the Local Defence Volunteers, and continued with the frantic rush to enrol and the scramble to establish some kind of broadly recognisable hierarchy. With only the minimum exercise of artistic licence – the timing of Eden's announcement was brought forward to a brighter, more television-friendly hour – this structure allowed each character to be introduced to the audience simply as a matter of course. George Mainwaring, Arthur Wilson and Frank Pike (the 'pompous man–passive man–young boy' comic triangle replacing Perry's earlier arrangement) would hear the radio broadcast inside the Walmington-on-Sea branch of Swallow[53] Bank; Mainwaring would assert his authority ('Times of peril always bring great men to the fore . . .'), and then, later that day, the action would shift to the inside of the church hall, and the arrival of the first few volunteers – Frazer, the fierce-looking Scotsman; Godfrey, the genial old gent; Walker, the cheeky spiv; Jones, the eager veteran; and Bracewell, the sweet-natured, wing-collared, bow-tied toff – as well as the rude intervention of a brash, bumptious ARP warden and an officious little fire chief. It was an eminently *productive* pilot script: lean and energetic (the only character who is allowed to sit down, and then only briefly, is Mainwaring: first to read out an important message from the War Office, and later to write down the names of the new recruits); informative (a remarkable number of historically-accurate facts, relating to the LDV's chaotic formation, are woven neatly into the narrative); socially suggestive (with a bank manager exploiting his position, a chief clerk exploiting his good looks, a butcher exploiting the demand for rationed meat and a 'wholesale supplier' exploiting the demand for everything else); and, unlike many opening episodes, encouragingly funny.

The right idea really had come to fruition. On 4 October 1967, Michael Mills not only confirmed that the pilot script had been accepted, but also announced that he was ready to commission an initial series of six programmes ('with an option for a further six').[54] On 25 November, Croft and Perry signed the contract and committed themselves to *Dad's Army*.[55] They were ready: ready for their finest half-hour. Now all that was needed was a cast.

believable little worlds rather than brilliantly big stars. Throughout the first half of the 1960s he had cherry-picked the choicest character actors in British television comedy until, in effect, he had assembled his own unofficial repertory company, his own private Ealing. All of the following actors were used by Croft in one or more episodes of both *Hugh and I* and *Beggar My Neighbour* and would go on to feature in one or more episodes of *Dad's Army*: Arnold Ridley, Bill Pertwee, James Beck, Edward Sinclair, Harold Bennett, Felix Bowness, Arthur English, Carmen Silvera, Robert Raglan, Queenie Watts, Robert Gillespie, Julian Orchard, Jeffrey Gardiner and Jimmy Perry. The familiarity bred contentment: the audience knew who was who, and the director knew who could do what. It was inevitable that the close-knit community of Walmington-on-Sea would be composed predominantly of Croft's people.

Jimmy Perry, however, was disappointed to learn that he would not, on a regular basis, be joining them. Michael Mills had argued that the show's creator and co-writer would have to make up his mind as to which side of the camera he most wanted to be, and David Croft had concurred: 'Jimmy, I knew, had set his heart on playing the spiv – he'd actually written it with himself in mind – but I felt that, as one of the writers, he would be needed in the production box to see how things were going. I also felt, I suppose, that it wasn't going to make for a particularly happy cast if one of the writers gave himself a role – the other actors would've been inclined to say that he'd written the best lines for himself.'[4] Perry was by no means the first writer to find that his cunning plan had suddenly gone awry. Back in 1960, for example, the American writer Carl Reiner had created his very own starring vehicle (*Head of the Family*), basing the leading role of Rob Petrie expressly on himself, only to be informed by his producer that Dick Van Dyke was much more suited to playing himself than he was (and the show, as a consequence, was relaunched as *The Dick Van Dyke Show*).[5] Perry's sense of disappointment, nonetheless, was immense: 'I always resented it. Always. I wrote Walker for myself. That's how it had all started. And I wanted to be on *both* sides of the camera. But Michael Mills didn't think it was a good idea and neither did David, and, in those days, I was in no position to argue. So that was that: very sad, but there you are – you can't have everything.'[6]

The casting process, from the first casual discussion to the final collection of contracts, lasted several months, beginning in mid-October 1967 and ending in early March 1968. The genealogy of the characters (who were little more, so far, than garrulous strangers on paper but already intimate friends within the minds of Croft and Perry) contained the clues. Mainwaring, for example, was a composite of three people from Perry's past: the manager of his local bank, the head of a Watford building society and Will Hay's chronically incompetent, permanently harassed, on-screen persona (there had been a 'Colonel Mannering' – 'known to the press as "the uncrowned king of Southern Arabia" '[7] – in *The Life and Death of Colonel Blimp*, but the name 'Mainwaring' was chosen for its comically ambiguous, class-sensitive pronunciation). Wilson was prompted by Perry's aversion to the stereotypical sergeant figure:

> I'd been a sergeant myself, you see, and one day, while I was serving in the Far East, this major had come up and said to me: 'Sergeant Perry, why do you speak with a public school accent?' And I'd replied: 'Well, I suppose because I went to a public school.' So he said, 'Oh. But still: a *sergeant* speaking like *that* – it – it's *most* strange!' Well, the man was an idiot. There were more than a million men in the Royal Artillery alone, and they came from all walks of life. So this cliché that a sergeant should always look a certain way and sound a certain way – it's *just* a cliché, and I wanted to get right away from that.[8]

Jones owed much to the elderly raconteur with whom Perry had served in the Home Guard, and a little to the bellicose sergeant at Colchester barracks who had taught him bayonet drill ('Any doubt – get out the old cold steel, 'cause they don't like it up 'em!').[9] Godfrey was a throwback to the Edwardian era, when discreet and deferential shop assistants would inquire politely if one was 'being attended to';[10] Walker was drawn from memory – not only of real wartime wide boys, but also, inevitably, of the still-vivid 'Slasher Green', Sid Field's kinder, gentler, comic parody; Frazer was formed from all of the old anecdotes about those Scots who had grown progressively – and aggressively – more 'Scottish' while in exile down south among the Sassenachs; and Pike was modelled on Perry's own youthful experiences as a movie-mad, scarf-clad, impressionable raw recruit.

Casting Mainwaring, Perry believed, would be easy. There was one actor in particular who, in his opinion, bore a striking family resemblance to Walmington-on-Sea's uppity little fusspot: Arthur Lowe. What impressed Perry most about Lowe was his technical brilliance: his timing – like that of Jack Benny or Robb Wilton – was flawless; his mid-sentence double takes – like those of Bob Hope or Cary Grant – were exquisite; and his control of crosstalk – like that of Will Hay or Jimmy James – was seemingly effortless. 'You just had to watch him,' said Perry. 'It takes an awful long time to learn how to do those things even moderately well, but he did them beautifully.'[11] Lowe had been acting professionally for more than twenty years, starting off in Manchester rep before graduating to West End musicals (including *Call Me Madam*, *Pal Joey* and *The Pyjama Game*), plays (*Witness for the Prosecution*, *A Dead Secret*, *Ring of Truth*) and movies (including a brief role as a reporter in *Kind Hearts and Coronets* and a more significant part in Lindsay Anderson's *This Sporting Life*). By the mid-sixties he was best known for his long-running role on television as the irascible and fastidious Leonard Swindley – first, from 1960, in *Coronation Street* (where he managed Gamma Garments boutique, unsuccessfully fought a local election as the founder and chairman of the Property Owners and Small Traders Party, and was jilted at the altar by the timid Emily Nugent), and then, from 1965, in a broader spin-off situation-comedy, *Pardon the Expression* (which saw him leave Weatherfield to become assistant manager at a northern branch of a department store called Dobson and Hawks). 'I'd seen him in those two things,' said Perry, 'and somehow he'd clicked with me. He was such a funny little man.'[12] By 1967, after appearing in yet another spin-off series called *Turn Out the Lights*, Lowe, having tired of being associated so closely with one long-running role, had left Mr Swindley behind and returned to the theatre. He was available, but, much to Perry's surprise, the BBC did not appear to want him.

'*Arthur Lowe?*' exclaimed Michael Mills when the name first came up. '*He* doesn't work for *us*!'[13] This was not entirely true – he had, in the past, appeared in the odd episode of such programmes as *Maigret* and *Z Cars* – but it was true enough to make Mills (ever protective of the BBC's distinctive identity) urge his producer to look elsewhere. David Croft had, in fact, already done so, and had settled on Thorley Walters – an actor whose most recent role on television had been that of Sir Joshua Hoot QC in BBC1's *A. P. Herbert's Misleading Cases*. Walters was no stranger to playing either stuffy or inept military characters – and in the Boulting Brothers' satire *Private's Progress* (1956) he had played Captain Bootle, who was both – although his movie career now centred on such Hammer horrors as *Dracula – Prince of Darkness* (1966) and *Frankenstein Created Woman* (1967). Croft went ahead and offered him the role. Walters turned it down. 'He thanked me very much for asking,' recalled Croft, 'but he said that he couldn't think why I'd thought of him. But he *would* have been very good.'[14] Perry, once again, suggested Arthur Lowe, but Croft, once again, already had someone else in mind: this time it was Jon Pertwee.

Pertwee was one of those actors who seemed almost too serviceable for their own good. Whenever a radio producer wanted someone to play a gibbering Norwegian, or a spluttering English aristocrat, or a windy Welshman, or just about any other comical accent, tic or turn, Pertwee invariably came top of the list (in *The Navy Lark*, for example, he supplied the voices for no fewer than six distinctive characters);[15] whenever a television show or movie required a piece of Danny Kaye-style verbal dexterity or a quirky characterisation, Pertwee would, inevitably, find himself in demand. Croft had worked with him on an episode of *Beggar My Neighbour*,[16] and had been very impressed: 'He'd played this major – quite similar, really, to the part [of Mainwaring] as it was conceived at that time – and he'd been very funny. So I sent him the script and offered him the part.'[17] This time, it seemed, Croft had succeeded in getting his man. On 13 November 1967, Michael Mills instructed the BBC bookings department to 'negotiate a fee with [the agent] Richard Stone for the services of Jon Pertwee', adding that 'Pertwee is in America at the moment, and has seen [the] script and wished to do [the] show. I would like him to be aware of the fee that we are offering, so that we can make a firm casting.'[18] What happened next remains unclear: it could have been the case that Pertwee, or his agent, judged the proposed fee (which would not, at best, have been many shillings more than £250 an episode)[19] too low, or he might have decided, on reflection, that he did not wish to risk being typecast in a series that might just possibly run for several years, or he might simply have been enjoying himself too much in New York (where he was appearing in the Broadway production of *There's a Girl in My Soup*) to seriously consider making an early return, but, whatever the real reason, the result was that he changed his mind and chose to drop out. Croft, once again, found himself back at square one.

It was at this point that Perry saw his chance. Knowing that Arthur Lowe was currently appearing in a play called *Baked Beans and Caviar* at Windsor, he persuaded David Croft to go along with him to see it. 'Unfortunately,' Perry recalled, 'Arthur was *dreadful* in it – it wasn't his sort of thing at all – but David, to his great credit, backed me and agreed to consider him for Mainwaring.'[20] Perry's persistence was about to pay off, but not without one final scare – courtesy of none other than Arthur Lowe himself. Croft had arranged for the actor to meet him and Perry at Television Centre:

> It didn't get off to a good start. We'd whistled him up to the Centre so that we could talk over lunch in the canteen, and the first thing he said was: 'I'm not sure, you know, about a situation-comedy. I hope it's not going to be one of those *silly* programmes. The sort of show I hate is *Hugh and I*.' So I had to tell him the fact that I'd done about eighty *Hugh and I*s! He quickly backed out of that one. After all, it *was* work, and he wasn't over-employed at the time.[21]

Croft forgave the *faux pas*; he knew that Lowe, so long as he could shake off the ghost of Mr Swindley, had both the wit and the ability to make the role his own. It was, he concluded, a risk, but a risk well worth taking. A fee was agreed of £210 per programme, and a contract was sent out on 21 February 1968. Lowe signed it immediately. Captain Mainwaring, at long last, was cast.

Sergeant Wilson, Perry would later reveal, could have been played by the portly and bespectacled Robert Dorning: 'I'd seen him with Arthur in *Pardon the Expression* – he'd played Arthur's boss – and I'd thought to myself: "Wouldn't they make a good couple to play the leads [in *Dad's Army*]?" So I was very keen on getting them both, and Dorning could certainly have been good as Wilson, but then, of course, Michael Mills stuck his oar in . . .'[22] Mills – who was indeed an ex-Navy man – announced that he was absolutely convinced about who was the right man for the role. David Croft – who was never surprised to hear that Michael Mills was absolutely convinced about anything – invited him to share this information. 'You *must* have John Le Mesurier!' barked Mills. 'He *suffers* so well!'[23] Croft found, on reflection, that he rather liked this idea. Le Mesurier *did* suffer well. No post-war British movie seemed complete without his furrowed brow, frightened eyes, sunken cheeks and world-weary sigh. He had been the psychiatrist with the nervous twitch in *Private's Progress*, the time-and-motion expert (also with a nervous twitch) in *I'm All Right Jack* (1959) and the City office manager (*sans* twitch) in *The Rebel* (1961), as well as innumerable other bewildered-looking barristers, bureaucrats, officers and doctors who together seemed to sum up a certain sense of home-grown *ennui*. He had reprised the role on television in both *Hancock's Half-Hour* (1956–60) and *Hancock* (1961), and more recently he had shown a little of the warmer side to his nature as the retired Colonel Maynard – 'a dear old stick'[24] – in the situation-comedy *George and the Dragon* (1966–8). Croft sent him the pilot script of *Dad's Army*. Le Mesurier, on reading it, thought it had the potential to become a 'minor situation comedy', but he was intrigued by the news that he was wanted for the role of the sergeant rather than the captain – 'casting directors usually saw me as officer material'.[25] He read the script again, and liked it a little more: Perry, he felt, 'knew how to turn a funny line', and Croft, he noted, was 'a theatre man who had brought to television a reputation for cool, calm organisation'. 'Promising,' he thought to himself, 'all promising.'[26] He informed his agent, Freddie Joachim, that he only had one real reservation: the fee. Joachim, who regarded the medium of television as beneath his calibre of client, proceeded, without the slightest sign of enthusiasm, to haggle on Le Mesurier's behalf.

Croft, in the meantime, was busy trying to persuade Clive Dunn to accept the role of Lance Corporal Jones. Jack Haig, an old favourite of Croft's from his time at Tyne Tees in the 1950s, had been first choice, but, after discussing the offer with the ultra-cautious Tom Sloan (who appears to have given him the impression that the show was by no means assured of a long run),[27] Haig had turned the part down in order to concentrate on a lucrative new vehicle for his popular children's character, 'Wacky Jacky'. Dunn, though a mere forty-eight years of age, was the obvious alternative: like Haig, who was nine years his senior, he knew how to portray elderly comic characters. An alumnus of the Players' Theatre, which was a well-respected club in Villiers Street, London WC2, specialising in Victorian/Edwardian-style music hall, pantomime and melodrama, Dunn had appeared in everything from Windmill revues to children's situation-comedies (such as *The Adventures of Charlie Quick*, broadcast by BBCTV in 1957), and had first made his name on television as Old Johnson, the aptly-named 83-year-old waiter and Boer War veteran in Granada's *Bootsie and Snudge* (1960–3), the popular follow-up to *The Army Game*. Like Croft, he came from an established showbusiness family – his maternal grandfather, Frank Lynne, had been a moderately popular music-hall comedian, his uncle, Gordon Lynne, was also a comic and both his parents, Bobby Dunn and Connie Clive, had been professional entertainers – and the two men had known and liked each other for years (Dunn's mother, in fact, had once had an affair with Croft's father).[28] Putting their friendship to one side, however, he had not jumped at the offer when Croft first made his approach: he had just started work on *The World of Beachcomber*, BBC2's fine adaptation of J. B. Morton's much-admired newspaper columns, and, as he would put it later, he 'wasn't particularly hungry'.[29] As a former prisoner of war – he had spent four harrowing years in a German labour camp in Liezen, Austria – he would have been forgiven for regarding the subject matter with suspicion, but, in fact, he found it quite appealing. The reason for his reluctance had more to do with the high casualty rate of new situation-comedies: 'The ups and downs of the profession had made me cautious.'[30]

He decided to phone a friend: John Le Mesurier. 'I'll do it if you do it,'[31] said Dunn. 'Yes,' replied Le Mesurier, 'but . . .', and suggested that they 'hung out a little' in the hope that the money might improve.[32] Dunn agreed with 'Le Mez' (as he was known to his friends), and delayed making a decision. Croft, however, had already enlisted a standby: an inexperienced but very promising 28-year-old actor by the name of David Jason. 'I didn't know him very well,' Croft explained, 'but my wife represented him and I'd used him fairly recently in an episode of *Beggar My Neighbour* and he'd been marvellous.'[33] Jason had just started work on the show that represented his first real breakthrough on television – the ITV/Redif-fusion teatime sketch show *Do Not Adjust Your Set* (1967–9) – but, even so, was quite prepared to commit himself to a high-profile David Croft comedy. Late in February 1968, Croft, who was now growing impatient, spotted Dunn in the BBC canteen, and took the opportunity to ask him if he had reached a decision yet about joining the cast; an embarrassed Dunn stalled again, and then slipped quietly away 'hoping that John would [soon] make up his mind and that David would not resent the delay'.[34]

Wheels began turning within wheels: Dunn's agent, Michael Grade, was a close friend of Bill Cotton, and spoke to him on an informal basis in order to ensure that someone at the BBC realised that his client really was predisposed to join the show. David Croft, meanwhile, had begun taking steps to resolve the matter once and for all. The following day, David Jason recalled, proved full of sur-prises: 'The order of events was as follows: I went to the BBC and read for the part at 11 a.m.; soon after, my agent received the message that I had the part; by 3 p.m., I was out of work! Over the lunch period Bill Cotton had persuaded Clive to take the part, and hadn't informed the producer. The rest is history!'[35]

Dunn, it seems, had just heard via Freddie Joachim that Le Mesur-ier had finally decided to accept, and the news had sparked him into action.[36] Once his billing had been secured – third, below Lowe and 'Le Mez' – and the assurance had been given that he would be handed the pick of the 'Joey Joeys' – the physical comedy – he proceeded to make a commitment. Both men received and signed their contracts on 29 February 1968 (although Le Mesurier's fee was set at a sum £52 10s higher than Dunn's – or Lowe's),[37] and the first tier of the cast was complete.

The remainder of the platoon proved somewhat easier to assemble. Croft cast Arnold Ridley as Private Godfrey. Up until this point, Ridley's life had been chequered with bad luck: he had been invalided out of the Army on two separate occasions (first in 1917, following the Battle of the Somme, then after talking his way back into service, in 1940, following the evacuation from Dunkirk); his production company, Quality Films, went bust after just one, well-received release (*Royal Eagle*, 1936), and he had been forced to sell the rights to some of his most enduringly popular – and lucrative – plays (including *The Ghost Train*, 1925) in order to stave off bankruptcy. There had been spells in various soap operas – including *Crossroads* (as the Revd Guy Atkins) and *Coronation Street* (as Herbert Whittle, the would-be wooer of Minnie Caldwell), as well as an ongoing role in *The Archers* (as Doughy Hood) – and undemanding one-off appearances in such series as *White Hunter* (1958) and *The Avengers* (1961 – as, all too predictably, 'Elderly Gent'), but, at the beginning of 1968, the septuagenarian actor was still performing primarily because he could not afford not to. 'He was another one who'd worked for me before,' Croft recalled:

> He'd been very good, very funny, and he was a lovely, gentle character. He looked right, sounded right. I *was* a bit worried about him because I think he was already 72 when I first interviewed him for the part. I'd said, 'I don't think I can save you from having to run about a bit now and then. Are you up for it?' And he'd said, 'Oh, yes, I think I'll manage.' As it turned out, of course, he couldn't, but we got an enormous amount of capital out of helping him on to the van and things like that, you know. So he turned out to be a very successful character.[38]

Casting Dumfries-born John Laurie as Private Frazer had been another one of Michael Mills' suggestions. Laurie, who at 71 was Ridley's junior by a single year, was a hugely experienced actor: he had played all of the great Shakespearean roles at the Old Vic and Stratford, and appeared in a wide range of movies, including two directed by Alfred Hitchcock – *Juno and the Paycock* (1930) and *The 39 Steps* (1935) – three by Laurence Olivier – *Henry V* (1944), *Hamlet* (1948) and *Richard III* (1954) – and four by Michael Powell (the most notable of which was *The Life and Death of Colonel Blimp*, in which he played the ever-loyal Murdoch), as well as one starring Will Hay – *The Ghost of St Michael's* (1941). He had been working intermittently on television since the mid-1930s, but it had only been since the start of the 1960s that he had begun appearing on a relatively regular basis (first as thriller writer Algernon Blackwood in Associated-Rediffusion's 1961 *Tales of Mystery*, and later as Dr McTurk in the 1966 TVS children's science-fiction series *The Master*, as well as several cameo roles in both *The Avengers* and *Dr Finlay's*

Casebook). David Croft was well aware of what Laurie could do – he had worked with him before in a 1965 episode of *Hugh and I*,[39] and had every faith in his ability to flesh-out the still-skeletal figure of Frazer – but was apprehensive about the actor's reaction to such an under-developed character:

> 'Frazer', at that time, was described in the script simply as 'A Scotsman'. It can't have been very inspiring to such an experienced actor. Michael Mills said, 'Make him into a fisherman.' So Jimmy and I made him into a fisherman for that first episode. No use to us at all, of course, as a fisherman never went out to sea in those days because it was the invasion coast. Later on, we started allowing him to make coffins in his workshop, and that developed into him becoming the undertaker – and then he became very useful indeed, a marvellous character. But we did find it difficult, at the start, to write for him, as this 'Scottish fisherman', and I doubt that John was too impressed either.[40]

Laurie, sure enough, was far from impressed, but he had a policy of never refusing offers of work, and so he agreed, somewhat reluctantly, to play a character whose lifetime he confidently expected to last no longer than six half-hour episodes.

James Beck was a far more willing recruit. The 39-year-old actor from Islington had been working extremely hard at establishing himself on television since the start of the 1960s – following a formative period spent in rep at York – but had not yet succeeded in securing a regular role in a significant show. At the end of 1963 he had written a typically polite letter to Bush Bailey, the BBC's assistant head of artists' bookings, asking if there was any chance of an interview ('as I don't seem to be making a great deal of headway').[41] Bailey did see him early the following year, and filed a favourable report, but nothing tangible came of the meeting except for more of the same old bits and pieces. By 1968, most viewers would have glimpsed him at some time or other in the odd episode of such popular police drama series as *Z Cars*, *Dixon of Dock Green* and *Softly Softly*, or in a one-off role in a situation-comedy such as *Here's Harry*, but few could have put a name to the face. The prospect of a major role in a new show such as *Dad's Army*, therefore, was precisely the kind of opportunity that Beck had been waiting for. Playing a spiv actually represented something of a departure for an actor who had grown used to being cast as characters on the *right* side of the law: even in his two previous appearances in Croft situation-comedies he had played a police constable on the first occasion and a customs officer on the second.[42] As someone who had grown up in the same working-class environment that had (with more than a little help from capitalism and rationing) formed such ambiguous characters, and also as a great fan – and gifted mimic – of Sid Field, it was a departure that Beck relished. 'He was obviously a talented actor,' Croft recalled. 'He just came to me, in fact, in an audition. I had used him before, and I fancied him very much for that particular part. There weren't any other real competitors for it – except Jimmy, of course, and we'd already ruled him out – so casting Walker turned out to be one of the easiest ones of the lot.'[43]

Ian Lavender had Ann Callender to thank for the part of Private Pike. Lavender – a 22-year-old, Birmingham-born actor whose fledgling career up to this point consisted simply of two years in drama school at Bristol's Old Vic followed by a six-month season playing juvenile leads at Canterbury's Marlowe Theatre – had recently become one of Callender's clients, and early in 1968, just before he was due to make his television debut on 5 March in a one-off ITV/Rediffusion drama called *Flowers At My Feet*, she urged her husband to watch him. 'So I did,' recalled Croft, 'and I was most impressed. He played a young juvenile delightfully.'[44] Croft had no qualms, as a BBC producer, about casting one of his wife's clients, partly because he had great faith in her – as well as his own – judgement, and partly because he already had the BBC's blessing to go ahead and do so:

I'd had a considerable number of interviews at this time with Tom Sloan, because of the fact that my wife was an agent. I said, 'Tom, look: we've got this corporate situation – my wife's an agent, she's got some good clients, but, at the same time, I don't want to use them if somebody is going to say, "He uses his wife's talent all the time."' So he said, 'Well, no, you mustn't *not* use them, David; you must also forbear to use them when somebody else of superior ability is available. But you must not deny her actors a chance for employment.' And that was fine; that was settled. He did go on to say, 'When you *do* use somebody in your wife's list, just drop me a note', which I always did.[45]

When Callender called Lavender with the news that he was wanted at Television Centre he had no idea that the man to whom she was sending him was her husband:

I was just sent along to see this man Croft. About a situation-comedy called *Dad's Army*. It was a bit terrifying, really, because at drama school I'd been playing Romeo and Florizel and all that sort of thing, and the only comedy I'd ever done was Restoration Comedy. I knew about the Home Guard, because my father had been station sergeant at a police station that served the Austin motorworks in Birmingham, and he'd had to go and inspect them and make sure they were doing everything right, so I knew what it was. But the thought of being in a comedy – I did find *that* daunting. Anyway, I went and read for David. Then I was called back again the following week, and then again at the end of the week after that. And then I heard I'd got the part.[46]

It was only after he had been hired that Lavender discovered just how well-connected his agent actually was:

Ann Callender said to me, 'I'm going to take you out to lunch, darling.' Which she did. And she said, 'By the way, I forgot to tell you that David Croft is my husband.' And my face obviously dropped, because then she said, 'Yes. That's *exactly* why we didn't tell you. But you got the part because *he* wants you. And I'd just like to point out – don't forget that he can always write you out!'[47]

Once Pike had been picked, Croft turned his attention to the supporting players. John Ringham, an experienced, self-styled 'jobbing character actor',[48] was chosen to play Private Bracewell, the Wodehousian silly ass from the City; Janet Davies, a bright, reliable performer whom Croft had used in a recent episode of *Beggar My Neighbour*, was hired as Mrs Mavis Pike;[49] Caroline Dowdeswell was recruited to play junior clerk Janet King (a hastily drawn character introduced after Michael Mills had declared that the show needed a *soupçon* of sex);[50] Gordon Peters, a former stand-up comic who specialised in playing Hancock-style characters, was drafted in for the one-off role of the fire chief; and several seasoned professionals – including Colin Bean, Richard Jacques, Hugh Hastings, George Hancock, Vic Taylor, Richard Kitteridge, Vernon Drake, Hugh Cecil, Frank Godfrey, Jimmy Mac, David Seaforth and Desmond Cullum-Jones – were engaged (at six guineas each per episode) to make up the platoon's back row.[51] One character now remained to be cast: the nasty, nosy, noisy ARP warden.

Croft thought more or less immediately of Bill Pertwee. Pertwee, in real life, could not have been less like the loud and loutish character Croft and Perry had created to darken Mainwaring's moods, but he was quite capable of investing such a role with a degree of comic vulnerability that would lift it far above the realm of caricature. Like his cousin, Jon, Bill Pertwee came to television after learning his craft both in Variety – first as a colleague of Beryl Reid, later in partnership with his wife, Marion MacLeod – and radio – as a valued and versatile contributor to both *Beyond Our Ken* (1958–64) and *Round the Horne* (1965–7). After catching the eye in a series of *The Norman Vaughan Show* on BBC1 in 1966, he found himself increasingly in demand not only for comic cameos but also as a warm-up man for various television shows, and he started to think more seriously about pursuing work in the medium 'to add another string to one's bow, as it were'.[52] In 1968, just as he was preparing for a season of performances at Bognor Regis, he heard from David Croft:

I'd worked for David the previous year. It was just a small part in an episode of *Hugh and I* with Terry Scott and Hugh Lloyd: I'd only had a couple of lines, but I had to shout at Terry Scott and push him around a wee bit in a cinema queue. That must have stuck in David's mind, because when he was casting *Dad's Army* he rang up the agency I was with [Richard Stone], found out that I was probably available and gave me a call. He said,

'I'm starting a programme about the Home Guard, and I've got these couple of lines for an air-raid warden. You just come into an office and shout a bit and then go out again.' And that was it – that was how he cast me in that.[53]

Even though the air-raid warden was not, at that stage, conceived of as a regular character, Croft knew that Pertwee could be relied on not only to turn in the kind of spirited performance he required to test the role's comic potential, but also to inject some welcome energy and good humour into a company of tough and occasionally testy old professionals. 'I booked Bill because he was good, of course, but I also booked him in order to keep everyone else happy and sweet. He was always very bubbly, very well liked by everyone, and he's marvellous fun.'[54]

The casting, at last, was complete, and Croft regarded the ensemble that he had assembled with a considerable amount of satisfaction: 'The cast that you started out thinking about is never the same as the one you finish up with, but I was pretty pleased with the line-up we'd managed to get. There was a great deal of quality there.'[55] He looked ahead at all the potential clashes of egos, all the possible conflicts of ambition, all the inevitable accidents (happy and otherwise), all the long drawn-out set-ups and last-minute revisions, all the budgetary worries, all the problems with props and people and performances, and he could not wait to get started. He was ready to make a television programme.

THE COMEDY

There's nothing funny on paper. All you are playing with is a bagful of potential. Even when the show's written you haven't got anything. Comedy is like a torch battery – there is no point in it until the circuit is complete and the bulb, which is the audience, lights up. It is how strongly the bulb lights up which determines how well you have done your job.

FRANK MUIR[1]

of good days or bad days to come. His spirits sagged when John Laurie turned to him and said in a voice of casual menace, 'I *hope* this is going to work, laddie, but to my mind it's a *ridiculous* idea!', but later, during a coffee break, they were revived when Bill Pertwee came over and assured him that the show was 'going to be a winner'.[5] He remained, nonetheless, over-sensitive and apprehensive; this had been his big idea, his personal project, and now it was set to be tested.

Preparations had certainly been thorough. David Croft was determined to make the programme seem as true to its period as was humanly possible. Any line that sounded too 'modern', such as 'I couldn't care less', was swiftly removed from the script. The services of E. V. H. Emmett, the voice of the old Gaumont-British newsreels from the 1930s and 1940s, were secured to supply some suitably evocative scene-setting narration. Two talented and meticulous set designers, Alan Hunter-Craig and Paul Joel, were brought in to create a range of believably 1940s-style surroundings, and, after researching the era at the Imperial War Museum, they either found or fabricated the right kinds of food – Spam, snoek, dried egg, fat bacon pieces, rabbit, potatoes, cabbages and carrots – brands – Camp coffee, Typhoo tea, Bird's custard, Brown's 'Harrison Glory' peas, Porter's 'Victory' self-raising flour, Orlox beef suet, Horlicks tablets, SAXA salt, Sunlight soap, Craven 'A' cigarettes – furniture – elderly desks, 'utility'-style shelves, sideboards, cabinets – portraits – of the King and Queen, and Churchill ('Let Us Go Forward Together') – and posters – bearing such advice as 'Keep it under your hat', 'Hitler will send no warning' and 'Keep it dark' – to ensure that every home, hall, bank and butcher's shop in Walmington-on-Sea would reach the screen reflecting a richly authentic wartime look. Sandra Exelby, an accomplished BBC make-up specialist, developed a variety of period hairstyles and wigs, while George Ward, the costume designer, searched far and wide for genuine LDV and Home Guard brassards, badges, boots, uniforms, respirators and weapons, ordering what other outfits were needed from Berman's, a London costumier (and he made a point of having Captain Mainwaring's uniform made from out of a slightly superior quality material in order to reflect the higher salary he would, as a bank manager, have received). Someone even managed to find an old pair of round-rimmed spectacles for Arthur Lowe to wear.

'It had to look *right*,' Croft confirmed, 'and, of course, people had to be able to really believe in the characters.'[6] Both he and Perry had worked hard to provide each major character with a plausible past – Jack Jones, for example, had been given a long and elaborate military career (which went all the way from Khartoum, through the Sudan, on to the North-West Frontier, back under General Kitchener for the battle of Omdurman, the Frontier again, then on to the Boer War and the Great War in France) to lend more than a little credence to his regular rambling anecdotes. Each actor was encouraged to draw on any memories which might help them to add the odd distinguishing detail (John Laurie remembered his time as a Home Guard in Paddington – 'totally uncomical, an excess of dullness' – and found an easy affinity with Frazer's strained tolerance of 'a lot of useless blather').[7]

The theme song was Jimmy Perry's idea. 'I wouldn't call myself a composer,' he explained, 'I'd call myself a pastiche artist. My aim is to write something that makes you know, as soon as the show starts, exactly what it's going to be about. For *Dad's Army*, I wanted to come up with something that took you straight back to the period and summed up the attitudes of the British people.'[8] His lyrics, when they came, could not have seemed more apposite:

> Who do you think you are kidding, Mr Hitler
> If you think we're on the run?
> We are the boys who will stop your little game.
> We are the boys who will make you think again.
> 'Cause who do you think you are kidding, Mr Hitler
> If you think old England's done?
>
> Mister Brown goes off to town
> On the eight twenty-one
> But he comes home each evening
> And he's ready with his gun.
> So who do you think you are kidding, Mr Hitler
> If you think old England's done?[9]

Everything about these words – their polite defiance, their frail ebullience, their easy grace – belied their belated origin. 'I was very proud of it,' Perry admitted.[10] He composed the music in collaboration with Derek Taverner, whom he had known since their time together in a Combined Services Entertainment unit in Delhi, and then resolved to persuade Bud Flanagan, one of his childhood idols, to perform the finished song. Flanagan (along with his erstwhile partner, Chesney Allen) was still associated firmly and fondly in the public's mind with such popular wartime recordings as 'Run, Rabbit, Run' and 'We're Gonna Hang Out The Washing On The Siegfried Line', and his warm and reedy voice was the ideal instrument to age artificially this new 'old' composition. Fortunately, although the 72-year-old music-hall veteran was not in the habit of recording songs that he had not previously performed, he agreed, for a fee of 100 guineas, to supply the vocal. On the afternoon of 26 February 1968, he arrived at the Riverside Recording Studio in Hammersmith and, to an accompaniment from the Band of the Coldstream Guards, he proceeded to sing: 'Who do you think you are kidding, Mr Hitler . . .' Jimmy Perry, standing at the back of the production booth, was visibly thrilled: 'It sent a sort of shiver up my spine. What a moment! To think that dear old Bud Flanagan, whom I'd sat and watched as a kid up in the gallery at the Palladium, was right there now, singing a song that I'd written. Marvellous!'[11] After eight takes – Flanagan had stumbled a few times over one or two of the unfamiliar lines – the song had been captured to everyone's satisfaction. It was a sound from a bygone era (the final sound, in a way, because Flanagan would die a few months later), and it set the tone for all that was to follow.

Location filming took place between 1 and 6 April. Harold Snoad, David Croft's production assistant, had selected the old East Anglian market town of Thetford as the regular base. It was a shrewd choice: inside the town itself, the neat rows of grey-brick and flinty houses implied just the right degree of close-knit intimacy. The surrounding area boasted a rich range of vivid natural sights – pine forests stretching out to the north and west, wide open fields, long meandering streams – and man-made contexts – the Army's Military Training Area was only six miles away at Stanford – in which to frame the fictional world of Walmington-on-Sea. Arthur Lowe travelled down to Thetford by train, Clive Dunn and John Le Mesurier together by car and the remainder of the cast and crew by coach. 'Everyone knew exactly what they were doing,' Ian Lavender recalled, 'except me':

> I didn't know *anything* about location shooting. I lived near Olympia in those days, and the journey to TV Centre wasn't very long, so I just wandered over in the belief that I was going to spend a few hours in Thetford and then come home on the coach. When I got to TV Centre, however, I noticed that everybody had brought their *suitcases* with them, so I had to invest several shillings for a taxi ride back to pack some clothes! It had never occurred to me that I wouldn't be coming home at nights – that was how green I was.[12]

Every external scene for the whole of the first series had to be filmed during that single (unseasonably chilly) week in Norfolk, and, as Lavender remembered, the pace was unrelenting:

> It was all a bit of a blur. The only thing I remember of the filming, quite honestly, was when I accidentally came up with Pike's voice. Most of the filming was mute – because it was going to be mixed in with stock newsreel footage – but one scene, featuring these circus horses going round and round, was done with sound. And all I said was, 'Have you got the rifles, Mr Mainwaring?' And this *voice* came out: '*Have you got the rifles, Mr Mainwaring?*' Pure shock, I think. And so I more or less stuck with that voice for the next nine years.[13]

The most surreal moment, said Clive Dunn, occurred when the cast was racing through a few light-hearted scene-setting motions: 'As we filmed our bits of comedy showing the Home Guard changing road signs to fool the German invaders, a staff car loaded with German NATO officers passed by . . . , smiling and unaware that we were about to launch into a long comedy series about the Second World War.'[14]

The evenings were reserved for socialising. 'There was a good atmosphere right from the very first day,' Ian Lavender recalled:

I'd been terrified at the start – *terrified* – but they were all so welcoming. I think I'd already been put through my 'initiation process' back in that pub at Chiswick by Arthur. He'd shown me how to smoke a cigarette 'Arabian style'. He had his own private supply of these cork-tipped Craven 'A' cigarettes, and he'd got me to hold one of them like he did, suck it – phew! – and I'd fallen off my stool. That was my first memory of Arthur, socially – making me fall off a bar stool. And then in the hotel at Thetford they were lovely. They'd sort of say things like, 'Come on, this is your bit as well', you know, 'Don't be afraid of . . .' It wasn't a matter of taking me under their wing and protecting me, but neither was it a matter of leaving me to sink or swim. They were just very, very, welcoming.[15]

After Thetford came the rehearsals: at 10.30 on the morning of Monday, 8 April, the cast, Croft and Perry reassembled at St Nicholas Church Hall in Bennett Street, Chiswick, to begin work on the pilot episode, which by this time had been given the title 'The Man and the Hour'. Some of the actors seemed well-advanced in their characterisations – Arthur Lowe, for example, was quietly confident that both his look (a compressed Clement Attlee) and manner (proud, pompous and pushy) would work rather well, and Ian Lavender (whose prematurely greying hair would be disguised on screen by a combination of colour spray and Brylcream) had decided to give Pike a long Aston Villa scarf (hastily replaced, in the opening credits sequence, by a blue towel because the wardrobe van had left Thetford early), a mildly quavering vocal manner and a childishly inquisitive expression – but one or two, it seemed, were still in need of some advice. Bill Pertwee kept being urged by David Croft to make Hodges even louder and more obnoxious, delivering each line in the music-hall style of 'on top of a shout', and Jimmy Perry was and would remain astonished by John Le Mesurier's unorthodox methods of assimilation:

Talk about casual! The previous week, on the first day of filming at Thetford, John was sitting there very nonchalantly in the lounge of the hotel, and he'd said to me: 'Oh, James: how do you want me to play this part?' Well, that was a laugh for a start!

As far as I knew, John Le Mesurier only had one performance. Anyway, I said to him: 'Look, John, it's all yours on a plate – just do it as you feel.' So he said, 'Yes, oh, all right, old boy', and then he lit a cigarette and said, 'Who are you going to bet on in the 2.30 today?' Make no mistake, he was very, very, good, but, really, that man just *swanned* through life.[16]

Gradually, however, Le Mesurier warmed to the role by warming the role up, moving away from the kind of stiff and stuffy figures he was so used to sleepwalking into existence, and resolving instead to model Arthur Wilson on none other than John Le Mesurier: 'I thought, why not just be myself, use an extension of my own personality and behave rather as I had done in the Army? So, I always left a button or two undone, and had the sleeve of my battledress blouse slightly turned up. I spoke softly, issued commands as if they were invitations (the sort not likely to be accepted) and generally assumed a benign air of helplessness.'[17] James Beck, meanwhile, was busy striving to make Joe Walker (who had inherited Slasher Green's rakish trilby, pencil-thin moustache, padded shoulders and two-tone shoes) seem not only real but also appealing: 'Trouble is,' he later explained, 'spivs weren't really very nice people to know. So I felt that if Walker was to be a true comedy character, he had to have some redeeming quality. Then I remembered a spiv from Barnsley I'd known in the Army, and liked. He had this great thing. He would cheat the world at large, but he'd never cheat his pals. And that's the jewel in Walker's crown too. He always looks after his mates.'[18] Countless small but significant things were falling slowly into place.

As with any rehearsal period, however, problems were created as well as solved. The character of Bracewell, for example, came to seem less and less relevant the longer the rehearsal went on. 'It had absolutely nothing to do with [the actor] John Ringham,' explained David Croft. 'He was excellent. It was the character. Jimmy and I both came to the same conclusion, which was that Bracewell was too similar in personality to Godfrey, so we decided to drop him after the first episode.'[19] Another character – the chief fire officer (played by Gordon Peters) – did not even reach the screen: '[W]e had written a hilarious scene,' Croft recalled,

where the chief fire officer had decided to hold a fire exercise
in the church hall. He proceeded to fill it with fire hoses at the
same time that Captain Mainwaring was trying to hold a parade.
It worked like a dream, but at the end of one of the last runs
of the rehearsal I was approached by a grave-faced Eve Lucas,
my production secretary, who said, 'It's very funny, but do you
realise that you're seven minutes too long?' Something had to
go and, sadly, the fire practice scene went in its entirety; and
so too did Gordon Peters.'[20]

It was during this period that the cast and crew received a very
important visitor: Huw Wheldon, BBC Television's current Controller of Programmes and its next Managing Director. Wheldon was
still very much a programme-maker at heart, and nothing gave him
greater pleasure than seeing genuine talent succeed, but a few months
before – as he himself would later freely admit – he had been 'one
of a small group of programme executives who became distinguished
for recognising that a script by David Croft and Jimmy Perry called
Dad's Army would not work'.[21] Out of respect for David Croft,
Wheldon had gone along with the decision to commission a series
of six episodes, and he had reacted positively to the news that the
leading roles had been given to Lowe and Le Mesurier: 'This pleased
me,' he acknowledged, 'but it did not change my mind. I knew it
would fail.'[22] Then, a few months later, he heard that rehearsals had
begun, and, as had long been his habit, he decided to drop in on
the proceedings unannounced in order to see how the programme
was developing:

They were doing a five-minute sequence and I could not make
head nor tail of it. I could not follow the action. Suddenly I
realised that I had done the casting wrongly in my own mind.
I had taken it for granted that John Le Mesurier, elegant, intelligent, sardonic and rather weary, was the officer; and that Arthur
Lowe, brisk, belligerent and bustling, was the sergeant. But [it
was actually] the other way round. Lowe was Captain Mainwaring and Le Mesurier was Sergeant Wilson. I was delighted.
It was the first note of unpredictability in a series that has been
fresh and unpredictable and creative ever since.

I should have known better. David Croft was a good producer. He and Jimmy Perry were and are brilliant writers; and good writing and good production are key factors in these matters.[23]

The show had found another ally – and, in the weeks to come, it would need every one of them.

The pilot episode was recorded (in black and white) on the evening of Monday, 15 April, in the relatively capacious Studio 4, Television Centre, before an audience of approximately 320 people. It seemed to go fairly well (as did the subsequent five episodes, which were rehearsed and recorded in sequence over the course of the following few weeks). Only John Le Mesurier, among the cast, appeared doubtful about how well the programme was progressing, but then the Eeyorish Le Mesurier ('I worry about every new series, every new play. I worry whether people will tire of my face, even whether the car will start . . .')[24] tended to appear doubtful about most things. 'I remember seeing him one day in the bar at Television Centre,' recalled his friend Barry Took:

> He was sitting there, having a drink, wearing this wartime outfit. I said to him, 'What are you up to?' And he said, 'Oh, it's a new series we're doing for the BBC. About the Home Guard. It's a *disaster*, my dear boy, I really can't tell you, oh, it's absolutely *appalling*, it can't *possibly* work, no, no, my dear boy, it's an absolute *disaster!*' And I looked at him and thought, 'I bet it isn't!' But that was Le Mez, that was his attitude – always thinking that the worst could happen.[25]

It was not long, however, before other people associated with the programme began feeling less than sanguine about its prospects. Early in May, Paul Fox, the Controller of BBC1, viewed a tape of the pilot episode, and had misgivings about what he saw:

> The thing – the one thing – that I objected to was the title sequence. In that original version, the opening credits featured actual shots of refugees fleeing the German army in France and Belgium, and the closing credits also featured authentic war

scenes. And I have to say I didn't like that. At all. The reason I didn't like it – you have to realise that I'd been brought up in factual television, in news and sport and then in current affairs – was that I was very much against this mixing of fact and fiction; film of actuality belongs to factual programmes and should not be used mischievously in comedy programmes. And I couldn't understand why David and Michael [Mills] were so keen on including the sequence in *Dad's Army*, because, to me, it seemed unnecessary, unfair, unrealistic and, well, silly, and as this was a comedy programme, and as there were plenty of people still around who'd been in the services and lived through that time, I did feel that one had to step just slightly carefully. I know it was only 15 or so seconds, and it was, let's face it, a piddling matter, but in the end it became an issue of principle, really.[26]

Fox was only doing his job – one of his responsibilities, as channel controller, was to anticipate the mood of the viewing public (as well, inevitably, as that of the press and various pressure groups), and judge which risks were (and which were not) worth running – but that was not quite how either David Croft or Michael Mills, in the heat of the moment, interpreted his intervention. 'We were bloody annoyed,' the normally equable Croft complained. 'They were wonderful captions. They depicted all the massed forces of the *Wehrmacht*, and the tanks and all the rest of it, contrasted with the individually marching members of the Home Guard. That, to me, was what the show was all about, and, by objecting to it, Paul Fox, in our view, was just demonstrating that he had the opposite of the Midas touch as far as comedy was concerned.'[27]

A meeting – attended by Croft, Mills, Tom Sloan and Bill Cotton – was hastily arranged and held in Paul Fox's office. Everyone present, it seemed, had a different theory as to how the 'piddling matter' had been turned so quickly into 'an issue of principle'. Bill Cotton believed that the catalyst had been Fox's aversion, in those days, to all things German: 'Paul had served in the war – in the Parachute Regiment – and he was Jewish, and he had a "reaction" against Germans. I mean, I once bought a German car, and Paul had said, "What are you driving *that* car for? It's *German*!" But he really was very, very, disturbed about the idea of those credits. He took the line that, "If *you* think the war was funny, there are a lot of people around who *don't*." '[28] Michael Mills, on the other hand, suspected that Fox's background in Talks and News and Current Affairs under the redoubtable Grace Wyndham Goldie had made him unsympathetic both to the needs and ambitions of the Light Entertainment department in general and of Comedy in particular. Fox himself, in turn, sensed that Mills was using the disagreement as an excuse to undermine the authority of a controller who had only been promoted to the position a few months previously:

> It was a test, I think. I mean, I'd only just arrived, I'd barely bedded down, and Michael was quite keen to test the new controller. Let's not kid ourselves: Michael had that sort of rebellious nature – he loved a fight – and I'm sure he thought to himself, '*I* know that these credits are a good idea. *I'm* Head of Comedy. Why is this silly bugger on the 6th floor trying to stop me from doing it?' So there was a bit of that. And it was a pretty heated meeting. Don't forget I was on my own: here were four guys from Light Entertainment, making a case for keeping these credits, and there was I, keen to prevent the programme from setting a bad example. And in the end, somebody had to win.[29]

In the end, Paul Fox won. 'Tom Sloan caved in,' claimed Croft. 'Just when it looked as if Paul was prepared to agree to let me keep my captions, Tom said, "Well, on the other hand, of course, if *you're* not happy, Paul, we won't do it", and he just sort of surrendered, having won the argument.'[30] Bill Cotton was not surprised: 'Paul is basically bullish – with a small "b", if you know what I mean. I don't mean it in a bad way, but in order to get his own way he would try to create an atmosphere in which people wouldn't argue with him. You'd end up having to just laugh and get on with it.'[31]

David Croft and Michael Mills got on with it, but neither man felt like laughing. Mills wrote a bitter note to Fox on 23 May, not only acknowledging that the offending shots would, as requested, be 'replaced by something entirely innocuous', but also registering his 'profound disquiet' over the decision:

The whole object of this comedy series is to contrast the pathetic, comic, but valorous nature of the Home Guard, who believed at the time that this (the Nazi hordes) was what they were up against. It seems to me to be not only right but essential that this fact is brought home to the viewers – and it is, surely, our justification for doing a comedy programme on this subject.

Looking, as I do, at the abrasive nature of some of the output of other departments in the BBC television service I cannot help wondering whether we, in the Comedy department, are controlled by different standards, i.e. clowns must stay clowns.

In any case this decision cannot help but have a depressing effect upon me and upon some other people working in this department. The thought that other departments in television are allowed to advance their output into new areas, while we, apparently, are not, can only have a bad effect in the long run.[32]

Fox replied four days later, rejecting the suggestion that the Comedy department was being held back from dealing with 'abrasive' subject matter – 'From the department that produced *Till Death*', noted Fox, 'that's pretty rich'[33] (indeed, it would soon seem even richer, as both the strikingly free-form *Monty Python's Flying Circus* and the notoriously saucy *Up Pompeii!* would reach the screen during the following year)[34] – and questioning the extent to which *Dad's Army* really was 'breakthrough territory'.[35] Fox advised Mills that 'it would be more profitable to continue our discussion from two armchairs',[36] but Mills continued to brood over the matter while a crestfallen David Croft supervised the creation of a new set of titles: an animated opening sequence (designed by Colin Whitaker), featuring a union flag and a swastika facing up to each other from opposite sides of the Channel, and a closing sequence, featuring shots of the principal members of the cast guarding over the English countryside.

Little, if any, lasting damage (aesthetic or dramatic) was done by the enforced changes, except, perhaps, to the *amour propre* of Mills and Croft[37] – and one could, in fact, contend that the title sequence was more apt and effective without either the dubious use of images of real wartime suffering and the visual representation of an enemy who, after all, was never actually encountered. It is not difficult, however, to sympathise with Croft's exasperation at the immediate disruption these revisions caused to his pilot episode:

It was a mess. Someone – I can't remember who, it could have been Tom [Sloan] – suggested that, in order to reassure viewers that the show wasn't going to be sending up our finest hour, we should add a 'prologue', showing the characters in the present day [1968] supporting the 'I'm Backing Britain' campaign. So now the first episode looked as if it started three times: first with the prologue, then with the credits, and then with the E. V. H. Emmett newsreel-style clippings. In other words – a real dog's dinner. But at least it got the show on the air.[38]

There was, however, still one more ordeal to endure before the show was finally able to go on air, and that was the preview. 'Oh dear,' sighed Jimmy Perry. 'Oh *dear*!'[39] The pilot episode was previewed on three consecutive evenings at Television Centre. David Croft recalled what happened:

We showed it to about three different audiences of about 150 people, and they were stopped from talking to each other. It was a Swedish lady [Kathryn Ernst], I think, who ran the sessions, and she had distributed questionnaires for them to answer and tick off and so on. She wouldn't let anyone discuss it until they had written all of their opinions down, and then it was thrown open to discussion. Well, they didn't like it. They didn't like it at all. People said things like: 'Why do we still have to have these things about the war?' and, 'Don't the authors know the war's over?' and, 'We've seen quite enough of this!' I think the best comment we got was, 'I quite liked it,' from one sleepy gentleman.[40]

Jimmy Perry, who attended each session alongside his co-writer, could only suffer in silence. 'You kept hearing the same thing,' he said. '"Rubbish!", "Don't like it!", you know, and this went on for *three* nights, and I was *dying*!'[41] Eventually, the results were all collated and a report was sent directly to David Croft:

I don't know whether Tom Sloan saw it as well. Perhaps he did. It had been his idea in the first place. He'd said: 'Look, we've got this organisation [the Audience Research Department], why don't we bloody well use it?' Well, we did. I never heard of them using it again! Anyway, it was not a good report – if people had heard about it there probably wouldn't have been a second series – so I'm afraid I suppressed the evidence and we went ahead just the same.[42]

Paul Fox scheduled the opening episode to go out on BBC1 on Wednesday, 31 July, at 8.20 p.m., and, in keeping with BBC Light Entertainment policy, the critics were denied a preview screening. 'There were two basic reasons for that,' explained Bill Cotton:

First of all, we believed that it was important that one saw a new show at home, in the evening, in a domestic environment, with all the usual distractions – the telephone ringing, little conversations, people coming and going, the cat and the dog, all those things – instead of seeing it at eight o'clock in the morning – which is not the best time to see comedy anyway – on your own or in a small group, and possibly nursing a hangover. We didn't want people to be *led* into a reaction by a critic; we wanted them to come to their own conclusions. Secondly, we didn't see any reason why we should make it easier for the critics to clobber us![43]

Viewers, however, did receive a friendly nudge in the show's direction from the *Radio Times*:

Dad's Army will bring memories flooding back for anyone who remembers the days of Dunkirk. It may even – as producer David Croft says – 'make father's wartime reminiscing respectable'.

But although *Dad's Army* is set firmly in wartime – the fun itself is timeless. Why not join the little community of Walmington on Wednesday as they face a probable invasion . . . and decide to answer the call?[44]

Fortune seemed to be favouring the show as the day of its debut arrived. A bitter and chaotic ongoing dispute between the contractually-reconstituted ITV companies and the Association of Cinematography, Television and Allied Technicians Union (ACTT)[45] was playing havoc with ITV's schedules: the union (which was not recognised by the BBC) had begun by blanking out the screen during advertisements, losing the ITV companies around £50,000 each night in revenue, and had then progressed to pulling the plug on a number of programmes as well. Audiences, as a consequence, were being driven over to the 'other side': 'We usually watch the commercial channel and hardly ever switch over,' complained one viewer, 'but with the strikes and my favourite programmes like *Coronation Street* going off, we have been forced to watch BBC.'[46] According to one newspaper poll, 62 per cent of the viewing public was watching 'more BBC programmes than usual'.[47] *Dad's Army*, it appeared, was about to find itself in the right place at the right time.

One or two of the cast and crew – such as Bill Pertwee – were working on that warm Wednesday evening when the show first went out, but most had settled down in front of their television sets to watch the world of Walmington-on-Sea finally reach the screen. 'I'd been in the most terrible state all day long,' Jimmy Perry revealed. 'We'd made all six shows by then of course, and I'd thought, "Well, it's *quite* good", but you never know how a sit-com's going to be received, so I *was* nervous.'[48] At 8.19 p.m., another episode of the popular western series *The Virginian* came to an end, and then, as a familiar revolving black-and-white globe appeared, a sombre male voice announced, 'This is BBC1', and, all of a sudden, there they were – Mainwaring, Wilson and all the rest of them – starting after they had finished, in 1968, with the announcement of a speech from 'a man of many parts – banker, soldier, magistrate, alderman and secretary of the rotary club – a good fellow all round': George Mainwaring. Rising proudly to his feet in front of a large union flag, this round little man began:

Mr Chairman, Mr Town Clerk, ladies and gentlemen. When I was first invited to be guest of honour tonight at the launching of Walmington-on-Sea's 'I'm Backing Britain' campaign, I accepted without hesitation. After all, *I* have *always* backed

Britain. I got into the habit of it in 1940, but *then* we *all* backed Britain. It was the darkest hour in our history: the odds were absurdly against us, but, young and old, we stood there, defiant, determined to survive, to recover and, finally, to *win*! The news was desperate, but our spirits were always high.[49]

The picture dissolved, the credits ran, Bud Flanagan sang the theme song, and then the E. V. H. Emmett-narrated 'newsreel' transported the audience back to the May of 1940. 'The massive Nazi war machine is pushing its way across Europe,' boomed Emmett as the screen filled with archival images of German tanks moving inexorably through virgin cornfields, 'laying waste neutral countries with a savagery unmatched in history.' Brave-looking British soldiers were pictured, and Churchill was shown inspecting the troops – 'Is Tommy Atkins downhearted? We'll say he's not! Why should he be, with a leader like this?' – followed by freshly filmed footage of the soon-to-be members of the LDV – Jones altering the direction of a road sign, Frazer sharpening the point of a wooden stick – and ending with the defiant declaration, 'So look out, Adolf! Every day our defences are strengthened! And, if they *do* come, let's give them a sharp word!' The sound of an 'all-clear' siren followed, accompanied by an establishing shot of the brightly polished front door of Swallow Bank, and then, inside, the camera caught sight of Mainwaring, standing by the window, smiling triumphantly to himself as the enemy planes departed. 'Ah!' he barked. 'Going home, are they?' The story, at last, had begun.

No time, from now on, was wasted, and everything flowed. One by one, each theme, each character, each connection, was introduced and established with rare speed and ease. Mainwaring, for example, sparked off the class struggle more or less immediately by boasting that he held a commission and had served in the last war:

WILSON	Somewhere in the Orkneys, wasn't it, sir?
MAINWARING	I was a commissioned officer, Wilson, and I served in France. During the whole of 1919.
WILSON	Yes, but the war ended in 1918, I thought, sir.
MAINWARING	Well, *somebody* had to clear up the mess!
WILSON	Oh, yes, of course.

Arnold Ridley,
Major.

Arthur Lowe,
Sergeant-major.

Bill Pertwee,
Schoolboy.

Clive Dunn,
Trooper.

David Croft,
Major.

Edward Sinclair,
Sergeant.

Frank Williams,
Schoolboy.

Ian Lavender,
Unborn.

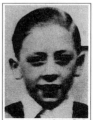

James Beck,
Schoolboy.

Jimmy Perry,
Sergeant.

John Laurie,
Home Guard.

John Le Mesurier,
Captain.

What they really did during the war.

The real Home Guard, lining up for inspection. Problems with ill-fitting uniforms dogged the Force through-out the war.

On guard. Britain was warned to expect the enemy in the most innocuous of disguises.

Weapons were a hard-won treasure for the Home Guard.

Michael Mills: the 'dark satanic' Head of Comedy at the BBC who spotted the show's potential.

From top right to bottom:

Tom Sloan: the BBC's prudent Head of Light Entertainment.

Paul Fox: the BBC1 Controller who clashed with David Croft over the opening credits.

Bill Cotton Jr: *'Dad's Army* was a surprise to me. A wonderful surprise.'

Huw Wheldon: 'The idea is not to avoid failure at all costs; the idea is to give triumph a chance.'

Cometh the hour, cometh the Mainwaring: the Walmington-on-Sea platoon cheer their leader.

Opposite:
Top: Jimmy Perry and his wife Gilda (*left*). David Croft (*centre*). Harold Snoad: David Croft's trusty assistant (*right*).
Bottom: 'Who do you think…': Bud Flanagan recording the theme song.

'Oh, it's *awful*!' cries Wilson of his captain's toupée.

'Ha-ha-ha!'

'No, no, no, no –'

'it's awfully *good*.'

Mainwaring and Wilson seldom see eye to eye.

Mainwaring and his frightfully common foe, Hodges.

The Vicar and the Verger.

'Don't tell him, Pike!': Mainwaring meets the enemy.

MAINWARING   Where were *you* during the war?
WILSON   Oh, Mons, Gallipoli, Passchendaele – I was a sergeant in the RA, sir.
MAINWARING   Oh, never mind that!

Wilson, in turn, sparked off the war of dispositions by issuing a decidedly limp introduction to the first group of volunteers:

WILSON   Would you, er, would you mind stepping this way, please?
MAINWARING   *Wilson!* Come here, come here! I intend to mould those men out there into an aggressive fighting unit. I'm going to lead them, command them, inspire them, to be ruthless killers. And I'm not going to get very far if *you're* going to invite them to 'step this way', am I? 'Quick march' is the order!

Frazer soon underlined his impudence:

MAINWARING   Occupation?
FRAZER   I keep a philatelist's shop.
MAINWARING   How do you spell that?
FRAZER   'S-H-O-P.'
MAINWARING   'S-H-' Ah! Thank you very much. I imagine you've not had any previous Army experience?
FRAZER   No. None at all.
MAINWARING   No. We can usually tell, can't we, sergeant?
WILSON   Yes, we can, sir.
MAINWARING   Once a soldier, always a soldier.
FRAZER   I'm a sailor. Chief Petty Officer, *R-R-*Royal Navy, retired.
MAINWARING   Sign there.

Godfrey's old Edwardian good manners came next – MAIN-WARING: 'Will you just sign there, will you?' GODFREY: 'Oh, I'd *love* to!' – followed by Walker's winking roguishness – MAIN-WARING: 'Any previous military experience?' WALKER: 'I got a girlfriend in the ATS!' – and Jones' reckless enthusiasm – MAIN-WARING: 'When did you leave the Army?' JONES: '1915, sir. I was invalided out, sir. The old minces – I couldn't quite make the focus, you see, sir.' MAINWARING: 'Presumably that's why you've signed the table.' There was just time for the fuse to be lit under the feud between the captain ('Are you out of your mind? Do you realise that *history* is taking place in there?') and the warden ('In five minutes' time an *ARP lecture* is taking place in this 'all!') before the arrival of the first parade, the first lecture, and the first 'uniforms' (LDV armbands) and 'weapons' (pouches of pepper). The episode closed with another speech from the round little man:

> Well, we're making progress. A short time ago, we were just an undisciplined mob. Now, we can deal with tanks. We can kill with pikes, we can make them all sneeze with our pepper – and, after all, even the Hun is a very poor fighter with his head buried in a handkerchief! But remember, men, we have one *invaluable* weapon on our side: we have an unbreakable spirit to win! A bulldog tenacity that will help us to hang on while there's breath left in our bodies. You don't get *that* with gestapos and jackboots! You get *that* by being British! So come on, Adolf: we're ready for you!

The credits rolled to the sound of the Band of the Coldstream Guards, and then it was all over: the end of the beginning.

An estimated audience of 7,171,000 had watched the programme (as opposed to the average audience of around 2,020,000 that had preferred BBC2's *Thirty-Minute Theatre* production of James Joyce's *Eveline*, followed by the *Europa* current affairs magazine, and the somewhat disappointing audience of 9,797,000 that had persevered with the heavily-publicised *Max* – a special hour-long edition of the Max Bygraves show – over on ITV).[50] The figure represented an encouraging start for a brand new situation–comedy, but, as David Croft realised more keenly than anyone, before the show could build on this promising foundation it would first have to survive the snap reactions of the television critics. 'You always turn to the papers with trepidation,' he admitted. 'It's always important to get good notices because the executives do read them and sometimes shape their views around them. Thankfully, the BBC, in those days, normally wouldn't be swayed by adverse criticism – they'd stick with a show, they'd allow it to grow – but, all the same, one could never take that for granted.'[51] In 1968, television critics had precious little time to form carefully considered judgements: 'There were no video tapes of course,' recalled Tom Stoppard (a 'fill-in' critic for the *Observer* at the time), 'and I don't think I went to a single preview screening . . . One "watched" at home.'[52] In those days, as the *Daily Mail*'s Peter Black observed, reviewers often had 'to cough up a notice as quickly as a theatre critic', dictating their copy over the telephone to their respective newspapers before 11 p.m.[53] It was not surprising, given the circumstances, that one or two experienced critics responded to the debut edition of *Dad's Army* in precisely the same way as they would any new situation-comedy; namely, with caution. Nancy Banks-Smith, for example, told readers of the *Sun* that the show seemed merely 'a nice little thing' – pointing out that the phrase was 'much used by women to describe someone who's no competition' – but she did concede that 'John Le Mesurier turns in a performance which is almost better than necessary. Nearly persuading you to keep a wary eye on the nice little thing. In case.'[54] Sean Day-Lewis, writing in the *Daily Telegraph*, was similarly circumspect, praising Croft and Perry's 'real gift for satire', but criticising the 'tendency to go for laughs at all costs, even if they punctured the atmosphere',[55] while Michael Billington of *The Times*, by contrast, felt that the show seemed 'afraid of making too much fun of a hallowed wartime institution', although he also acknowledged that Arthur Lowe's 'true, touching performance' was one that he would 'return to with pleasure'.[56]

What *was* surprising was the number of critics who were prepared, after viewing just one episode, to predict that the series would be a success. 'Who could resist,' declared Mary Malone in the *Daily Mirror*, 'the sight of little home guard commander, Mainwaring, harnessing his raggle-taggle fireside fighters into a force bent on the fight to a finish in the true Dunkirk spirit? This make-do-and-improvise war effort is funny and human and nostalgic. This war I'll watch.'[57] The *Sunday Telegraph*'s Philip Purser praised the programme for 'the brimming possibilities' of its subject matter, the 'nice period style' and 'a set of characterisations that have been maturing over a dozen years and in some of the greatest cellars in comedy',[58] while Tom Stoppard said in the *Observer* that the show was 'liable to bring a smile and a tear to every lover of England and Ealing'.[59] The most positive – and prescient – critic of all, on this occasion, was Ron Boyle, who wrote the following review in the *Daily Express*:

I cannot say I cracked a rib, split my sides, or even raised a good hearty belly-laugh, but some instinct is telling me that the BBC is about to come up with a classic comedy series.

The trouble here with the opening episode was that it had to set a stage for better things to come. I mean – ask anybody under the age of 30 about the LDV and they would probably guess it was some Iron Curtain secret police or a new ingredient that adds magic to soap powder. But now everything is established. The time is shortly after Dunkirk. Britain is ready to fight in her own backyard. Dustbin lid for a shield and broom handle for bayonet. Young viewers are going to treat it as a marvellous send-up. On a par with *Batman* and *Adam Adamant*. And then dad is going to clip everybody round the ear and tell them the Local Defence Volunteers really did exist – and so did the spirit of let's-get-at-them which now raises chuckles, but at the time was so deadly serious.

The more I think of it I don't see how this series can fail . . .

As the fusspot commander of the local pitchfork brigade, Arthur Lowe immediately scores. A pair of John Lennon spectacles, a toothbrush moustache, a high wing collar and we can forget all about Swindley . . . and begin to find a soft spot in our TV hearts for Mainwaring, the scourge of the Nazis.

The script mercifully avoided all the tempting cliché traps. Already I am ready to root for doleful Sergeant Wilson from the bank, Lance Corporal Jones, the doddering old local butcher, Joe Walker, the black marketeer, and all the rest of this motley gang.

Give it a week or two and I'll tell you whether this is really comedy's finest half-hour. All I say now is that the possibilities are tremendous.[60]

No new situation-comedy has ever received a more welcoming review from a national newspaper critic. The BBC was entitled to consider *Dad's Army* an immediate critical success.

The public, it seemed, also approved. Letters in praise of the programme began to trickle in, and the BBC's own sober-minded and scrupulous Audience Research Department produced a positive report. Although some members of the sample audience felt that the script was overly irreverent ('Very true to life,' commented one middle-aged viewer, 'but I didn't care for the lampooning of the LDV. Everything in the early days of the war had its funny side, but not buffoonery like this'), the majority judged the opening episode to have represented 'a very promising start to a series whose basic theme had considerable potentialities for comedy'. The report noted that viewers seemed particularly impressed by the programme's exceptional attention to detail: 'Such a true picture of village and small-town preparations against Hitler,' said one; 'Typical of what went on in those days,' observed another. 'Settings, costumes ("complete with gas masks") and make-up were also exactly right,' the report added, 'and the episode caught the 1940 atmosphere well, with many "authentic touches" . . . (As one delighted viewer remarked: "this play forgot nothing".)'[61] The show received a Reaction Index – a figure, based on the results of completed questionnaires, which the BBC took as a sign of the general reaction of an audience to one of its programmes – of 63 (out of 100) which was good for a brand new situation-comedy (the very first episode of *Hancock's Half Hour*, for example, only received a Reaction Index rating of 52),[62] and virtually assured the series of considerable internal encouragement.

The circuit had been completed: the bulb had lit up. *Dad's Army* had arrived.

CHAPTER V

Series One

*There are difficulties and there are failures. The aim, however, is
not to avoid failure – the aim is to give triumph a chance.*
HUW WHELDON[1]

They came, they saw, they laughed. Leave it alone.
NAT HIKEN[2]

'It didn't *feel* as if we'd made a particularly auspicious start,' Ian
Lavender remarked. 'There was no sudden realisation – "Oh! People
like it! We're a massive success!" – it was more of a slow dawning.
Like Topsy, it "just growed".'[3] None of the cast and crew was
willing to take anything for granted. The transmission of the first
series, in the minds of those who made it, was like a six-week-long
trial: all that they could do, now that the run had begun, was to sit
back, be patient, and hope for a favourable verdict.

Croft and Perry had been prudent: they had written the series in
such a way that, in terms both of tone and of structure, it would
make as much sense (in the unhappy event of a cancellation) as a
self-contained six-part story as it would (in the happy event of a
second commission) as the start of an open-ended sequence of episodes. The time-frame they had chosen ran from mid-May to late
August 1940 – in other words, from the formation of the LDV to
the climax of the Battle of Britain. Each programme – prefaced by
the same style of explanatory 'newsreel' – moved the action on a
little further into that first uncertain summer: the opening episode
marked the sudden birth of the volunteer force; the second focused
on the subsequent scramble to find or design a range of makeshift
weapons; the third – set near the end of July – featured the change

of name from 'LDV' to 'Home Guard', as well as the late arrival of a limited supply of First World War rifles; the fourth covered the methodical scanning of the skies for signs of imminent invasion; the fifth saw the belated delivery of uniforms, as well as the introduction of stricter controls over training and battle drill; and the sixth and final episode came to an apt but imaginary conclusion with a visit to Walmington-on-Sea from none other than Winston Churchill himself. 'If I'd had any conception that the show was going to run for nine series,' Croft reflected, 'I would have moved things forward at a slower pace. I would have held back the acquisition of arms, for instance, because it was very funny when all they had were picks and shovels and forks and carving knives on the end of sticks and all of those sorts of things. I could have run that theme for three or four more programmes at least. But one wasn't sure how long the series was going to last – in fact, the general feeling was that, at best, it probably wouldn't run for more than three series – so one had a sense of urgency to get on with it.'[4]

The BBC, however, was quick to reassure Croft that, as Bill Cotton put it, the show 'would be given plenty of time in which to breathe'.[5] The most tangible sign of this commitment came on 7 August 1968 – the date of the second broadcast – in the form of a contract for a second series. It was precisely the kind of well-timed encouragement – and well-placed publicity – that any programme-maker craved.

The second episode, entitled 'Museum Piece', went out earlier than usual at 7 p.m. (BBC1 had won the rights to screen a high-profile football match, the European Fairs Cup Final, later that evening), but, thanks in part to the disruption the ACTT's industrial action was continuing to cause to the schedules over on the commercial channel, the programme still managed to attract an audience of 6,817,500 – more than twice the size of that drawn to the movie *Ride the High Iron* on ITV.[6] That week's plot revolved around 'Operation Gun Grab', Mainwaring's impetuous plan to requisition a cache of antique firearms from the town's Peabody Museum of Historical Army Weapons; much of the comedy came from the fact that, before the guns could be grabbed, the platoon first had to find a way past the obstinate and surprisingly devious caretaker, one George Jones, the 88-year-old, thrice-married, irascible father of Jack. The critical response was, once again, encouraging – Richard Last, writing in the *Sun*, judged the show to be 'as good a comic idea for television as anyone has had recently'[7] – and so, increasingly, was that of the viewing public.

The approving letters continued to arrive on a daily basis at Television Centre. Many simply congratulated the BBC on the quality of the series: 'Each edition of this programme gets better,' enthused one correspondent. 'At last we have something that all the family can watch, delightful humour, and at the same time drawing attention to the British characteristics of which we all can be justly proud. I watch with my teenage family. They know nothing of these daft days but they enjoy the programme just the same.'[8] Others complimented the programme-makers on their attention to detail: 'Unless you were actually a member of the H.G. in its early stages,' remarked one old soldier, 'I can't think where you got the ideas.'[9] David Croft even received an admiring note from a fellow professional, Barry Took, describing *Dad's Army* as 'one of the funniest shows I've ever seen on TV': 'The script, casting, and direction are absolutely great,' Took wrote. 'Hope the series gets all the success it deserves.'[10] Only a couple of letters, at this early stage, were in any way critical of the programme, and both of these objected only to the volume of the studio audience's laughter.[11]

The most striking, and gratifying, aspect of this early correspondence was the extent to which the show seemed to have captured the imagination of so many people so quickly. Some of these viewers wrote in to say how much the character of Captain Mainwaring, or Sergeant Wilson, or one or more of the other members of the platoon, had reminded them of someone they had served alongside, or under, in the real-life Home Guard. Others sent in story suggestions – and in some cases full-length scripts – as well as offers of old uniforms, brassards, buttonhole badges and even authentic wartime vehicles.[12] 'That was all very heartening,' reflected David Croft. 'It certainly made one feel one was on the right track.'[13]

Episode 3 – broadcast on 14 August back in its regular 8.20 p.m. slot – was in many ways the strongest one yet. Entitled 'Command Decision', it concerned Mainwaring's often risible but sometimes rather touching desire to win the respect of his men. Realising that the absence of any arms other than pikes, pitchforks and catapults

('They'll be using *conkers* next!') is prompting morale to plummet right down to rock bottom, he instructs a sceptical Wilson to assure the platoon that proper weapons will arrive 'before the week is out'. Jones, upon hearing this, is almost overcome with emotion: 'I don't know what we'd do without you, Mr Mainwaring. You're our inspiration!' Mainwaring, clearly touched by this response, smiles benignly. Alone inside his office, he allows himself to sport the suspicion of a self-satisfied smile: 'The hour, and the man,' he says to himself softly. The following day, at the bank, he shows off his growing sense of self-assurance to his irritatingly irenic assistant: 'We're very slow to rouse in this country,' he informs Wilson. 'We don't like wars and bloodshed. But once we knuckle down to it, we fight better than anyone else in the world!' Wilson reminds him that it was, nonetheless, really rather rash of him to gamble on getting any guns before the end of the week, but Mainwaring remains unrepentant. Then, however, the blustering and brashly aristocratic Colonel Square (Geoffrey Lumsden) makes the first of what will prove to be many rude interventions, promising the platoon twenty rifles provided that 'Mainwearing' steps down and hands over the command to him. Mainwaring, grudgingly, agrees, only to find himself back in control once the combined shock of Square's wildly dictatorial demeanour and his ancient-looking muskets has driven the men back in his direction. Almost immediately, he slips once again into an acceptance of his old sense of destiny, reciting Kipling to himself and sounding more Churchillian with each passing inflexion. He knows, however, that unless those rifles arrive he faces abject humiliation. When, just in time, a modest supply is delivered, he is ecstatic: 'Their trust in their leader was not misplaced!' he declares, and, with his chest puffed up with pride, he rushes out to his men and receives their cheers.

Arthur Lowe's performance was as accomplished as anyone was likely to have seen on any channel, and in any genre, during the whole of that week. It was clever, crafty, entirely lacking in vanity and thoroughly *generous*: in every scene, in every line-up, he *listened* to each character as they spoke, reacting silently with arched eyebrows, rounded eyes, a weary rub of the face or a sudden moue of the mouth, highlighting the humour in each of the shots where he was absent. 'He *was* thoughtful,' Ian Lavender confirmed. 'He'd help you. In fact, after the first series, Arthur came over to me, very discreetly, you know, and said: "I know you don't have a lot to do, so get yourself a funny costume and just come and stand next to me." So in those early episodes you can see shots of me standing next to Arthur, saying nothing and looking stupid!'[14] It was in shots such as these, occurring most often as Mainwaring came to pause during his walk along the line, that the audience first came to know, and understand, and believe in each character:

MAINWARING	Pike! I told you yesterday: no mufflers on parade! You don't see Grenadier Guards wearing mufflers, do you, sergeant?
WILSON	Well, I never really thought to *look*, sir.
MAINWARING	Of course you don't!
PIKE	Well, I got a note from me mum, sir.
MAINWARING	*Note?* I'm not interested in *notes!* You're in the Army now, Pike!
WILSON	(*sheepishly*) Sir, I *think* perhaps you *ought* to read it.
MAINWARING	Oh! Very well! (*reads out loud*) 'Frank is starting with his chest again. He ought to be in bed. If he can't wear his muffler he's to come home or he will catch his death.' (*turns to Wilson*) We can't have him wearing that thing on parade! It makes the whole platoon look ludicrous!
WILSON	Well, perhaps he could wear it on patrol, sir? (*turns to Pike*) What time do you go on?
PIKE	Ten till twelve, sir.
WILSON	It'll be dark by then, sir.
MAINWARING	Oh, very well.

Lowe worked his way through these line-ups with all the skill and subtlety of a seasoned comedy straight-man: he looked at the likes of Pike, Jones, Godfrey, Walker and Frazer in much the same way as Oliver Hardy looked at Stan Laurel, or Jerry Desmonde looked at Sid Field, or Jimmy James looked at Hutton Conyers, or Ernie Wise looked at Eric Morecambe, or Jack Benny looked at just about everyone – a unique mixture of bewilderment, exasperation and uncontainable curiosity. The bewilderment makes one long to move aside, the exasperation makes one long to move on, but the curiosity – against one's better judgement, against one's will, against all reason – makes one stay rooted firmly to the spot. Mainwaring, Lowe understood, is the kind of man who is destined to make the same mundane mistakes over and over again – forgetting, for example, not to ask Walker how he came by some welcome but rare commodity, or forgetting not to invite Jones to reminisce about that other supposedly remarkable occurrence in the Sudan, or forgetting not to urge Frazer to repeat that recently snarled remark – and so, every time it happens, he just stands there, a sad but stoical figure, and waits for the whole sorry thing to blow over.

It would not be long before Michael Mills began advising Croft and Perry to lose the device of the line-ups – 'Don't do any more,' he boomed one night in the bar of the BBC Club, 'the viewers will get bored with Arthur walking up and down inspecting the platoon. There's a limit to the amount of laughs you can get with the same joke, you know!'[15] – but the co-writers wisely took no notice; the line-up, they understood, was as useful to an ensemble as the tableau curtains were to the solitary comedian – each one, in its own special way, marked out a moment in which to shine. The happy ritual drew one in and warmed one up – it was surely one of the reasons why, as the *Yorkshire Post* put it, the show had already, after just three episodes, 'become a "must" for a vast viewing public'[16] – and the deft role that Arthur Lowe played within it ensured that the scene would always seem real – 'So many comedies are all talk,' wrote Mary Malone in the *Daily Mirror*. 'Here, to say is to do.'[17] Even the *Morning Star*, by this stage, was ready to confirm the programme's broad appeal: 'Well worth watching,' Stewart Lane declared, 'for half an hour's respite from the day's cares.'[18]

Before any further progress could be made, however, the run was interrupted the following Wednesday (21 August) when BBC1 cleared its schedules in order to respond to the dramatic breaking news of the invasion of Czechoslovakia by the forces of the Warsaw Pact. Episode 4 ('Enemy Within the Gates') finally arrived a week late, on 28 August, but, reassuringly, it seemed to have held on to most of its regular audience, attracting a fairly healthy 8,080,000 viewers (compared to the 8,635,500 who had seen the previous edition), and receiving a solid Reaction Index rating of 65 (exactly the same as its predecessor).[19] In spite of the unexpected break, and the fact that ITV – having finally resolved its dispute with the ACTT[20] – was now offering a more competitive schedule,[21] *Dad's Army* continued to flourish.

The series finished strongly. Episode 5 ('The Showing Up of Corporal Jones'), broadcast on 4 September, was a spirited affair, notable in particular not only for Clive Dunn's assured performance as the desperately keen Jack Jones ('I'm perfectly fit, sir! I can still get the old cold steel in there, sir!') but also for the first, fleeting, appearance by Edward Sinclair as the meddlesome caretaker of the church hall ('If I tell the Vicar, he'll turf you out!'). As in previous weeks, there was something agreeably ironic about the fact that this prime-time programme, broadcast in the most youth-oriented decade of the century, was inviting one to identify with the plight of a septuagenarian. Following a visit from the sinister Major Regan (Patrick Wyldeck) – 'I think we're going to have to watch him, Wilson. His eyes are too close together' – Mainwaring is obliged to break some bad news to the most devoted of all his men:

MAINWARING I've got something to tell you, Jones.
JONES I'm going to get my second stripe, sir?
MAINWARING Well, no. Not exactly. I had a letter from GHQ, and, ah, they feel that, ah, well, the fact is that they feel –
JONES Yes, sir?
MAINWARING They feel that you're over age, Jones.
JONES *Over age?* I'm only 70!
MAINWARING Well, that's just the point. You see, *they* feel that 70 *is* over age.
JONES But that's not fair! I can do anything the other blokes can do! I bet it's that snooty major. I bet it's him. I only wish I had 'im registered with me for meat – he'd get it, but I'd cut it off the gristle!

Thanks in part to his own determined efforts – 'They don't call me "up 'em Jones" for nothing, you know!' – and in part to the cunning of others, a solution is found, and the crisis is overcome. The story, which, once again, was rooted in broad historical fact, worked well, and the humour flowed without any signs of force. More viewers than ever before – 8,837,500 – tuned in to see it, and the programme received an impressive Reaction Index rating of 70. An Audience Research Report on the episode noted that it had been 'even more favourably received than the previous four', appealing not only to those who had lived through the war years but also to younger viewers 'who could apparently believe in the situation and join their elders in "one long laugh"'.[22] The *Guardian*'s Stanley Reynolds reassured his readers that the programme 'is played in such an easy-going natural fashion that one imagines even the most hard-bitten professional anti-patriots must find it amusing,' and added that 'while in a lot of comedy one can see the seams between acting and directing, in *Dad's Army* things were so well balanced that no seams were visible'.[23] Even the most cautious critics were coming around: Maurice Wiggin of the *Sunday Times*, for example, had, after the opening episode, predicted nothing more than the possibility of an 'interesting' series,[24] but, after viewing the penultimate programme, he expressed the opinion that the show had 'settled down well . . . It wasn't too clear at first whether it was going to be weighted on the side of humour, or documentary nostalgia. Well, it *is* funny, and perhaps that's the best approach after all.'[25]

The sixth and final episode ('Shooting Pains'), was even more rewarding, with an effective guest appearance by Barbara Windsor (as Laura la Plaz, a small but strikingly supple sharpshooting artiste – 'The crack shot of the pampas' – whom Walker attempts to 'recruit' for an important interplatoon marksmanship contest), plenty of smart, funny dialogue, some well-honed physical business and a memorable cameo performance by Jimmy Perry. The clash of dispositions between Mainwaring and Wilson was, by this stage, a keenly anticipated highlight of each show, and, on this occasion, it was exacerbated by Wilson's wry observation that his superior's snug-fitting home-made pistol holder was, well, 'a little bit unorthodox':

MAINWARING   You know, the trouble with *you*, Wilson, is that you have a Blimp mentality. Of course it's unorthodox! If we're going to beat the Hun, we've

	got to be unorthodox! Can't get into a rut. Got to be flexible!
WILSON	Yes, sir.
MAINWARING	Why hasn't that girl brought my coffee? She *knows* I like it at 10.30 every morning!

Perry's contribution – as the Max Miller-ish stand-up comic Charlie Cheeseman ('The Cheerful Chum'), whom the whole platoon watches during a visit to the local Hippodrome Variety theatre – was the co-writer's belated, and brief, moment of glory in front of the camera ('And brilliant he was, too,' said David Croft).[26] What made the scene work so well was the way in which Croft cut away from Cheeseman after each ancient joke – 'My *wife*! My wife, she's so *fat*! She's so fat, I 'ave to put a bookmark in to remember where 'er mouth is!' – in order to focus on its stony-faced reception by Mainwaring ('I don't think this was a very good idea, do you?') and Wilson ('No. I don't think it was').

The story, and, indeed, the series, drew to a close just at the moment when the proud platoon, having won a highly improbable victory in the shooting contest, stood to attention as the guard of honour for the very distinguished visitor. The final frames were filled with the broad back and Homburg hat of Churchill, the smart salute by Mainwaring, and the sound of Monte Ray singing 'There'll Always Be An England'. It was all over. 'You have been watching . . .' the screen said, and 9,746,500 viewers[27] saw the credits for Lowe, Le Mesurier, Dunn, Laurie, Beck, Ridley and Lavender roll by one last time. The trial was over, and the verdict could hardly have been more favourable.

'I'm very sorry,' wrote one reviewer, 'to see the last (for the time being) of *Dad's Army*. It was that rare article, an excellent idea splendidly carried out. You can't say more for any programme than that.'[28] The sentiment, in fact, turned out to be a common one, as the critics queued up to celebrate the six episodes that they had seen. On 16 September, five days after the run had ended, Keith Smith, BBC TV's Chief Publicity Officer, sent another batch of clippings to David Croft, along with the following note: 'More newspaper reviews for you. Just for the record there has been no comedy series in the last twelve months which has attracted anywhere near the number of reviews *Dad's Army* has. Nor has any comedy series received this kind of universal praise.'[29]

Now, surely, there was no reason left to doubt it: *Dad's Army* was no ordinary situation-comedy. *Dad's Army* was something special.

CHAPTER VI

Success

A comedy show is an organic thing.
DENNIS MAIN WILSON[1]

*Creating a show is a very symbiotic relationship. You create this thing,
and then it starts creating you. Then it becomes like wrestling. You
kind of roll around on the floor together. Sometimes it's on top,
sometimes you're on top.*
JERRY SEINFELD[2]

'You know,' John Laurie remarked to Jimmy Perry early on in the
life of the show, 'I have played every major Shakespearean role in
the theatre and I'm considered the finest speaker of verse in the
country, and I end up becoming famous doing this crap!'[3] Perry was
not remotely offended by this observation, because by this stage in
their relationship he understood that it was merely Laurie's own
peculiar way of acknowledging something positive: *Dad's Army* had
indeed become a very successful situation-comedy. The first five-year
period of its existence was one of uninterrupted progress: the audience kept getting larger (rising from an average of around 8.2 million
in 1968 to one of around 16.3 million by the end of 1972)[4] and the
applause kept getting louder. David Croft won a BAFTA[5] award in
1971 for the Best Light Entertainment Production and Direction,
Jimmy Perry won an Ivor Novello award in the same year for the
best theme from any film, television or stage show, and both of them
won Writers' Guild of Great Britain awards (in 1969, 1970 and 1971)
for the best comedy script; and the entire cast was honoured in 1971
by the Variety Club.

The show seemed to be everywhere – on television (not only in its regular slot, but also in 'guest spots' on BBC1's annual *Christmas Night With the Stars*,[6] a one-off *Royal Television Gala Performance*[7] and an edition of *The Morecambe & Wise Show*: 'Do you think this is wise?' asked Eric. 'No,' answered Arthur, '*this* is Wise – the one with the short, fat, hairy legs!'),[8] in the cinema (a feature-length movie version was released in 1971),[9] in comic strips (featured each week from 1970 in *Look In* magazine), in the market place (colouring, dot-to-dot and 'activity' books, board games, a bubble bath, a set of sweet cigarette cards, a souvenir magazine and a series of annuals),[10] in an increasing number of countries overseas (beginning in 1970 with New Zealand, Australia, Holland, Belgium, Sweden, Spain, Malta, Finland, Sri Lanka and Tanzania),[11] and the show would be adapted for BBC Radio 4 in 1974. The cast seemed equally omnipresent. Arthur Lowe, for example, provided voiceovers for Spam, Lyons pie mix and Gold Blend coffee commercials, acted in a succession of Lindsay Anderson movies, stole the show as a drunkenly anarchic butler in Peter Medak's satirical farce, *The Ruling Class* (1971), co-starred with Ian Lavender and Bill Pertwee in the BBC Radio 2 situation-comedy *Parsley Sidings*,[12] and selected his favourite recordings for BBC Radio 4's *Desert Island Discs*;[13] John Le Mesurier supplied the reassuring voice behind both the Homepride ('Because graded grains make finer flour') and Kattomeat (with Arthur the sure-pawed cat) commercials, chose his own *Desert Island Discs* and contributed a BAFTA-winning performance to Dennis Potter's 1971 BBC1 play *Traitor*;[14] while Clive Dunn outdid them both during 1971 alone in terms of prime-time ubiquity by appearing as the subject of *Desert Island Discs*, *This Is Your Life* and his own BBC1 special, *An Hour With Clive Dunn*, as well as spending three weeks at number one in the charts with his novelty single 'Grandad'.[15] The success was infectious – which was just as well, because, as Clive Dunn acknowledged, so was the insecurity: 'We were always expecting to be told that the joy ride was over and that they had decided to stop "while we were winning" or some such nonsense.'[16]

The industry of the two co-writers during this period was particularly prodigious. As if the task of producing one script after another for a high-profile situation-comedy such as *Dad's Army* was not considered to be sufficiently stressful in itself, both men also busied themselves with a variety of other challenging personal projects.

Jimmy Perry, for example, wrote two more situation-comedies on his own: *The Gnomes of Dulwich* (BBC1, 1969) and *Lollipop Loves Mr Mole* (ATV, 1971–2).[17] David Croft produced and directed the first series of *Up Pompeii!* (BBC1, 1970) and the pilot episode of a situation-comedy (starring James Beck and Ronald Fraser) called *Born Every Minute* (BBC1, 1972), in addition to assisting (along with Richard Stone, Ray Cooney, John Chapman and Martin Shute) in the establishment of a new production company called Not Now Films and also producing and co-writing (with Jeremy Lloyd) yet another situation-comedy, *Are You Being Served?* (BBC1, 1972–85).[18] 'I think all of that [other activity] actually helped *Dad's Army*,' said Croft. 'It certainly helped as far as I was concerned, because with *Are You Being Served?*, for example, I had Jeremy Lloyd, a different writer, and a different cast, a different atmosphere, so it was like a sort of holiday in a way. It kept you fresh.'[19]

The BBC's attitude to the Croft–Perry partnership was one of enlightened indulgence. 'We had total control of everything,' Jimmy Perry recalled. 'We were *trusted*. There was such an air of *confidence* about the BBC in those days. You know, every now and again [an executive] might come over to us in the canteen and say, "What are you chaps up to?" And we'd tell him and he'd just sort of say, "Well, good luck with it!" And that would be that. Such a wonderful atmosphere in which to work.'[20] It helped, of course, that one of the writers also happened to be the show's producer-director – and a very canny producer-director at that. 'One never *invited* interference,' David Croft confessed. 'As far as I was able to arrange it, I wouldn't let anything – scripts, tapes, whatever – out of the office. Of course, if they were called for then you *had* to let them out, but there were still ways of dealing with that. I mean, if someone had ever asked me, "Can we see some scripts?" I would have said, "Oh, yes, of course, no problem at all", and then I would have got my secretary to wrap them up in several envelopes, put sellotape round them, you know – so they'd take a quarter of an hour to open. One could always resort to that sort of thing – gentle discouragement. I got away with it, fortunately, throughout my career. I had no interference at all.'[21]

Previous notable British situation-comedy writing partnerships – Muir and Norden, for example, or Galton and Simpson – tended to settle at the start on a particular mode of collaboration – usually face-to-face, in an office – and then stick with it, but Croft and Perry switched from a fairly detached, businesslike approach to something far more intimate and engaged midway through the run of *Dad's Army*. 'In the early days,' explained Perry, 'we'd meet up, work out a couple of plots, and then go our separate ways: I'd write one programme, David would write the other. Then we'd meet up again to sort them both out.'[22] Later on, he noted, they experienced a change of habit: 'We altered our style of writing completely. We decided that the best way to do it was for me to go round to his place, where we would just sit down and face each other, taking it in turns to write things down, and do each script together, line by line. I'm not sure *why* this was better, but I *think* it was.'[23] Croft believed that the success of the switch had something to do with their common background: 'Both of us had been actors. I think that was significant. When we were writing in the same room together, we'd sort of get up and play all of the parts and spark the dialogue off between us.'[24] In spite of working under pressure in such close proximity to one another over so long a period – 'two human beings', acknowledged Denis Norden of such a context, 'weren't really meant to gaze at each other for that number of hours across such a small space'[25] – their efforts were seldom undermined by anything worse than the mildest of disagreements. 'David and I never had a row in the whole time we were together,' Perry insisted. 'I don't really think our relationship would have survived a row – not when you were working as closely together as we were – but no, we never had any bust-ups.'[26] Each script, it seems, was constructed slowly, carefully, with each line, speech and scene slotting into place only after it had been subjected to a painstaking process of appraisal and editing. 'We worked on it and worked on it until both of us were happy with it,' said Perry, 'and when *we* were happy with it – that was it. There was none of this "first draft, second draft, third draft" stuff. We very rarely did rewrites. In fact, we very, very, rarely changed anything.'[27]

A Croft and Perry script was there to be read, not revised. 'Oh, they all wanted to change it,' Perry said of the actors. 'Of course they did. But that was something we would never tolerate. We had great strength, David and I, and we never tolerated any actor changing the lines. Mind you, there were some tough old pros among them, I can tell you, and they were good, they were smart – they'd try to separate David and me, get in between us, you know, but it never worked. We stuck together.'[28] One reason why the writers saw no reason for revisions was the fact that so much of each script – the scenes, the lines, the attitudes and the actions – had been shaped to suit the strengths, and the weaknesses, of each individual member of the cast. 'It wasn't a case of them bringing themselves more and more to the characters,' Croft explained. 'It was a case of *us* writing the characters more and more towards their own personalities. As soon as you've got the actors – got to *know* them – then you can adapt the material to match the way they act and react.'[29]

Not all of the actors bore a particularly close family resemblance to the characters that they portrayed – Ian Lavender, for example, may have been the least experienced member of the cast, but he was no 'stupid boy'; Clive Dunn did tend to panic sometimes, but, unlike his chronically respectful alter ego, his sympathies were firmly on the side of the socialists; Bill Pertwee was as pleasant and popular as the horrible Hodges was loutish and loathed; and Arnold Ridley (in spite of the fact that well-meaning assistants went to great lengths to assign him a dressing room within easy reach of the lavatory) was not incontinent – but in some cases the similarities were much too pronounced to be missed. John Le Mesurier, for example, was more than happy to blend in with Wilson's air of lazy elegance. James Beck had all of Walker's charm, and more than a little of his cheek. John Laurie, according to Jimmy Perry, was 'just like' Frazer: 'He'd start work on each programme muttering, "I'm worried about this one, laddie, I don't know if it's going tae work", and then he'd end it by saying, "Well, I never doubted that it would be all right!"'[30] Arthur Lowe, perversely, used to solemnly insist that 'there was nothing of my own personality in Mainwaring'[31] – a claim that, as David Croft confirmed, caused many a jaw to drop: 'Arthur was *enormously* like Mainwaring. No doubt about it at all. And Jimmy and I took all kinds of things from his own personality and wrote them into the part. Somehow, he never seemed to notice.'[32]

No one, not even his closest friends and family, denied that Lowe was indeed a somewhat pompous little man. 'He was very conscious of his position,' Ian Lavender recalled. 'He saw himself as the senior man on the set, the leader of the cast as well as the captain of the platoon.'[33] Clive Dunn was not alone in thinking of Lowe as 'a true blue Conservative' – 'They should take them out and shoot a few,' he once said of some striking dustmen, 'that would teach the monkeys'[34] – and he was certainly something of a snob – 'He's not our sort,' he once said dismissively of Dunn, 'he's Variety, you know.'[35] He was also rather prudish: the topic of trousers (the removal of) was guaranteed to get him hurriedly tut-tutting. 'Trousers are very personal things, you know,' Croft and Perry had Mainwaring say during one episode. 'Not to be bandied about.'[36] Lowe, they knew, agreed wholeheartedly with such a sentiment. Anything to do with the dropping, losing or doing without of the full set of conventional nether garments was deemed by Lowe to be far too suggestive and therefore completely unacceptable. He felt so strongly about this subject, recalled David Croft, that he ended up insisting upon the insertion of a clause in his contract which forbade his employers from forcing him to go trouserless in public:

> That came about when we were making the film [in 1970]. Jimmy made the mistake of telling Arthur about this idea he had to denote the passage of time between the formation of the platoon and its emergence as more of a coherent unit. He saw them marching along as a mob, you know, and then gradually their clothes would come off – they'd be marching in their long johns – and then the uniforms would go on. So he told Arthur about this and how hilarious it was going to be – Jimmy had a habit of telling people ahead of time about how hilarious certain features were going to be – and Arthur, of course, got straight on to his agent [Peter Campbell] and said, 'I'm not going to do *that*!' And so he actually had it put into his contract – that he would not be required to remove his trousers! Why he was so sensitive, I don't know, but that was Arthur – very much like Mainwaring.[37]

Preparations for the second series went well. The writers were more comfortable with the actors, and the actors were more comfortable not only with their roles but also with each other; the world of Walmington-on-Sea now seemed more familiar, more convincing, more real, on both sides of the camera. Rehearsals, however, were not without their problems. 'One of our big worries,' said Jimmy Perry, 'was Arthur Lowe. Although when it came to the recording in the studio he was magnificent, it was a struggle to get him to learn his lines during rehearsals.'[38] There was always the danger that the innumerable delays and diversions caused by Lowe's generally limp grasp of the script could have created serious tensions within the cast, but, according to Ian Lavender, the other actors were unusually understanding:

> It wasn't off-putting as such. Arthur did seem only to learn it on the rehearsal room floor, but it wasn't exactly an onerous process. It wasn't that *long*, for heaven's sake. We were rehearsing 27 minutes, split up between all the actors, so no one had really huge chunks of dialogue to work on. But yes, an awful lot of time was spent whilst Arthur learnt his lines. If you didn't like Arthur, or you didn't like the end result, you would've resented it, but that was the way Arthur worked, and the end result was worth it.[39]

It hardly helped, however, that an unrepentant Lowe made a point of declining to take his script home with him – 'Oh, I'm not having that rubbish in the house!'[40] – and never seemed aware of the chaos that he was causing. 'I remember one time,' said Lavender, 'when I thought we'd *never* finish the scene':

> It was in this episode ['Everybody's Trucking'] where Mainwaring had to inspect Jones' van, and, every time he'd put his hand or foot on some part of it, something fell off. Now, this had to be planned *very* carefully, because there weren't miniature cameras or anything wireless like that in those days [to enable a member of the crew to see when to trigger the 'accidents'], so it all had to be done on word cues. When Mainwaring said so-and-so, the running board falls off. When he said so-and-so, the headlight falls off. And so on. Well, there was Arthur, not exactly ad-libbing but slightly fluffing his lines, and bits of the van were falling off without him being anywhere near them. The guys [in the crew] were going, 'Er, that's the word – *off*!'

And there was Arthur, still searching for a word, some distance away from the bit that had just dropped off. So it all had to be done over and over again. It was mayhem![41]

David Croft, who was left to cover up the mess, probably had most cause, most often, to feel exasperated:

He never got any better. A lot of those hesitations that you see on the screen are actually Arthur thinking to himself, 'What the hell am I supposed to say next?' Sometimes, of course, that sort of thing helps an actor, because it means that the thought process has to be there – you know, if an actor knows the part inside out they can be inclined to push the line in too quickly, whereas if there's a slight hesitation, although it's only a fraction of a second, it's an important fraction. So sometimes it worked to our advantage. On the other hand, he did paraphrase some very good lines; we didn't get quite what we wanted and there was no hope of doing a re-take once the line had gone. So it could be very frustrating.

John Le Mesurier was quite different from Arthur in that respect. He had a photographic memory – he used to say, 'Don't tell me, don't tell me, it's on top of page 82', and he could 'see' the picture, see the page. And he was always in rehearsal a quarter of an hour before we started, and he always knew his part. Quite extraordinary.

Arthur just wouldn't take away his script. He always kept it in a desk in the rehearsal room. I think his problem was that during his days in repertory he'd *had* a more or less photographic memory and later on it had begun to fail him. So he didn't realise that he needed to actually get down and *study* the part. John Le Mesurier would call me and say, 'Can't you get him to *learn* the bloody thing?' So I started sending him *two* copies of the script. I told him, 'You can leave one in the rehearsal room and perhaps you'd like to place the other one under your pillow in the hope that some of it will percolate through the feathers during the night!' But all he did was go up to Jimmy and say, 'David seems to be in a foul mood these days. What do you think caused it?'[42]

Croft forgave him, just like everyone else forgave him, because of the innumerable occasions when he did everything right, and made an unfunny line seem funny, or a funny line seem even funnier, with a sublime piece of timing, or a sly arch of an eyebrow, or a sudden gasp of indignation, or some other smart little technical trick that only the finest kind of comedy actor could execute without the slightest sign of effort. He was good, and that made up for everything.

Quality was what counted. Everything about the show – not just the script and the acting, but also the sound and the images – had to be of the highest possible standard. The choice of studio, for example, was, as David Croft explained, always an important consideration:

> We tried, whenever possible, to avoid the big studios [at Television Centre]. Studio 1, for example, was massive – you could get lost in there. Also, in those days, there were no curtains around the audience to contain them – I had to introduce that – and they were not lit at all; they were in a dark limbo, like a sort of operating theatre, really. And we had enormous problems getting the right balance between the position of the microphones over the audience and the speakers. I did a lot of work with the sound engineers to get that balance right, because it's a very tricky thing: if you had a good sound engineer – and we had [from the third series onwards] a great one, Mike McCarthy – he would understand where the laughs were and wind up the microphones, because you can't have them up all the time – you'd get echoes. That sort of thing actually makes a real difference to how a show comes across on the television.[43]

Croft also ensured that the camera captured the essence of the comedy:

> In those days, the picture wasn't all that big, and so therefore you needed your close-ups. The art of direction involved choosing which shot to draw the attention of the audience to. You had to know where the laugh was. You had to study the scene in rehearsal, look at the person giving the feed-line, and the

scene-setting 'newsreels', however, were dispensed with, and the structure of the series was made a little more flexible than before (with the emphasis switching from the evolution of the Home Guard to the development of the individual characters), but otherwise the format remained the same. It was unfortunate, however, that the second series more or less coincided with the brief but destructive period at the BBC when, as part of an ill-conceived cost-cutting exercise, all but a few Light Entertainment shows were wiped after being broadcast so that the videotape could be reused. 'One of the factors which [normally] helped to save my programmes from destruction,' commented David Croft, 'was that I was on the staff and, therefore, always present when a piece of paper came round requiring a producer's agreement for a show to be wiped. I always contrived to withhold consent. I can only conclude that when the necessary form appeared for these six programmes I must have been on holiday.'[48] Only one episode – 'Sgt Wilson's Little Secret' – was thought, initially, to have survived the subsequent carnage (copies of two more would be uncovered more than thirty years later),[49] but it appears, on the evidence both of the scripts and the record of contemporary reactions, that the series picked up rather neatly where its predecessor had left off. Episode 1 ('Operation Kilt') saw the platoon commence the long and arduous process of semi-professionalisation (fifteen minutes of PT before parade and a testing sequence of Regular Army-style training exercises), while Episode 6 ('Under Fire') focused on the anxious watch for incendiary bombs. The episodes in between tended to centre on particular characters and relationships: there was one on Godfrey along with his two sisters, Dolly – 'Charles, dear, it's that nice bank manager, Mr Mainwaring. He's got a big gun with him' – and Cissy – 'Have a little word with that nice Mr Walker tonight, will you Charles? We need some more chocolate drops'; one on Jones – 'Ah, a competition like. Well, that seems fair, don't it, Mr Frazer?' – and Frazer – 'It will be if you stop bribing them with steak'; one on the awkward *ménage à trois* of Wilson, Mrs Pike – 'He does look pale, doesn't he, Frank?' – and her curiously fatherless son – 'You know what they say, Mum: pale and passionate!'; and one on Walker and the rest of the platoon – 'Walker is just one of millions . . . but to us he's an important counterstone in our organisation!'. Three of the shows were directed by Croft's very able assistant, Harold Snoad, but both the tone and the style remained constant.

The opening episode – broadcast on 1 March 1969 in the more high profile slot of 7 p.m. on a Saturday – was seen by 13,887,500 people: about 6.5 million more than had watched the competing programmes on ITV, and over four million more than had seen the final show of the previous series.[50] '[I]f this was a sample of what was to come,' the BBC's Audience Report declared, the viewers 'were in for a real treat.'[51] The prediction, it seems, was proven right: subsequent episodes attracted similarly sized audiences (the average was 12.2 million), and similarly positive responses.[52] The final episode – broadcast on 5 April 1969 – received a particularly enthusiastic internal report: 'Over two-thirds of [the sample audience] again found themselves laughing "immoderately and out loud" at these characters and their antics which, although larger than life, were basically so true to the spirit of the Home Guard', with some viewers adding that 'their youngsters wouldn't miss it for anything!', and the 'majority . . . described [*Dad's Army*] as the "best current comedy series on either channel"'.[53] Both the cast and the crew were in Norfolk at the time, shooting external sequences for the next set of shows, and Bill Cotton travelled down to congratulate the entire team on its current success: 'It was just a little gesture,' he said, 'to let everyone know they were being properly appreciated.'[54]

The message got through. The work that followed was more confident, more ambitious, more assured than before. The third series, the first to be broadcast in colour, was notable both for the length of its run – fourteen weeks rather than the usual six – and the depth of its characterisations. Mainwaring became bolder, but also more vulnerable; Wilson was a little less submissive, and, in his own sly way, slightly more sardonic; Frazer, who would soon be securely ensconced as the town's undertaker, grew even spikier, as well as – thanks to all of those candle-lit tales of the countless terrible ways to die on and around the gloomy Isle of Barra – spookier; Godfrey was frailer than ever and, once his rifle had been replaced with a first-aid kit, more sleepily pacific; Walker's rough diamond seemed to have received a furtive little polish, and Jones was still Jones, only more so. A more prominent role for the remorselessly crude (but newly promoted) chief ARP warden Hodges ensured that

Mainwaring's social pretensions would from now on be under fire not only from above but also from below, and his patience on parade was set to be strained even further by the introduction of two more irregular irritants: the vicar and the verger.

Frank Williams – best known to viewers in those days for his long-running role as the dithering Captain Pocket in *The Army Game* – was cast as the fussy and epicene Revd Timothy Farthing, while Edward Sinclair, yet another Croft original, was invited back to play the part of the permanently gurning Maurice Yeatman. 'I'd worked for Jimmy Perry before [in Watford rep],' Williams recalled, 'and I'd also done a couple of episodes of *Hugh and I* for David Croft, but when I first came into [*Dad's Army*] I thought it was just going to be for one episode.'[55] Right from the start, however, it was clear that there was a real rapport between Williams – a bright, gregarious, genuinely religious Londoner – and Sinclair – a somewhat reserved and rather studious Mancunian – as well as an obvious comic bond between their on-screen characters. 'Teddy and I got on so well together,' Williams remembered. 'We became very close friends. In fact, socially, Bill [Pertwee], Teddy and myself developed into something of a trio, just like, in the show, the warden, verger and vicar teamed up to provide Mainwaring and the Home Guard with a sense of conflict.'[56]

When the third series began on Thursday, 11 September 1969, at 7.30 p.m., *Dad's Army* was regarded within the BBC as, in the words of Paul Fox, 'a banker'.[57] Its role now was to win the ratings war, and, during the following few months, that was precisely what it did: scheduled straight after the well-established *Top of the Pops*, the show regularly drew in an additional two million viewers to BBC1, and averaged a weekly audience of around 12.1 million (three times the size of that attracted to ITV).[58] From start to finish, the run was remarkable.

It was a lively and varied series. Some episodes – such as 'The Day the Balloon Went Up' (which saw Mainwaring float high and helplessly over the verdant English countryside) – made good use of scenes shot on location, while others – such as the BAFTA-winning 'Something Nasty in the Vault' (which saw Mainwaring and Wilson sit side by side with an unexploded bomb on their laps) – exploited the intimacy of a carefully-lit studio. There was also room for gently comical character studies: 'Room at the Bottom' revolved around the discovery that Mainwaring was not, in fact, a commissioned officer, and 'Branded' revealed that Godfrey had been a conscientious objector during the previous campaign. Other shows were fairly broad, sometimes near-farcical, romps, such as 'No Spring for Frazer' (a Croft personal favourite in which the platoon became convinced that a missing butterfly spring had been dropped by the Scot inside the coffin of Mr Blewitt's recently departed brother. The series finally came to a close on 11 December with 'Sons of the Sea', a typically well-constructed episode which began with the usual kind of tension – MAINWARING: 'Wait a minute – I've had an *idea*!' WILSON: 'Now be *careful*, sir! Please, please, be careful!' – evolved into an intimate comic escapade – the men bundle together inside a boat, proceed to get lost in thick fog and end up convinced that they have drifted across the Channel – and concluded with the captain finding himself, once again, on the receiving end of a typically English punchline – '*Quelle est la gare?*' he inquires anxiously of a bowler-hatted man whom he assumes to be an unusually smartly-dressed Frenchman. 'Eastbourne, actually,' the man replies politely.

The final episode received the exceptionally high Reaction Index rating of 77, although, as the BBC's internal report acknowledged, the score was probably intended as a tribute not just to that one particular edition but also 'to the series as a whole'. It appears that recent, highly improbable, press speculation concerning the BBC's supposed reluctance to commission another set of episodes had encouraged some viewers to believe that what they had just witnessed was very likely to have been the last of *Dad's Army*: 'It had been an entertaining, warm-hearted series, one that the whole family could watch and enjoy,' the report concluded, 'and if this was, indeed, the last show, it was a great pity, as there still seemed plenty of situations to be exploited.'[59] Rumours of the show's imminent demise would, of course, soon prove to be unfounded: Tom Sloan, it is true, had indeed intended, as a routine matter of policy, to sit down after the third series had ended and assess the progress that the programme had made, but, as one of its staunchest supporters, there had never been any serious doubt about his readiness to commission another run.[60] Even Paul Fox, the show's supposed *bête noir*, chose this moment to confirm in a letter to David Croft his enthusiasm for the programme:

I am sorry it has taken me so long to write a note of thanks to you for *Dad's Army*. You made an enormous success of it and, like millions of others, I am only sorry it has come to an end. Temporarily, I hope.

Looking back to that first programme, I am glad to say you were right 100 per cent. Thanks to your persistence – and despite that title change! – the show became a great hit.

To you – and all who've been associated with this splendid series – many congratulations and grateful thanks.[61]

A fourth series duly followed in the autumn of 1970.[62] Each member of the platoon, from this point on, would sport a small rectangular badge, bearing the legend 'CP1', on the sleeve of his tunic: rather than standing (as it would have done in the real-life Home Guard) for the unit's location, it served instead as a sly authorial signature – these characters were the property of Croft and Perry. This telling little gesture could not have been better timed, because among the thirteen episodes in this series were examples of Croft and Perry's writing at its best. In the bitter-sweet 'Mum's Army', for example, Mainwaring was made to live out his very own version of *Brief Encounter* when, after enduring years of marriage to the unseen, unloving and unlovable Elizabeth, he suddenly meets the fragrant, elegant, gracefully flirtatious Fiona Gray (played by Carmen Silvera). Everything she says and does convinces him that, at long last, he has found his soul mate, and so, when he learns that she is set to leave, he opens up, for the first and probably the final time in his life, and pleads with her to stay:

MAINWARING   But – but – I don't *want* you to go! The whole pattern of my life has changed. I just live from one meeting to the next.

MRS GRAY   I know. And I'm just the same, but it's the only thing to do. People are talking.

MAINWARING   People always talk! Who cares about that?

MRS GRAY   But there's your wife.

MAINWARING   Nobody'll talk to *her*! Hasn't left the house since Munich!

MRS GRAY	Be sensible, George. You can't afford scandal and tittle-tattle.
MAINWARING	I tell you I don't care!
MRS GRAY	But there's the bank.
MAINWARING	Damn the bloody bank!
MRS GRAY	George!
MAINWARING	I'm sorry. Look: *don't* get on that train. Look, we'll meet once a week –
MRS GRAY	George, you're making this very difficult for me, but I've made up my mind. It's the only way. *(the next departure is announced)* There's my train.
MAINWARING	Look, Fiona, I've never begged anything from anybody in my life, but I'm begging you not to go.
MRS GRAY	I'm sorry, George.[63]

It was the kind of story, and the kind of tone, that the writers of a situation-comedy will only try when they feel absolutely sure not only of themselves but also of their audience.

'A. Wilson (Manager)?' was another episode – equally audacious in its own quiet way – that had a beautifully judged script. One morning in the bank, Mainwaring receives two telephone calls: the first is from Head Office, informing him that Wilson has been made manager of the Eastgate branch of the bank; the second is from Area HQ, informing him that Wilson's commission has come through. While he is still reeling from these two unexpected blows, the telephone rings again. This time it is the vicar. 'What are *you* going to tell me about Wilson?' snaps Mainwaring. 'That he's been made Archbishop of Canterbury?' When Wilson finally, belatedly, glides in to begin work, Mainwaring is positively apoplectic:

MAINWARING	Judas!
WILSON	I beg your pardon?
MAINWARING	*Judas!*
WILSON	I'm awfully sorry but I don't quite follow you.
MAINWARING	You follow me all right, Wilson – you've been following me for years, waiting to step into my shoes![64]

Suddenly, all of the resentment that has long been simmering within Mainwaring comes rushing to the boil:

MAINWARING   Just because you went to some tuppenny-ha'penny public school!

WILSON   Yes, well, I wouldn't call Meadowbridge *that*.

MAINWARING   Meadowbridge! You know where *I* went, don't you? (*bitterly*) Eastbourne Grammar!

WILSON   Well, what's wrong with that?

MAINWARING   Oh, don't be so patronising about it! I had to fight like hell to go there – and I had to fight even harder to *stay* there!

WILSON   Well, that's all to your credit.

MAINWARING   *You* never fought for anything in your life! Brought up by a nanny, father something in the City – all *you* had to do is just sit back and let everything come to you!

WILSON   Yes, well, it wasn't *quite* as simple as all *that*.

MAINWARING   I've been the manager of this bank for over ten years now. I ought to have gone on to better things *years* ago. Yet every time I've gone for an interview for a promotion it's always been the same thing: 'What *school* did you go to?' And as soon as I told them, that was that!

WILSON   Well, I'm sure *that* didn't really influence them!

Things proceed to fall apart: Mainwaring grows increasingly spiteful, Wilson increasingly smug ('Ambition's turned his head,' complains a tearful Mrs Pike), and, as the day of their separation arrives, the two men, like some old warring, soon-to-be-divorced couple, seem intent on saying all of those things that are best left unsaid:

MAINWARING   Why are you going now? It's only Wednesday. You don't take up your position in Eastgate until Monday.

WILSON   Yes, well, I know, but they've been having a lot of difficulty over there, sir, you see. The manager's been called up, and Mr West from the

116

	Head Office is going to stay on in Eastgate in order to show me the ropes.
MAINWARING	Mr West of Head Office, eh? We *are* honoured! Why are you travelling in uniform?
WILSON	(*casually*) Well, I don't know, just sort of, kind of *handy*, you know.
MAINWARING	*Rubbish!* You're travelling in uniform so that you can parade up and down the platform looking for salutes!
WILSON	(*suddenly rattled*) And why not? *You* did!
MAINWARING	How do you mean?
WILSON	The day you got your new uniform, I followed you.
MAINWARING	You followed me?
WILSON	Yes, I did! And I watched you go up and down the high street *three* times looking for a serviceman to salute you, and in the end you had to make do with a sea scout!
MAINWARING	Say what you have to say and go.
WILSON	(*calming down*) Well, I've just come to say goodbye, sir. I wondered if you'd like to come up to the station and see me off.
MAINWARING	I certainly would not! Our relationship ends here and now.
WILSON	Oh, really, sir! After all we've been through together, for heaven's sake, can't we let bygones be bygones?
MAINWARING	Don't try to soft soap me!

Wilson reaches out to shake Mainwaring's hand, but Mainwaring fails to respond. They salute each other in silence, and then Wilson departs. Mainwaring, however, cannot resist shouting out after him: 'And if I *did* look for salutes, at least *I* did them properly – that salute you just gave me was *rotten!*'

Wilson's independence turns out to be brutally brief. On his very first morning as manager, just after he has settled down behind his imposing desk inside his impressive office, the air-raid siren sounds, he leaves to enter the shelter, and then later, when he returns, he finds that the very first bomb to have been dropped on Eastgate has landed on the bank. Searching through the ruins, he comes across the portion of the door that bore his name. He picks it up, reads the plate, 'A. Wilson, Manager', thinks to himself for a moment, then tosses it aside and moves on. Mainwaring sounds contrite when he hears the news from Head Office: 'At nine o'clock the poor chap was manager of a bank and at five past he had no bank to manage.' He calls Wilson into his office: 'It's most unfortunate,' he tells him. 'Yes, it is,' says Wilson. 'Most unfortunate.' Mainwaring is clearly sorry, but not that sorry: 'No – don't sit down,' he says coolly. 'I'm rather busy.' He hands his sergeant back his stripes – 'Get 'em sewn on by tonight. That's all' – and then Wilson, once he is back on the outside of Mainwaring's office, looks up wistfully at the name on Mainwaring's door, sighs softly to himself, and then goes off to serve, once again, in Mainwaring's platoon.

Both of these episodes dared to make explicit what would normally remain implicit: namely, that *Dad's Army*, like any other great situation-comedy, told tales about trapped relationships. Just as Hancock will never shake off Sid, and Harold Steptoe will never extricate himself from Albert, neither Mainwaring nor Wilson will ever be free of the other, nor will either ever escape from the prosaic constraints of Walmington-on-Sea. '*Dad's Army* needed that enclosed atmosphere,' David Croft remarked. 'It forced the characters to keep bouncing off each other.'[65] Croft and Perry usually lit this cramped little world from above, so that only the comedy was visible, but, from this fourth series on, they felt confident enough, in certain well-chosen episodes, to light it slightly from an angle, so that, for a moment, the prison bars were free to cast their shadows.

The programme, in many ways, was approaching its peak. There was only an hour-long special in 1971, the delightful 'Battle of the Giants' (watched by a record 18,735,500 viewers[66]). The following year, at 8.30 p.m. on Friday, 6 October, the fifth series commenced. Everything about this remarkable thirteen-week run of episodes – the quality of the writing, acting and direction, the pace, the tone, the rich variety of themes and moods, the carefully choreographed set-pieces, even the choice of locations – seemed to confirm that the show had reached a new level of maturity. The opening episode,

'Asleep in the Deep', set the standard for all that was to follow. The conception was simple – most of the platoon (along with Hodges) become trapped in an underground room at the local pumping station ('We're entombed!' cries Frazer); the execution was brilliant – a well-disguised water tank, an obediently leaking pipe and some glorious ensemble acting; and the effect was sublime. When Mainwaring and his men, with the sole exception of the sleepily recumbent Godfrey, responded to the crisis by performing a spirited burst of 'Underneath the Spreading Chestnut Tree' (complete with the full range of gestures), it was funny, but, so real had this comic world become, it was also, in a strange but meaningful way, entirely appropriate. The BBC's Audience Report on the episode was, unsurprisingly, full of positive remarks about 'one of the funniest series on television': 'Quite hilarious; the best laugh we've had for ages'; 'This is what the public wants . . . just good, clean fun'; 'It may be the script – or the cast – or a combination of both – but this show is witty – really funny stuff!'. There was plenty of praise for each aspect of the 'polished' production, including the performances of the cast as a whole ('Good old troopers – and very good to watch!') and Lowe and Le Mesurier in particular ('their facial expressions need no words'), the costumes, the sets, the general air of authenticity ('the facts are always so correct'), and even the standard of the make-up.[67] It was, quite simply, a programme of the highest quality.

Each subsequent episode in this run was watched, admired, discussed and then cherished as a memory. There was 'Keep Young and Beautiful', for example, which saw Mainwaring try on a toupee ('Oh, it's *awful*!' cries Wilson. 'Ha-ha-ha! No, no, no, no – it's awfully *good*. Awfully good. Oh, dear, oh, dear!') and Wilson squeeze into a 'gentleman's abdominal support' ('Watch it,' Mainwaring retaliates, 'you might snap your girdle!'). Then there was 'A Soldier's Farewell' (in which Mainwaring occupied the bunk beneath the bulge that was his wife and dreamed that he was Napoleon); 'Getting the Bird' (an ultimately rather touching little tale about a mysterious young woman whom Wilson appears to know); 'The Desperate Drive of Corporal Jones' (a simple but suspenseful comedy about a soon-to-be bombed barn); 'If the Cap Fits . . .' (featuring Frazer's brief but harrowing spell in charge of the platoon); 'The King Was in His Counting House' (in which Mainwaring invited his men to visit his home – 'Tonight, you may call me "George"' – for an hour or two in 'a happy carefree, relaxed atmosphere'); 'All Is Safely Gathered In' ('a joyous thing',[68] in the words of David Croft, which saw the platoon help gather in the harvest before succumbing to some particularly potent potato wine); 'When Did You Last See Your Money?' (involving Jones, £500 and Mr Blewitt's recently-stuffed chicken); 'Brain Versus Brawn' (which saw Mainwaring's men endeavour to outwit the 'younger, fitter chaps' during a training exercise by disguising themselves as firemen); 'A Brush with the Law' (in which the warden, the verger and Captain Square conspired against their mutual wartime enemy – Mainwaring); 'Round and Round Went the Great Big Wheel' (featuring an elaborately unreliable War Office invention); and, finally, 'Time On My Hands' (about a Nazi parachutist entangled on the town hall's clock tower).

These were the episodes that charmed the broad community. 'Brain Versus Brawn', for example, was seen by 18,634,500 people, which would turn out to be the biggest audience, for a regular half-hour edition, in the whole of the show's nine-year run, and an average of 16.3 million tuned in each week to watch.[69] It was excellence – more so than period, or genre, or limited choice – that was responsible for this rare popularity. Adults recognised the real-life roots of the relationships and relished the intelligence of the performances, children warmed to the characters and repeated the catchphrases, and everyone – regardless of age, or sex, or class – understood that this admirably entertaining show was an example of television at its best.

The following year, during the making of the sixth series, both the cast and the crew would be shaken by the premature death of James Beck,[70] and, as a consequence, the programme's near-perfect pattern of progress would suffer some disruption. The close of 1972, however, was a time of celebration: *Dad's Army*, that improbable idea, that 'nice little thing', had climbed its way right up to the summit.

THE
CHARACTERS

The missus looked at me and she said: 'What are you supposed to be?' I said: 'I'm one of the Home Guards.' She said: 'Well, what d'you DO in the Home Guard?' I said: 'I've got to stop Hitler's army landing.' She said: 'What – YOU?' I said: 'No! There's Harry Bates, and Charlie Evans, and . . . There's seven or eight of us altogether . . . We're in a GROUP!'

ROBB WILTON[1]

Be friends, you English fools, be friends!

HENRY V[2]

CHAPTER VII

An Officer and a Gentleman

*Other men are lenses through which
we read our own minds.*
RALPH WALDO EMERSON[1]

*Impelling power and restraining wisdom are as opposite as any two things,
and are rarely found together.*
WALTER BAGEHOT[2]

When, as a consequence of the exceptional success of *Dad's Army*, David Croft and Jimmy Perry agreed to publish a selection of scripts from past series,[3] they decided to include a potted biography of each one of the leading characters. It seemed, in the circumstances, a perfectly natural thing to do: after all, to those who tuned in to watch the world of Walmington-on-Sea on a regular basis, these fictional individuals had been alive for some time.

Mainwaring and Wilson were very easy to believe in. Whenever Mainwaring put down the telephone, summoned up the sickliest of grins and said, 'Just chatting to the little woman', and whenever Wilson responded to Mrs Pike's audible inquiry, 'Will you be around later, Arthur, for your usual?' by wrapping a hand over his eyes and whispering, 'Oh, *Mavis!*', nothing more needed to be said, or shown, because one already knew. Just by watching these two men each week, listening to their stories, following their exchanges, studying their asides, it was possible, without even trying, to compile brief biographies of both of them in one's mind:

George Mainwaring: Born in Eastbourne in 1885. His father, Edmund, was either – depending on whose account one chooses to believe – a well-regarded member of the Master Tailors' Guild who ran a high-class gentleman's outfitters on the Parade, or the beleaguered proprietor of a modest little side street draper's shop most easily identified by the assortment of workmen's trousers that used to hang and flap outside the window. George's childhood – unlike that of his brash, sporty, effortlessly popular brother Barry – was one long struggle, but he did manage to win a scholarship to his local grammar school, where he took a cold bath every morning, buried his nose in books, and did all that he could to cultivate a clear brain and a sharp eye. After school, he joined the Eastbourne branch of Swallow Bank, slowly and methodically working his way up from office boy to assistant chief clerk. When war broke out in 1914, he volunteered at once – only to be turned down on account of his poor eyesight; four years later, following several more unsuccessful attempts to join up, he was commissioned as a 2nd lieutenant in the Pioneer Corps, and arrived in France just in time to clear up the mess, but just too late to qualify for any medals. Shortly after returning to civilian life, he met and married Elizabeth, a nervous, big-boned, sensitive-nosed, reclusive vegetarian from a relatively well-connected family in Clagthorpe. The couple's childless but 'almost blissful' marriage received a welcome boost in the early 1930s when George was promoted to the position of Manager at the Walmington-on-Sea branch of the bank; he proceeded to immerse himself in his work, while she proceeded to hide herself away inside their modest little home at 23 Lime Crescent. In 1940, just when George seemed to have resigned himself to a life of quiet desperation, fate intervened, and he seized his chance to answer his country's call with his own special brand of bulldog tenacity.[4]

Arthur Wilson: Born in a large, rambling country house in Gloucestershire in 1887. His father was something in the City, his great uncle was something in the House of Lords. His childhood, thanks to an excellent and attentive nanny, was idyllic, and his education, at the medium-sized Meadowbridge public school, was also perfectly pleasant. After failing the exam to enter the Indian Civil Service, he began his working life in the City, where he soon acquired a reputation for romance rather than banking. He served in the Army from 1915 to 1918, securing a commission as a captain, and was in an excellent position to witness at first-hand all of the great wartime British disasters. Shortly after returning to civilian life, he met and married one of Sir Charles Cochran's Young Ladies; she left him soon after the birth of their only daughter, who would grow up to serve in the WRNS. In the early 1930s, while working at the Weston-super-Mare branch of Swallow Bank, he encountered an attractive young widow, Mrs Mavis Pike; when promotion to chief clerk took Wilson to work under George Mainwaring at Walmington-on-Sea, Mrs Pike, along with her young son, Frank, chose to follow him. In 1940, just when Arthur was waiting patiently for more good fortune to land in his well-tailored lap, Mainwaring intervened, and he resigned himself to at least a year or two of quiet desperation.[5]

One reason why these two characters were so easy to believe in was the fact that they seemed to believe in each other; it was obvious, from the way that Mainwaring studied Wilson and Wilson studied Mainwaring, that each man was the other's most devoted critic, biographer and social anthropologist. Mainwaring, for example, would analyse Wilson's appearance and demeanour, itemising his faults – the overlong hair ('You're not a violin player, you know!'), the unfastened collar and cuffs, the 'dozy' level of alertness, and the fact that his right hand had sometimes been known to come to rest on his hip ('It only needs a couple of inches more and you could be taken for one of those nancy boys!') – and then exclaim: 'Why must you give yourself *airs* all the time? Why don't you behave *normally*, like me?' Wilson, in turn, would make a mental note of each one of Mainwaring's many insecurities, and then, when the time seemed right, he would smile, give a knowing little look, and offer words of comfort ('Your face doesn't look nearly so round and moonlike') or commiseration ('How awfully embarrassing for you, sir'). Whenever the two of them were together it was the relationship – rather than merely the men – that one watched.

'It is no coincidence,' wrote one critic at the time, 'that each role was interpreted by a man who knows what real acting is, and not by some clumsy egomaniac.'[6] Arthur Lowe and John Le Mesurier were, in many ways, as unlikely a couple as George Mainwaring and

Arthur Wilson. Lowe's background was northern working class (born in Hayfield, Derbyshire, in 1915 – the only son of Arthur, a railwayman, and Mary Ford – brought up in Levenshulme, South Manchester, and educated at Alma Park Central grammar school); Le Mesurier's was southern upper middle class (born in Bedford in 1912 – the only son and youngest child of John Halliley, a well-known family solicitor, and Mary Le Mesurier – brought up in Bury St Edmunds in Suffolk, and educated at Sherborne public school in Dorset). Lowe's route to success was long, indirect and arduous. There was a spell as a stagehand at Manchester's Palace of Varieties (where he stood in the wings and studied such gifted comedians as Robb Wilton and Will Hay), and then, while serving in the Middle East as a sergeant-major in the Army, there was an important formative period spent performing in plays and revues for the troops. After the war had ended he made his professional stage debut in Manchester rep, then came years of hard toil in the provinces, the odd small role in British movies, a West End debut in 1950, and finally, from the early 1960s, regular work in television. 'Oddly enough,' he once reflected, 'it was never my ambition to be a star; I simply wanted to be the best character actor going, but stardom obviously came through television. I don't think I'd have done it without television.'[7] John Le Mesurier, on the other hand, ambled his way to fame: after allowing himself 'to be guided ever so gently into the occupation my parents knew best', as an articled clerk in an old and respected Bury St Edmunds firm of solicitors called Greene and Greene, he eventually summoned up the courage to inform his family 'that the law was about to lose an unpromising recruit'.[8] He took his mother's maiden name and began training to be an actor at the Fay Compton Studio of Dramatic Art in London (Alec Guinness, one of his contemporaries at the school, would say that Le Mesurier – 'whose brilliant comic timing was evident even then' – was the 'most distinguished of my fellow students').[9] A subsequent uneventful spell in repertory was rudely interrupted by the war (Le Mesurier startled his commanding officer by rolling up at Tidworth barracks in a taxi, with a set of golf clubs among his personal baggage and the smell of champagne cocktails on his breath, but he ended his period of active service as a captain in the Royal Armoured Corps on the North-West Frontier of India), and then, upon being demobbed, he drifted into movies and never looked back – or, indeed, forward. 'It might have been nice to have been a star for a while,' he once remarked. 'But I really don't mind. You know the way you get jobbing gardeners? Well, I'm a jobbing actor. I don't mind whether I spend a day on a film or two months. As long as they pay me, I couldn't care less whether my name is billed above or below the title.'[10]

The two men differed from each other markedly in terms both of taste and of temperament. Lowe, for example, made the following selections when appearing on *Desert Island Discs*:

1. Tosti, 'Parted' (Peter Dawson)
2. 'Love Is The Sweetest Thing' (Al Bowlly/Ray Noble and his Orchestra)
3. 'At Last' (Glenn Miller and his Orchestra)
4. Litolff, Concerto Symphonique No. 4 in D minor (scherzo) (Clifford Curzon *piano*/LPO/Boult)
5. Berlin, 'It's A Lovely Day Today' (from *Call Me Madam*) (Shani Wallis/Jeff Warren)
6. Bach, Concerto in C minor (Paul Badura-Skoda and Jorg Demus *pianos*/Vienna State Opera Orchestra/Redel)
7. Debussy, 'La Mer' (NPO/Boulez)
8. 'Who Do You Think You Are Kidding, Mr Hitler?' (theme from *Dad's Army*) (Bud Flanagan)

FAVOURITE RECORDING: Debussy, 'La Mer'.
BOOK: A book on tropical plants.
LUXURY: Claret.

Le Mesurier chose these:

1. 'Take The "A" Train' (Duke Ellington and his Famous Orchestra)
2. 'Spring Is Here' (from *Spring Is Here*) (Bill Evans Trio)
3. 'Setting Fire To The Policeman' (Peter Sellers)
4. 'Come Rain Or Come Shine' (from *St Louis Woman*) (Judy Garland)
5. 'Easy Living' (Rob Burns *clarinet*/Alan Clare Trio)
6. 'What's New?' (Annie Ross)
7. 'After You, Who?' (from *The Gay Divorce*) (Fred Astaire)

8. Bach, Double Concerto in D minor (BWV 1043) (David and Igor Oistrakh *violins*/RPO/Goossens)

FAVOURITE RECORDING: Bach, Double Concerto in D minor.
BOOK: Samuel Pepys' *Diary*.
LUXURY: A small distillery.[11]

Lowe was a dapper little man of inflexible habits and fixed routines, whereas Le Mesurier was something of a suede-shoed libertine who liked nothing more than to ring up a friend and inquire in a hopeful murmur, 'Playtime?'[12] Lowe lived in Little Venice with his actress wife Joan Cooper, and the two of them spent most of their leisure time either restoring or relaxing on board their Victorian steam yacht *Amazon* (which rarely left the security of the jetty). Le Mesurier was twice divorced. His first marriage, to June Melville, had collapsed soon after the war, partly as a result of her alcoholism,[13] while his second, to Hattie Jacques, ended when she left him for another man.[14] He shared a home in Ramsgate with his third wife, the vivacious Joan Malin,[15] but, whenever he stayed in London at his flat in Baron's Court, he would while away the evenings – and the early hours of the mornings – at The Coach and Horses in Romilly Street (Jeffrey Bernard was a favourite drinking companion) or at Ronnie Scott's jazz club in Frith Street ('Listening to artists like Bill Evans, Oscar Petersen or Alan Clare always made life seem that little bit brighter').[16]

Lowe was relatively easy to ruffle. He dreaded, when 'off-duty', hearing someone shout out at him, 'How's Mr Swindley, then?' or ''Ow yer goin' on, captain? All right?' (in response he would stiffen up and say, 'My name is Arthur Lowe').[17] On one occasion, when assorted members of the cast had joined him and Joan on board *Amazon* for an informal lunch party, he startled his guests by suddenly shouting, 'Weigh anchor!', moving the boat out a mere 100 yards on the river, and then promptly dropping the anchor straight back down again, simply because he had spotted a 'snotty-nosed kid' staring over at them from the bank – 'We don't want to have our lunch with that sort of thing going on,' he explained.[18] Little ruffled Le Mesurier, however, apart from his wife Joan's torrid year-long affair with his close friend Tony Hancock (to which he responded by behaving, in his words, 'tolerably well').[19] He appeared to relish all that was odd or unexpected in life, wandering into out of the way bars in the hope of encountering some woozy little eccentric, travelling miles for the chance to hear an expletive-speaking parrot and reacting with calm good manners when an attractive female fan demanded one evening that he take her straight out into a ditch and make love to her ('Well, my dear, I'd like to oblige you,' he told her, 'but it's rather late and dark, and I really can't see myself clambering about at this time of night looking for a ditch. Perhaps we ought to do it by daylight').[20]

There were times during the making of *Dad's Army* when Lowe seemed to regard Le Mesurier's adventures with the same strange mixture of censoriousness and envy that Mainwaring reserved for those of Wilson. On one occasion, for example, Le Mesurier arranged for Bill Pertwee to give him a lift down to Thetford (he had grown bored with his own car and had abandoned it, on a whim, beneath the Hammersmith flyover). Setting off from London on a Friday, Le Mesurier persuaded Pertwee to take a detour to Newmarket in order to visit the National Stud and converse with an interesting assortment of trainers and jockeys; then he proposed another detour, this time to Bury St Edmunds, where he and Pertwee toured the local pubs and eventually spent what was left of the night in one of the town's hotels; the two men finally completed their journey – which would normally have taken no more than four hours – when they drove in to Thetford on Sunday evening. Lowe, noticing their arrival at the hotel, came over and asked what kind of trip they had experienced. 'Fine,' smiled Le Mesurier, 'it took two days.' Lowe merely looked at his colleague, muttered 'Extraordinary', and walked away.[21] Things were no different during make-up sessions, in which Lowe would sometimes find himself temporarily unattended while one woman was busy giving Le Mesurier a manicure, another was brushing his hair and a third was fetching him a sandwich. 'John could get those women to do anything for him,' Ian Lavender recalled. 'I mean, I actually saw him persuade – no, "persuade" is the wrong word – I saw him *charm* a make-up girl into taking the watch off his wrist, winding it up and then putting it back on again! "Oh," he'd say, "it's *far* too much *trouble,* could you *possibly* do it for me, my dear?" And she'd do it, as if it was the most natural thing in the world for her to do!'[22] There was, for Lowe, only one meaningful way in which to react to such a scene: an arch of an eyebrow, a quick puff of the cheeks, and another mumbled 'Extraordinary.'

In spite of all their differences, the two men genuinely liked, admired and trusted each other, and, when they acted together, they shared a rare and special rapport. 'So well attuned were we,' Le Mesurier once observed, 'that often an exchanged glance between us was enough to make a point in the script. One critic was kind enough to say that we did not really need dialogue – it was quite evident what we were thinking simply by studying our expressions.'[23] It was true: Lowe – a sublime bridler – could sum up a dozen lines of text simply by sitting up and inhaling sharply as if he had just been scorched by a piping hot potato, as could Le Mesurier merely by sliding the tip of his tongue along his thin-lipped, lopsided smile. No word, when it *was* used, was wasted: Lowe, for example, managed, by varying his intonation, to make 'Wilson' sound not only like a name but also, whenever the situation called for it, a question, a cry for help or a threat, whereas Le Mesurier never uttered a single 'yes, sir?' without having first marinated it in sarcasm. There were no false notes. Each actor drew not only on his own disposition but also on his own wit to bring his character smartly into life.

Lowe described Mainwaring as, above all else, 'a very brave little chap': 'When he says "He who holds Walmington-on-Sea holds England", he means it. It's bloody ludicrous, but he means it . . . and all the other Captain Mainwarings in the Home Guard meant it too. That's part of the appeal of the series. There's truth in it all the way through.'[24] Mainwaring, Lowe felt, had something in common with two other characters he had portrayed – Leonard Swindley from *Coronation Street* and Mr Micawber from Charles Dickens' *David Copperfield*: 'They are all of them a mess. Swindley was. Mainwaring is a good little bank manager, but, as an army officer, he's a mess. And have you ever seen anything like the utter hopelessness of Micawber?'[25] The other fictional character with whom he had most in common, however, was the hapless hero of George and Weedon Grossmith's *Diary of a Nobody* (1892), the harassed middle-class City clerk Charles Pooter.

Both Pooter and Mainwaring are loyal, if somewhat taken for granted, servants of staid but respectable employers; both crave respect but generally fail to attract it (Pooter has to put up with Pitt – 'a monkey of seventeen' – who takes great delight in calling out 'Hornpipe' whenever he catches sight of his superior's rather broad-bottomed bespoke trousers,[26] Mainwaring must endure Hodges' regular rude and raucous gibes); both are blessed with friends who often seem worse than their enemies (Pooter has Cummings, who can easily take umbrage, and Gowing, who is 'sometimes very tedious with his remarks, and not always cautious',[27] Mainwaring has Wilson); and both, on a daily, sometimes hourly, basis, find their personal dignity subject to the most appalling vicissitudes. It was, for example, Pooter – but it could just as easily have been Mainwaring, or, indeed, 'Mainwearing' – who made matters worse for himself by notifying his local paper of his omission from its brief record of the guests at a recent ball:

> *May 12.* Got a single copy of the *Blackfriars Bi-weekly News*. There was a short list of several names they had omitted; but the stupid people had mentioned our names as 'Mr and Mrs C. Porter'. Most annoying! Wrote again and I took particular care to write our name in capital letters, POOTER, so that there should be no possible mistake this time.
>
> *May 16.* Absolutely disgusted on opening the *Blackfriars Bi-weekly News* of today, to find the following paragraph: 'We have received two letters from Mr and Mrs Charles Pewter, requesting us to announce the important fact that they were at the Mansion House Ball.' I tore up the paper and threw it in the waste-paper basket. My time is far too valuable to bother about such trifles.[28]

Both men are just bright enough to realise, deep down, that they are not bright enough. Rarely does either man dare to tell a joke, and, whenever one of them does, it invariably rebounds straight back in his reddened face (GOWING: 'Hulloh, Pooter, why your trousers are too short!' POOTER: 'Very likely, and you will find my temper "*short*" also.' GOWING: 'That won't make your trousers longer, Juggins').[29] There is something desperately inevitable about Pooter's discovery, immediately after having sent off a carefully worded letter of thanks, that there are actually two, rather than one, 'p's in 'appreciate' ('Awfully vexed at this'),[30] or Mainwaring's premature return from placing the town hall under martial law ('It was closed. Doesn't open till nine in the morning'), or Pooter's shiny-soled slip-up on the dance floor ('I expressed myself pretty strongly on the danger of having a plain polished floor with no carpet or drugget'),[31] or Mainwaring's ill-timed encounter with Pike's gravy boat ('You *stupid* boy!'). Each man's future, clearly, is littered with banana skins both physical and spiritual.

The one significant difference between these two characters stems from the fact that Pooter is lucky enough to be married to Carrie, a woman whom he genuinely loves, whereas Mainwaring is unlucky enough to be married to Elizabeth, a woman whom he genuinely fears. Carrie Pooter – 'my dear, pretty wife'[32] – forgives her husband his failings ('You, dear old Charlie, are *not* handsome, but you are *good*, which is far more noble'),[33] laughs at most of his painfully laboured puns, allows him to seize her round the waist and launch into a 'wild kind of polka',[34] and is 'not above putting a button on a shirt, mending a pillow-case, or practising the "Sylvia Gavotte" on our new cottage piano.'[35] Elizabeth Mainwaring, in stark contrast, forgives her husband nothing, never laughs, never dances, never goes out, and is above doing far too many things to mention.

Starve Pooter of affection and one ends up with Mainwaring: the hope has grown a little leaner, the heart a little harder. Wilson – the only member of the platoon to have had the misfortune to have met Mainwaring's spouse – considers her to be 'well, er, a bit *odd*, you know', while Pike, who has spoken to her on the telephone, notes that she is 'always cross'. Even Mainwaring himself, who does his best to be discreet, has been known to confess that his wife is 'a very highly strung woman': 'Slightest noise, she tosses and turns till sunrise. Dustbin lid blew off last night, and before you could say "Jack Robinson" she was under my bunk with a gas mask on. Took me twenty minutes to persuade her to come out.' When Mainwaring plans to treat his cheddar-loving wife to a toasted cheese supper – 'I might have a little surprise for you tonight', he tells her cheerily on the telephone – she misreads his intentions and lets him know in no uncertain terms that she is absolutely appalled. When he attempts to give her 'a very good dressing down' for burning all of his sausage rolls, he ends up receiving a nasty black eye (the result, he later claims unconvincingly, of having 'bumped into the door of the linen cupboard'). He longs for romance – his chaste, cherished affair with Fiona Gray was proof of that – but his marriage brings him nothing but misery, and sometimes, in spite of his brave face, the sad soul within shows through: 'You can't have Mrs Mainwaring eating broken glass', Jones exclaims after Pike has accidentally smashed Elizabeth's latest bottle of sleeping tablets. 'That could be fatal – that could mean instant death!' Mainwaring is silent for a moment or two while he ponders this remark, and then, distractedly, mutters: 'Yes . . . Just . . . just dust them over a bit.'[36] Bereft of real companionship at home, he seeks it out in the Home Guard.

Mainwaring has wed himself to the war effort. It has become his grand passion, his one true vocation, and he simply cannot understand why the grip it has on others is often so much looser than the one it has on him. 'I mean, fancy men not *wanting* to come on parade! It's the highlight of my day! Do you know, once I'm having my tea, I can feel the excitement mounting inside of me. I put on my uniform, and I march down here to the parade, and I feel a warm glow of pride in what we're doing and what we've achieved. We're doing something for *England!*'[37]

He is the kind of Englishman who takes a particularly great sense of pride from the thought that St George was far smaller than his dragon. Even when a bomb lands on his bank, and all of the windows have been smashed, and the door of his office is jammed, and part of his wall is missing, and water has started dripping down from the ceiling on to his desk, Mainwaring merely puts up his umbrella and refuses to budge:

> You see that chair? Well, that's *my* chair; the Manager's chair. This is *my* desk; the Manager's desk. *My* office; the Manager's office. I wasn't made Manager overnight, you know, it was a long, hard struggle: office boy, clerk, Assistant Chief Clerk, Chief Clerk, Assistant Manager and, finally, Manager. It's taken me twenty-five years to get this office, and there's no red-necked, beer-swilling foreigner going to throw me out of it![38]

What he knows – or rather, what he *thinks* he knows – of the outside world could be scribbled down in stark black and white on the back of a postage stamp. He is not too keen on the French ('They're never very much good after lunch, you know'), exasperated by the Italians ('a shambles'), suspicious of the Russians (although he acknowledges that 'they can't be all *that* bad otherwise they wouldn't be on our side'), quietly contemptuous of the Americans ('a few extras', he calls them, 'a second eleven, as it were') and, of course, he detests the Germans ('a nation of unthinking automatons' who do not respect the laws of cricket). Mainwaring does know what he loves, and what he loves is England – his very own green and pleasant, proper, prudent, not too posh, not too common, hat-tipping, hard-working, game-playing vision of England – and he is prepared to give his all in order to defend it. 'I *have* to be a hard man,' he insists, 'otherwise we'd all be under the Nazi jackboot by now!'

Wilson, Mainwaring believes, is a soft man. 'You worry me,' he moans. 'You'd do anything rather than face up to your responsibilities. You've never really grown up, have you? You're not a middle-aged Chief Clerk at all – you're a sort of Peter Pan!' Nothing seems more great an obstacle to Mainwaring's dream of creating a 'well-oiled fighting machine' than his sergeant's obdurate over-politeness:

MAINWARING   Wheel them in.
WILSON   All right sir. (*goes to doorway*) Would you, er, would you kindly, er, step this way, please?
MAINWARING   Oh, Wilson! *Bark* it out! *Bark* it out!
WILSON   Right. (*raises his voice*) Would you kindly step this way please![39]

John Le Mesurier played Wilson like a thorn that had found a side:

It seemed to me that Arthur, on screen, identified a central, but rarely performed, character in the British class system – the product of the lower middle class – essentially conservative, fiercely patriotic and strong on the old values – but a natural opponent of idle aristocrats as much as of upstart workers. Naturally, Captain Mainwaring disapproved of Sergeant Wilson, whose accent and manners suggested a comfortable background, one that had evidently removed any sense of ambition or daring. Indications of sloppiness or excessive caution ('Do you think that's wise?') were met by explosions of indignation and a frenzy of activity signalling another usually hopeless adventure for the Walmington Home Guard.[40]

Mainwaring knows that, in spite of all of his huffing and puffing, he will almost certainly remain stuck on the same rung of the social ladder, whereas Wilson, in spite of his chronic reluctance to huff and puff, will continue to rise blithely from one rung to the next, acquiring along the way such privileges as membership of the exclusive golf club ('I've been trying for *years* to get in there!' Mainwaring protests), lunching on hard-to-find smoked salmon ('*I* had snoek fishcake at the British Restaurant!') and inheriting an eye-catching aristocratic title. The only thing stopping Mainwaring from becoming a revolutionary, Wilson realises, is the fact that he is such a snob:

MAINWARING   Things'll be very different after the war, you mark my words! The common man will come into his own. This country will be run by *professionals*: doctors, lawyers . . . bank managers . . .

WILSON   You mean people like you?

MAINWARING   All right, yes: people like me.

WILSON   (*smiling mischievously*) You mean 'common?'

MAINWARING   Now *watch* it, Wilson!

WILSON   I didn't know you were a socialist, sir.

MAINWARING   How *dare* you! You take that back!

WILSON   But you just said that, after the war, the country was going to be run by common men like you.

MAINWARING   I said nothing about 'common men'! I said '*the* common *man*'! People who've got somewhere by their own efforts – not because their father had a title. *Their* day's over!

WILSON   Well! I wonder what will happen to them?

MAINWARING   Ha! They'll go to work – *that's* what'll happen to them! We shall have true democracy.

WILSON   Well, supposing they don't *want* to go to work?

MAINWARING   Well, *they* won't have any say in the matter![41]

Wilson's aristocratic matter-of-factness, his disinclination to shake his imagination out of its slumbers (save for those occasions when someone likens his looks to those of the dashing Jack Buchanan – 'Do you really think so?'), stands in stark contrast to Mainwaring's wild idealism ('We are in the front line every minute of our lives here!'). It is not that Wilson is incapable of authentic thoughts and emotions; it is just that, as a somewhat enervated pragmatist, he is not prepared to rehearse them:

INSTRUCTOR   Right! Now, I'm a gestapo officer. Now you, sergeant –

WILSON   Mmm? Yes?

INSTRUCTOR   What are you doing in France?

WILSON   I'm not *in* France.

INSTRUCTOR   Oh, yes, you are! You got there by parachute. I've captured you, and now I'm interrogating you.

WILSON   Oh, I see. Well: 'Bonjour.'

INSTRUCTOR   You're not supposed to tell me anything! Now: What are you doing in France?

WILSON   I don't know.

INSTRUCTOR   You're trying to blow up a munitions factory.

WILSON   (*sounding bored*) All right: I was trying to blow up a munitions factory.

INSTRUCTOR   So! You admit it!

WILSON   Oh, *really*! This is too absurd!

INSTRUCTOR   I'll show you how absurd it is! (*gets hold of Wilson's hand*) I'm putting matches underneath your fingernails! I'm setting light to them! They're burning down! Now they've reached your fingers! You're in *agony*! How do you like *that*?

WILSON   Well, to be absolutely *honest*, it isn't really *bothering* me very much![42]

It takes a great deal to rouse Wilson from his well-bred placidity (even the persistent Mrs Pike, who continues to harbour hopes of a marriage proposal, has to make do with the loan of his ration book); bad manners, however, will always rattle him:

WILSON	Oh, now, *really*, sir!
MAINWARING	What's the matter?
WILSON	Well, I really *must* protest, sir. Just because you're the officer you don't *have* to take the hammock! I mean, you just *strut* over there, put your hand out and say, '*I'm* taking that!' I mean, it's just the sort of behaviour I cannot *stand*!
MAINWARING	(*sounding shaken*) Well, I'm very sorry, Wilson. Perhaps it *was* a little unthinking of me. A little undemocratic. But *you* know I'm the last person in the world to take advantage of my position.
WILSON	Oh, really, sir?
MAINWARING	We shall take it in turns, of course.
WILSON	Thank you.
MAINWARING	But I shall use it first.[43]

Wilson, unlike Mainwaring, is clearly unsuited to times of war – his class has conditioned him to shilly-shally, whereas Mainwaring's has conditioned him to scrap – but, at the right moment, in the right circumstances, he is quite capable of confounding his critics: 'When the occasion demands', he assures his sceptical captain with one of his wry little smiles, 'I *can* bawl and shout – just like you.' The Germans, from a distance, fail to fire his fiercest feelings: while he acknowledges the fact that some of them have 'rather an abrupt manner', their uniforms strike him as 'awfully smart' ('they really do something for one, don't you think?') and he cannot stop himself from observing that they seem 'awfully well-disciplined'. He finds more than enough to motivate him, however, in the contemplation of his own heartfelt English idyll:

Every day, I walk up the high street to work, and, as I pass those little shops, a nice, friendly, *warm* atmosphere seems to come wafting out – I mean, even from that *dreadful* fellow Hodges' greengrocer's – and then I stroll on a little bit further and I pass Frazer's funeral parlour, and then before I cross the road to come to the bank there's Jones' butcher shop – white tiles all gleaming and shining, and old Jones standing there with his straw hat on and wearing his striped apron, and giving me a cheery wave – and do you know, sir, it sort of, I don't know, it sort of sets me up for the day. I feel it's my time, you see.[44]

It made for a strange relationship, this marriage of the right stuff and the real thing, but, somehow, it worked. Each man knows, in his heart of hearts, that he needs the other. Wilson knows that, if Mainwaring was not there to push him, he might very well stagnate, whereas Mainwaring knows that, if Wilson was not there for him to push against, he might very well fall flat on his face ('They recognise authority when they see it. Er, you'd better come with me'). When one of them comes up with the answers, the other comes up with the questions; when one orders Pike to prime the grenades, the other persuades him to load them with dummy detonators; when one praises his platoon for having guts, the other prays that he will never get to see any. It is, in the circumstances, a most appropriate partnership: unorthodox, edgy, amateurish, improbably effective and very, very, English.

CHAPTER VIII

A Scot, a Spiv and a Stupid Boy

To be attached to the subdivision, to love the little platoon we belong to in society, is the first principle (the germ as it were) of public affections.
EDMUND BURKE[1]

A single expression, boldly conceived and uttered, will sometimes put a whole company into their proper feelings.
THOMAS PAINE[2]

Frazer, Walker and Pike: every time Mainwaring saw them he sighed. Each one, he believed, undermined his ideal of a well-managed uniformity: Frazer was not English, Walker was not respectable and Pike was not very bright. It took only one tart remark from the Scot – '*R-r-r*-rubbish!' – one furtive little favour from the spiv – 'Psst! Oi – I got your cheese!' – or one piece of unsolicited advice from the stupid boy – 'Shoot him, Mr Mainwaring – go on, you've got the authority!' – to upset the captain's foolish consistency. He was stuck with them, and sometimes he had no choice but to rely on them, but he never stopped thinking of them as problems posing as solutions.

Each one, in his own way, is an outsider. James Frazer, for example, is a solitary Scot, the sole member of Walmington-on-Sea's Caledonian Society, a man whose only company outside of the platoon is the flickering light from his single candle. He was born, according to Croft and Perry,[3] a long time ago on the Isle of Barra, a wild and lonely place just off the west coast of Scotland. He joined his first ship at the age of fourteen, and spent the next 35 years sailing the seven seas (amassing in the process a veritable treasure trove of tales concerning strange, exotic lands and dark, supernatural happenings).

The First World War saw him rise to the position of chief petty officer in the catering branch of the Royal Navy, and then slide back down the ranks after he was found guilty of hitting another officer with the crooked end of a boat hook during a moment of intoxication. When he retired from his nautical career he chose to settle in Walmington-on-Sea, where, after a brief flirtation with philately, he opened up a funeral parlour next door to Jones' butcher's shop in the high street. He remains a bachelor, although he was once engaged to a 'long-legged Scottish lass' called Jessie (she disappeared – he assumed that she had been blown off a cliff and was carried out to sea – only to reappear some time later in Singapore, from where she wrote to him, requesting what he considered to be an exorbitant sum of money to pay for her return fare), and he continues to admire, from a distance, 'soncy' young women with 'big, strong thighs'. He is not a great optimist.

Joe Walker, the genial outlaw, was born in Plaistow, East London. He learned, at an early age, to live on his wits, and he served his apprenticeship on some of the city's shadiest streets and stalls. He moved down to Walmington-on-Sea, rather suddenly, as soon as the Second World War broke out, and promptly registered his occupation as a banana salesman and supplier of illuminated signs. His business is based in Slope Alley, where he makes use of two old garages at the bottom of a friend's yard, but he has also been known to secrete some of his 'wholesale supplies' in a variety of other locations scattered around the town. His time in the Home Guard was interrupted early on by a short spell at an artillery training base, and, ever since his return (he was discharged after it was discovered that he was allergic to corned beef), he has served the platoon in a number of unorthodox, but often rather ingenious, ways.[4]

Frank Pike, the unworldly youth, was born in Weston-super-Mare, where he was brought up by his mother and his 'Uncle Arthur'. He is, according to Mrs Pike, an exceptionally fragile young man who is plagued by such multiple ailments as croup, hay fever, sinusitis, sensitive skin, vertigo, a delicate chest, weak ankles and 'nerves'; outside of her house, however, he displays a surprisingly healthy appetite for adventure. He is an avid reader, taking *The Hotspur*, *Wizard* and *Film Pictorial* each week, a regular listener to *The Happidrome* on the wireless, and he is a devoted – some might say obsessive

– fan of the movies (he models himself, he likes to think, on such suave, romantic stars as Ronald Colman and William Powell). He works, by day, as a clerk at the bank, and, by night, as the youngest private in his platoon, and he is never happier than when he is entrusted with the town's one and only tommy gun.[5]

It was Frazer, out of the three of them, whose oddity gave Mainwaring most cause for concern. Right from the start, when the self-appointed leader launched into his maiden speech, there, right in front of him, was the bushy-browed, wild-eyed, beaky, unsmiling Celt, daring him to turn something crooked into something straight: 'We Englishmen,' Mainwaring begins, only to check himself as Frazer growls menacingly beneath his breath. 'We-we Britishers,' the captain nervously extemporises, 'um, w-we here . . .' From this point on, Frazer is Mainwaring's fiercest critic, regularly casting doubt upon his judgement, maligning his character and keenly anticipating his come-uppance. Whenever a distinguished visitor is to be found in the commanding officer's office, Frazer, invariably, is the member of the platoon who comes bursting through the door: 'Hey! We're all lined up out here waiting, waiting, and if you don't come soon we're all off home! I thought ye'd just like tae know!' Mainwaring, smiling weakly, does his best to explain away such rude behaviour – 'Rough diamond, that one. Heart of gold!' – but privately he is seething. 'He has the look of a communist about him,' he tells Wilson. 'I've noticed that when we're on night duty he never plays Monopoly with the rest of the men.'

John Laurie was certainly nostalgic for his classical actorly past (when John Le Mesurier once asked him who, in his memory, ranked highest of all the Hamlets, he snapped back, 'Me, laddie, me!').[6] In spite of this he clearly relished playing such an irascible, outspoken and deeply devious old creature. It had been half a century or so since Laurie had left his native Scotland – he and his wife, Oonah, had settled in England in a smart mock-Tudor house at Chalfont St Peter in Buckinghamshire – but he only needed to crank his old Dumfries accent up a notch or two in order to sound as if he had just come down, grudgingly, from some cold stone home in the auld country. Although he had played a Home Guard before – in the later scenes of *The Life and Death of Colonel Blimp* – and innumerable lugubrious Scots – such as Jamie, the doom-laden caretaker in *The*

Ghost of St Michael's, who regularly claims to have heard 'the sound of the phantom pipes *wailing* through the castle' – Frazer would prove to be his definitive comic caricature.

It was as if Mainwaring, the parochial little Englishman, had unwittingly conjured up this craggy Scot, stooping like a question mark, from out of his own nightmares: the jealously guarded stock of gold sovereigns, the old pre-Union phrases, the chatter about haggis, whisky and bagpipes, the secretive nature, the morbid occupation, and the eyes that are just a little too close together ('denoting,' according to Mainwaring, 'a mean streak') – each hoary cliché combined to create a formidably foreign figure, an exotic old gainsayer whose sole *raison d'être*, it sometimes seemed to Mainwaring, was to see his master '*r-r-r*-ruined'. The Scot's storytelling does not help: whenever the captain calls for a morale-boosting contribution, Frazer can always be relied on to come up with something that seems to have been designed expressly to serve the opposite purpose: 'I mind the time when I was a wee, wee laddie on the lone Isle of Barra. A submarine got sunk in Castle Bay, and seven *b-r-r-r*-ave men were trapped in it. The water got higher and higher and higher, until it got up to their necks, and then . . . *Terrible way tae die!*'[7]

The pedantry always niggles (MAINWARING: 'We have one invaluable weapon in our armoury: ingenuity and improvisation.' FRAZER: 'That's two!'), the rumour-mongering ('I'm not one for tittle-tattle or gossip of any kind, but . . .') never fails to annoy, and the heckling ('What a lot of *blather* he comes out with!') is guaranteed to grate. The most worrying of Frazer's traits, however, is his ill-disguised desire to dominate. He not only harbours hopes of supplanting Jones as lance corporal, he also dreams of taking over from Mainwaring as captain. On one occasion, for example, he startles his commander by revealing just how closely – and critically – he has been monitoring his performance:

FRAZER	Cap'n Mainwaring, sir, I'll come straight to the point: during the period we've been together you've wasted far too many hours of our precious time, and tonight's lecture was the last straw!
MAINWARING	Now look here, Frazer –
FRAZER	Let me finish! I've made some careful notes of

	it all (*puts on spectacles*) and if you just ho'd on a wee (*reaches into pocket for notebook*) I'll give you one or two items that might interest ye. (*reading from notes*) On November 6, 1940, you wasted *thr-r-ree* hours giving us a lecture on 'Why the Germans Don't Play Cricket'. On January 28, 1941, you gave us a lecture telling us how Hitler, when he is in a rage, 'bites the carpet'.
MAINWARING	It's a well-known fact that he does!
FRAZER	Maybe, but you *then* proceeded to waste two hours working out a plan on how to send him a poisoned hearth rug! According to my notes, it comes to a total of four hundred and thirty-eight hours wasted on useless blather! (*removes spectacles*) Well, that's how I feel, and I had to come in and tell ye so to your face – er, no offence intended, you understand.[8]

Mainwaring rates this diatribe as 'rank insubordination', and even Wilson admits that it had been 'rather strong', but the decision to teach the troublemaker a lesson by allowing him, temporarily, to see for himself how hard it is to be in charge of the platoon only succeeds in revealing just how dictatorial, given the chance, he can be.

Frazer usually falls a fraction short, however, of outright rebellion. 'I'm a simple man,' he protests disingenuously whenever he fears that he has gone a little too far. 'I speak ma mind and what's in this hard auld Scottish heart.' The irony is that his various snarls and schemes serve only to strengthen the status quo, reminding the other members of the platoon that even when things, under Mainwaring, are at their worst, they could always be worse still under the man waiting impatiently in the wings.

Things would certainly be worse for everyone without Walker – the man who supplies the platoon with such scarce wartime resources as alcohol, cigarettes, petrol coupons and the odd 'stray' item of equipment – which is why Mainwaring, the self-styled paragon of middle-class respectability, feels so uneasy in his presence. Walker reminds him that he is just as morally fallible, in certain circumstances, as the rest of his men: whenever Mainwaring has just finished administering a stern lecture to someone on the need for integrity, frugality and Olympian self-control, Walker, without fail, will stroll in bearing some incriminating little treat and spoil the sober effect ('Ah. Yes. Er, that will be all, thank you, Walker').

Mainwaring does not know how to respond to such a shamelessly ambiguous figure. Walker has no firm attachment to any particular industry, but he is undeniably industrious ('That whisky you get every week don't fall off a lorry on its own accord – it has to be pushed!'); he has a harshly modern mind (MAINWARING: 'You'd sell your own grandmother, wouldn't you?' WALKER: 'Well, there's no market for 'er'), but has held on to an old-fashioned heart (he would much rather commit a good deed than a dirty trick); and he operates at the rim of society but still exerts an influence at the hub. Mainwaring simply cannot work out the reason why he, a pillar of the community, should find himself being leaned on by this louche individualist. When, for example, the rule-abiding bank manager attends a much-anticipated local black-tie Rotarian dinner – 'That's what I like about these gatherings: everybody here represents a profession or a craft' – he does not expect to rub shoulders with a rule-bending spiv:

WALKER	Evening, Cap!
MAINWARING	What are *you* doing here?
WALKER	Well, why shouldn't I be 'ere?
MAINWARING	Well, I wasn't aware that under-the-counter dealing's a profession!
WALKER	No – but it's a craft, isn't it? Anyway, if it hadn't been for me you wouldn't be knockin' back that sherry. And those chicken croquettes you're going to 'ave later would've been made of whale meat – instead of rabbit.[9]

Walker, much to Mainwaring's chagrin, can always be trusted to lower the tone: not only does he undermine every lecture with his flippant, and sometimes rather crude, interventions ('You're being very tedious today, Walker!'), he also insists upon bringing his awfully common girlfriend, the brightly coloured Edith Parish, to all of the platoon's social occasions ('I don't think *that's* the class of girl we want here at all!'). Walker can also be trusted, however, to come up with, when it really matters, the kind of unconventional, inspired ideas that can turn a demoralising defeat into a brave little victory. He is, in short, the most reliable of rogues, and even Mainwaring, although he will never truly understand him, knows that he will always need him.

Mainwaring is by no means so sure that he needs someone quite like Pike. Every day in the bank, and every evening on parade, the gawky youth manages to elicit the same sharp exclamation: 'You *stupid* boy!' Mainwaring, whose marriage has not been blessed with the presence of children, is unsure whether to tame or train this strangely malleable, impressionable and unruly adolescent. He could do without the vague air of scandal that he discerns about the boy ('Well, it's no business of mine,' he tells his queasy-looking sergeant, 'but this is a very small town, Wilson. Tongues wag. People put two and two together . . .'), and he could certainly do without the over-protective matriarch who countermands so many of his most solemn orders ('Now look here, Pike: *I'm* running this platoon – not your mum, er, your mother!'). The root of Mainwaring's unease runs deeper still than that: what he could most do without is a boy who behaves as if he is merely *playing* at being a soldier.

The war, to Mainwaring is deadly serious, but to Pike it is only a game. The Home Guard, to Mainwaring, is part of the proper Army, but to Pike it is simply an extension of the Scouts. Hand Pike a gun and he will run around the church hall shouting '*Nya-ah-ah-ah!*' Send him anywhere near a stream and he will end up stumbling in ('I'm all wet, Mr Mainwaring!'). Invite him to visualise the enemy, and his mind will wander off to that movie he saw last week in which Alan Ladd was held captive by William Bendix and Eddie Marr. Dress him up, for the purposes of a training exercise, as a Nazi officer, and he will be off, strutting about, saying such things as, 'So! *Ve* are ze masters now, eh?' and ordering 'Sixteen shandys mit der ginger beer.' To a man like Mainwaring, who thinks of his platoon as fighting on the front line, a boy like Pike, who still seems to be playing in the sandpit, is a particularly embarrassing kind of irritant.

Even Wilson, the indulgent 'uncle-sergeant', sometimes appears distinctly ill at ease in the company of this undisciplined but chronically inquisitive young character. It is not just the tried and tested threats that he dreads ('I'll tell Mum!'), it is also, and even more so, those occasional intimations of something bordering on a fully-grown insight:

PIKE Anyway, if you've got an 'eadache it's your own fault. By the time we've finished supper it's always so late you never leave our house until after I've gone to bed, and then you're back early for breakfast in the morning before I'm awake.

WILSON Well, you know, Frank, I always come round to your house for *meals*, because your mother has my ration book.

PIKE Yeah, well, what I can't understand is: I never hear you leave and I never hear you come back again in the morning.

WILSON Yes, well, you see, I let myself in and out very *quietly*.

PIKE (*sotto voce*) You never do anything else quietly.[10]

Whereas Mainwaring fears that Pike will never mature ('I can't help thinking that boy's slightly retarded!'), Wilson fears that it is only a matter of time before he does.

Nothing can be done. Pike, like Walker, like Frazer, is not the kind of crease that can ever be ironed out. Mainwaring might think of them as misfits, but at least they are his misfits, the local misfits, and they are in, like him, for the duration.

CHAPTER IX

The Old Fools

It's not that age brings childhood back again,
Age merely shows what children we remain.
GOETHE[1]

Why aren't they screaming?
PHILIP LARKIN[2]

Frazer calls them 'the old fools': Jack Jones and Charles Godfrey, the mangy lionheart and the doddery gent. One of them is rolling back the years, the other one is reeling from them, but both are faithful, and neither will shy from the fight.

Jones was born in 1870. His extraordinary military career began in 1884, when he signed on as a drummer boy, and continued more or less uninterrupted until 1915, when, having risen to the rank of lance corporal, he was invalided out on account of his myopia. He then proceeded to open up a small butcher's shop in Walmington-on-Sea, and found another use for the old, cold, steel, but he remained, at heart, a proud and passionate soldier. He built up his business, hired a young boy named Raymond to serve as his assistant, became an enthusiastic secretary of the local Darby and Joan Club, overcame the occasional attack of malaria and acquired a well-deserved reputation as the town's most indefatigable raconteur. In 1940, just when even he seemed resigned to the fact that his fighting days were well and truly over, the call came again, and, after slipping his new commanding officer a couple of pounds of steak ('compliments of the house, sir'), he entered the Home Guard with all of his many medals on display and his old rank intact.[3]

Godfrey is politely imprecise about the year of his birth – as, indeed, he is about anything else of a personal nature – but it is certainly clear that he came into the world an awfully long time ago. The Great War was not really his cup of tea – he was actually a conscientious objector – but he still managed to win the Military Medal for bravery while serving with the Medical Corps as a stretcher bearer at the Battle of the Somme. After working for more than thirty-five years behind the counter in the gentleman's outfitting department of the Army and Navy Stores, he returned to live a leisurely life alongside his two spinster sisters, Cissy (a keen knitter) and Dolly (a dedicated maker of exceedingly good upside-down cakes), in Cherry Tree Cottage, Walmington-on-Sea. The idea of the Home Guard appealed to his chivalrous spirit, and although his weak bladder, coupled with his regular appointments at the local clinic, meant that he would sometimes have no choice but to ask to be excused, he signed up without the slightest hesitation, and soon found a cosy niche for himself as the platoon's medical orderly.[4]

Mainwaring is prepared to indulge these two elderly men, because both of them share his commitment to the cause (and neither of them questions his authority). They, in turn, are prepared to indulge him, because, as Jones puts it, he is 'our brave leader, our salvation', and because, as Godfrey puts it, 'I don't like to let him down, you know, because he wouldn't let *me* down.'

There was, Clive Dunn would admit, 'an element of wartime revenge'[5] in his portrayal of the Hitler-hating, bayonet-waving, Lance Corporal Jones. His own memories of being a prisoner of war, he noted, gave his performance 'an added *grrr*':[6]

> Those years weren't much fun. I remember one day when they took all our clothes away and stuck them in a big oven to delouse them, then marched us completely naked in just our boots five miles to the sea, right through the middle of the village. We were sprayed with carbolic, had a quick dip and were marched five miles back again the way we'd come . . . I just told myself it was another part. I only hoped that tomorrow I'd get a better one.[7]

He also relished the opportunity, via Jones' rambling military anecdotes, to hint 'at the failings of great men such as the terrible Lord

Kitchener'.[8] The only thing about the character that Dunn, at least initially, was unsure of was the line that became one of his most popular catchphrases: 'That was the one expression I didn't want to use. I thought the audience might find it a bit offensive [of me] to say, "They don't like it up 'em!" But they *loved* it, of course. They love anything that's a bit rude.'[9]

There was something rather poignant about Arnold Ridley's performance as Godfrey. The veteran actor, who in his youth had not only been a keen and competent cricketer but had also played rugby for his home town of Bath, was in a constant state of discomfort due to the legacy of the wounds that he suffered at war (a serious injury to his left arm – sustained on the Somme – had rendered it virtually useless, his legs were riddled with shrapnel and a blow on the head that he received from the butt of a German soldier's rifle had left him prone to occasional blackouts). Much of his on-screen frailty was still, despite all that, gamely exaggerated in order to create all of the requisite comic effects (when the pubs opened, Clive Dunn recalled, the normally slow-moving Ridley was capable of showing 'a turn of speed worthy of the rugby three-quarter he once was').[10]

Each actor appreciated the fact that his character was meant to matter. Jones and Godfrey, more so than any of the other members of the platoon, epitomise the essential ethos of the Home Guard: age may have withered their bodies, but it has failed to weaken their spirit. One lags a beat or two behind the younger men, and the other lacks more than a little of their virile self-control, yet neither man's courage can be questioned. Jones needs no prompting in order to volunteer to crawl out along a flag pole, or cling to the sail of a windmill, or to have grenades tossed down his trousers, while Godfrey, even though his mobility is somewhat limited, will not hesitate to risk his life in order to assist in the defence of his country and his cottage.

Jones, in particular, is a man on whom Mainwaring plainly dotes. 'I admire his spirit,' the proud captain purrs. 'You can see the light of battle in his eyes. Very exhilarating.' The deferential old campaigner can usually be relied on to make his relatively inexperienced and under-qualified commanding officer feel a little more authentic, even if, in the course of doing so, he also succeeds, inadvertently, in making him feel a little more uneasy as well:

JONES   Oh, Captain Mainwaring! That's the sort of talk I like to hear, sir! You know, you remind me of a major we had in the trenches in 1916. He was *just* like you. His name was Major Willoughby-Darcy, sir, and he didn't like skulking, either. He couldn't *bear* skulking. He didn't like crouching and skulking at all, sir. He was a *marvellous* man! You ought to have seen him! He had his top-boots polished like glass, and he had a monocle in his eye glistening away there. Anyway, one day, we was all crouching down in the trench, and suddenly he says, 'Look here, boys! I've had about enough of this!' He says, 'I'm going up on the parapet and walk about and show those damned Jerries I am not afraid of them!' And he got up on the parapet, and —

MAINWARING   Yes, I think I know what you're going to tell me, Jones. He walked about on the parapet and never suffered a scratch.

JONES   No, sir. He got shot. And he got shot in a very awkward place. He did a lot of crouching after that.[11]

The relationship is not without its tensions – Mainwaring can sometimes be cutting with his comments ('No, I think you're getting into the realms of fantasy again, Jones'), and Jones can sometimes be stingy with his sausages ('There he goes again with his "realms of fantasy"! He's playing with fire, you know – I control his meat!') – but each man's respect for the other ensures that no enmity will ever be allowed to fester. There are some, it is true, who regard the lance corporal's inimitable brand of befuddled belligerence as a distinct liability: Frazer, for example, considers his comrade to be 'a woolly-minded auld ditherer', and Wilson, who is well aware of the fact that Jones has an unfortunate tendency to 'get rather over-excited', fears that he sometimes acts as a bad influence on his battle-starved captain. Mainwaring, however, continues to take great comfort from the knowledge that, if the Nazis ever *do* arrive, Jones will be right by his side, nostrils flaring, bayonet fixed, shouting, 'Hande hoch! Hande hoch! Keep those handeys hoch!'

Godfrey, in such a circumstance, is likely to be a little further back; Mainwaring knows, however, that he, too, will stand up, or perhaps sit down, and be counted. There was a time, early on in the existence of the platoon, when Mainwaring tended to side with Frazer when the cruel-tongued Scot dismissed Godfrey as the kind of half-hearted soldier who was 'as soft as a cream puff', and this negative perception seemed to be confirmed when Godfrey confessed that he could not bring himself to harm a humble mouse, let alone a fellow human being ('I can't stand cranks!' the outraged captain complained. 'Can you imagine a man not *wanting* to fight? It isn't *normal*!'), but it was not long before Mainwaring had the true measure of the old man:

MAINWARING	Why have you never worn your medal?
GODFREY	Well, it, er, seemed rather ostentatious.
MAINWARING	Ostentatious? Well, if *I'd* won the MM, I should have been so proud I would have worn it on my chest for the whole world to see!
GODFREY	Oh, *that* would've been all right, because you *look* like a hero.
WILSON	It just shows, sir – you can't go by appearances.
MAINWARING	No, er, ah.[12]

Mainwaring likes to think of Godfrey as 'a sort of father figure for the younger ones to lean on', and Wilson, in this particular instance, is happy to concur ('as long,' he warns, 'as they don't lean on him too heavily'). In his youth, it appears, Godfrey was quite the gadabout, all wing-collar, white tie and cherubic smiles as he flitted from one festive function to the next, but he now leads a thoroughly unsensational life in retirement, rising at 7.30 a.m. each morning to brew the tea for his two sisters, tending to various chores in his garden, listening to a little light opera on the wireless and, of course, attending, whenever possible, the regular evening parades. He may give the impression of being resigned to his own decrepitude – his days are dogged not only by his weak bladder, but also by rheumatism, gout, headaches, indigestion and a drowsiness that borders on narcolepsy, and he has long given up trying to straighten his stooping back (because, he says, 'at my age it's already decided which way it wants to go') – however, he is still sufficiently vain to refuse to wear his spectacles on the grounds that they make him look old.

The one thing about Godfrey that no degree of infirmity can ever change is the fact that he is a genuine English gentleman: dapperly dressed (at least when out of the drab denim uniform), discreet, magnanimous and honourable, he is completely impervious to all external pressures when it comes to doing the decent thing. When, for example, the platoon, in a moment of collective weakness, elects to remain in the pub and play darts rather than arrive on time for parade ('The Nazis aren't coming just at this minute,' one of them laughs), it is Godfrey, alone, who decides to set off for the church hall:

FRAZER   No you don't! We're in this together and we're going
             to see it through together! I'm not going tae stand by
             and see any namby-pamby, creeper-crawling back!
GODFREY   I'm sorry, Mr Frazer, but that sort of talk, you know,
             doesn't influence me in the slightest bit. I'm going to
             do what is right.[13]

Godfrey will always endeavour to do what is right, even if the act of doing so exhausts him, and it is this, above all else, which makes him quietly inspirational.

He, like Jones, like Frazer, Walker and Pike, like Mainwaring and Wilson, is a thoroughly believable character, inhabiting a thoroughly believable world, real enough and rich enough to withstand the weekly examinations. Regular viewers could pause between each episode and map out the local landmarks – Swallow Bank, St Aldhelm's Church Hall, the Novelty Rock Emporium, the Jolly Roger Ice Cream Parlour, Stone's Amusement Arcade, the Plaza cinema, the Marigold Tea Rooms, the British Restaurant, the Red Lion pub, all of the shops along the high street. They could imagine the actions of the inhabitants – not just the members of the platoon, but also Hodges, and the vicar and the verger, and Mrs Pike, and the frighteningly flirtatious Mrs Fox, the frightfully common Edith Parish, the ever-shaky Mr Blewitt, the permanently scowling Mrs

Yeatman, Alderman Bickerstaff the mayor, Mr Gordon the bald-headed town clerk – and even debate such patently unprovable issues as the nature of Mrs Mainwaring's looks, the ration-friendly recipe for Dolly Godfrey's upside-down cakes and, inevitably, the 'truth' of the relationship between Pike and his 'Uncle' Arthur. The fact that it all seemed to matter, even though it was just a fiction, was due not to mass delusion, but rather to mass affection.

THE
COMPANY

We really did love working together. We all came from different walks of life. We all came from different areas of the business. We all contributed. Some of us weren't natural playmates, but we were all great workmates.

IAN LAVENDER[1]

CHAPTER X

Thetford

Most of the British countryside, especially in the most vulnerable areas, is ideal for the kind of defence which you are called upon to organize. It is exactly the sort of country which is a nightmare to the Nazi.
Home Guard Training Manual[1]

Assuming that the production manager has tied up all the loose ends . . . you should find yourself and the crew at the right place, at the right time and, with any luck, on the right day.
BBCTV Training Manual[2]

They used to call it 'Croft's weather':[3] every summer, when the cast and crew arrived in the little Norfolk town of Thetford for the annual fortnight of filming, the sun, in spite of the inevitable vagaries of the season, always seemed to be shining. The clement conditions would then continue, invariably, until all of the exterior shots for the forthcoming series had been gathered safely 'in the can'. The world of Walmington-on-Sea, as a consequence, would always – regardless of what time of year the show went out – look brightly green and pleasant.

Location shooting revolved around a cluster of tried and trusted routines and rituals. The Bell Hotel, a former coaching inn situated in the heart of the old part of the town, served as the base for the principal members of the cast, while the smaller Anchor Hotel, which was just across the river, accommodated the remainder of the team. Saturday saw the arrival of the production crew, along with several caravans full of costumes and equipment, and the actors followed, via various routes and diverse modes of transport, on Sunday. The initial sights and sounds remained, year in, year out, much the same: David Croft and his production manager, Harold Snoad, could be seen attending to details both minor and major; Jimmy Perry could be heard reassuring people that his battered old medicine chest contained everything from throat sprays to senna pods; Arnold Ridley would be double-checking that his room overlooked the quiet river rather than the noisy courtyard; John Laurie and Ian Lavender would be chatting in the reception area; James Beck would be asking someone to spare him a cigarette; John Le Mesurier, Clive Dunn and Bill Pertwee would be busy exchanging short jokes and tall stories; Arthur Lowe would be inquiring anxiously if the local corner shop still stocked his precious cork-tipped Craven 'A's; and Frank Williams and Edward Sinclair would be bustling about in a manner that was strongly reminiscent of the vicar and the verger. Keys were collected, rooms explored, bags unpacked, and then, in the evening, old friendships were rekindled.

Each morning began with Arthur Lowe's notoriously detailed analysis of the breakfast menu: 'I see you have kippers,' he would say to the worried-looking waitress. 'Tell me, are they boil-in-the-bag or are they' – at which point his left hand would essay a friskily undulating motion – 'real swim-about kippers?'[4] He would also ask if the cold ham was tender – *really* tender – and note that, while he was perfectly happy to have his coffee strong, he preferred to take his tea weak – and that meant depositing only one tea bag in his pot rather than the two that the tea-boy seemed intent upon giving him. The other actors, who grew to relish this regular performance, were by this stage already finishing off their own meals and were starting to study the day's itinerary and discuss their forthcoming scenes. John Le Mesurier, in spite of having stayed up most of the night telling stories and sipping spirits, would appear well prepared for the day's work, whereas James Beck, because he had stayed up most of the night with 'Le Mez', would appear somewhat the worse for wear. A production assistant would eventually appear and announce that the coach was due to leave for the latest location in five minutes, and then the cast and crew would rise and make their way out of the hotel. Lowe, more often than not, would be the last to leave, and, when he did finally emerge, it was not uncommon for him to discover that the coach had departed without him. 'These early morning starts play havoc with my lavatorial arrangements,'[5] he would grumble to Jimmy Perry, who usually found himself having to wait behind in order to chauffeur the dilatory actor to the next site. (Perry bought him some packets of All-Bran, which, after some initial resistance – 'I'm not touching that muck! It's like eating the stuffing of a mattress!' – alleviated the problem considerably: 'You know,' Lowe would sigh, sounding like some cheap advertisement, 'All-Bran has totally changed my life!')[6]

The daily shooting schedule, like all shooting schedules, involved lengthy periods of inactivity punctuated by brief but intensive bursts of action. Most of the cast would while away the idle time by sitting back in their chairs and reading – Arnold Ridley, for example, would lose himself in the theatrical and sporting columns of the *Daily Telegraph*, while John Laurie and his fast-learning protégé, Ian Lavender, would compete with each other to see who would be first to complete *The Times* crossword. Arthur Lowe's focus, however, rarely seemed to be far away from food: elevenses, for example, called for at least a couple of rounds of sandwiches (usually bacon and sausage, but sometimes ham if it was 'genuine Wiltshire' and not that 'packeted muck'[7]), which would then be followed by a full traditional English lunch and an afternoon tea that consisted of several rounds of cucumber sandwiches and a choice selection of Mr Kipling – and they really *had* to be Mr Kipling – cakes. Dinner, inevitably, was a topic that Lowe first began to ponder well before the end of the afternoon (there was wine to choose – a crisp, light, dry Ruffino, perhaps, or possibly, depending, of course, on the food, a soft, buttery, Mâcon – and another menu to peruse), but then again, as Ian Lavender confirmed, this was one meal that everyone came to cherish:

> It was like a family gathering. There was the crew, the cast, the extras – who, incidentally, were never called, or treated like, 'extras'; they were always referred to as the 'extra-specials', and were made to feel part of the team – and we'd all come back to the hotel and join up for this evening ritual. It actually really did serve an important purpose, because it gave us all the chance to *talk*. I remember asking David Croft why filming always took a fortnight even though, essentially, everything could probably

have been wrapped up neatly enough in eight or nine days, and he said: 'You haven't seen each other for nine months. These two weeks aren't just about filming; they're also about all of you sitting around before, during and after dinner and talking, getting rid of all of your stories from last year – what you've been doing, what jobs, where you've been, what happened to so-and-so, all of that – so that by the time we get to rehearsals you haven't got anything left to talk about and I've got your undivided attention.' And, of course, it worked. A very canny man, David, very canny indeed.[8]

These regular periods of relaxation also helped the more mature members of the cast to recharge their batteries after spending so much of each day playing out in the fields at being soldiers. David Croft – whom some of the actors referred to affectionately as 'the one-take major'[9] – moved from one set-up to the next at what by normal film-making standards was a remarkably rapid pace: 'I had to. We could only afford, I suppose, one-and-a-half days filming per episode, so we had to pack quite a bit into one fortnight, and I needed to be very efficient. I never, for example, took a safety shot – because once you did, and it didn't work out quite right, you'd be up to take 7 or 8 in no time at all and you're wasting an awful lot of time – and I rarely went further than take 3. I had to drive very hard, because if I didn't keep going it all would have stopped completely.'[10] It helped that Croft had, in Harold Snoad, such a reliable and well-organised 'right-hand man'. 'David and I got on extremely well and he had complete faith in me,' recalled Snoad (who would later be responsible, as a respected producer-director in his own right, for such situation-comedies as *Ever Decreasing Circles* and *Keeping Up Appearances*).[11] 'For instance, on the whole he seldom saw any of the locations . . . before turning up on the actual filming day. I would then say "I thought we could put the camera here" – only one camera on location – "and they could come round that corner and we could pan them to the bridge . . ." etc., and nine times out of ten he would totally agree with me and that is how he would shoot it.'[12]

Sequences were shot in a wide variety of East Anglian sites during the show's nine-year run – including, for example, an old railway station in Weybourne (for 'The Royal Train'), a farm in Witney Green (for 'All Is Safely Gathered In') and a sand quarry in King's Lynn (for 'The Two and a Half Feathers') – but the two most common locations were the town of Thetford itself and the Military Training Area in nearby Stanford. Each year, Snoad remembered, certain parts of the town had to undergo a routine transformation in order to pose as wartime Walmington-on-Sea.

> Whenever we had to do any filming in the streets of Thetford it was necessary for the windows of any houses we saw in the background (and this could be quite a large number in some of the platoon marching sequences) to look correct – i.e. criss-crossed with sticky tape as they would have been during the war. When we first started filming the series we used to spend many a long hour trudging up the road visiting each house with rolls of sticky tape, explaining what we wanted and often having to do the job ourselves. We very quickly decided that this was far too time-consuming, so when the second series came along we duplicated copies of a letter explaining what we wanted, with a diagram of a typical finished window, and these were dropped through the letter boxes in envelopes along with a roll of brown sticky tape and a pound note for their trouble. And everybody obliged![13]

The first time that Snoad saw Stanford – the parish of which had been appropriated by the War Office in 1942 as a base for Army exercises – he knew that he had found an extraordinarily serviceable site:

> Not only was there some lovely countryside but there were some proper roads (which would pass as public roads – indeed, originally they had been public roads). There were also various buildings which had originally been part of small hamlets, but which had then been taken over by the MOD when they acquired the whole area, including cottages and a church. Some of the buildings had suffered somewhat having been used for target practice, but on the whole there was enough left to provide most of what we needed. There was also a river (which

had gates which allowed us to flood the surrounding area when we needed Pike to be rescued having fallen into a bog) and a bridge. Colonel Cleasby-Thompson [the commanding officer of the camp] was extremely helpful and we were virtually given a free hand to do anything we needed.[14]

Snoad and Cleasby-Thompson liaised on a daily basis in order to ensure that the shooting schedule of *Dad's Army* did not clash with that of the real Army, but there were, perhaps inevitably, one or two occasions over the years when, as Snoad put it, 'things went slightly wrong':

We were at a stables (disused but it still looked OK) filming a complicated sequence with the platoon trying to learn to ride (Captain Mainwaring had decided that with strict petrol ration-ing the platoon's transport would be equestrian) when suddenly there was a rustle in the bushes alongside our camera and a young officer in full camouflage uniform (blackened face, the lot) politely informed me that he and his men had orders to blow up this area in 10 minutes! At this a large degree of frenzied conversation ensued and, after I had made an urgent telephone call to the authorities, it was agreed, with only three minutes to go, that they could come back and blow it up the next day![15]

Most problems, however, were of a far more prosaic nature. The combined age of the cast, for example, was, at the start of the 1970s, 524,[16] and David Croft was well aware of the fact that, whenever the time arrived for him to say 'Action!', some of the actors, through no fault of their own, would not be quite as active as the others. He was particularly anxious to ensure that the ensemble's two septuagen-arians, Arnold Ridley and John Laurie, never felt compelled to over-exert themselves – and he always provided both of them with sturdy chairs in which they could relax while the others were obliged to stand – but whereas Ridley, for understandable reasons, welcomed such solicitude, Laurie, although only one year younger, seemed determined to do without it. On one occasion, for example, he and Bill Pertwee were being filmed on horseback, riding at a leisurely pace, when, in the distance, the sound of two practice shots cracked through the air and caused Laurie's horse to bolt: 'He managed after a time to bring it under control,' remembered Pertwee, 'but I knew he was shaken by the mishap. I asked him if he would like to go back to the caravans for a rest and a cup of tea, but he said, "No, laddie, I'll be all right, and don't mention it to the others, I don't want any fuss." And that just about summed John up. I think he believed he might break down and not be able to carry on at all if anyone had started showing concern.'[17] The sight of Ridley settling into his special chair, said Ian Lavender, was usually the cue for Laurie to stagger past with some weighty piece of equipment, or break out into a gentle little jog, or stride briskly back and forth while 'assuring' his semi-recumbent colleague, 'You just take it easy there, son!':

It was a game, really. There was always a sense of competition – friendly competition – between the two of them, because they were the oldest members of the cast. Arnold was very conscious of the fact that he wasn't very fit – I mean, he hadn't known a day without pain since the First World War – and both David and Jimmy, therefore, were very considerate towards him, giving him the first-aid bag instead of the heavy rifle, the galoshes instead of the boots, all of that, and, very sensibly, they didn't write that Arnold should be picking up a telegraph pole. But John Laurie, wicked old man that he was, would be watching Arnold and muttering, 'Ah, the silly auld fool! See what the auld duffer is doing now!' And if there *was* a telegraph pole to be picked up, John would be the one who rushed over to pick it up. To show how fit he was. He wasn't fit – the chest had gone – so he huffed and puffed. We all knew exactly why he was doing it: to get Arnold worried, to see that the other man in his seventies was still running about and help-ing. It wasn't actually meant to make Arnold think that he was old and decrepit and on the verge of being written out. It was just John being a mischievous old man. And he *loved* doing it. I'd be saying, 'John, what are you *doing*?' 'Oh, I need to be seen doing something.' 'John, go and sit down, you fool!' He'd try to pick up the telegraph pole: 'I can do it.' 'No, you can't, sit down!' 'You can't lump me in with *him*!'[18]

One year, Lavender remembered, Laurie was distinctly rattled when Ridley rolled up a little late for the start of location filming in a sleek limousine:

Arnold had broken his hip, and his leg, which was covered in plaster, was sticking straight out in front of him, so he'd needed to travel in something that gave him plenty of leg room. Naturally, he instantly became the centre of attention – which *enraged* John. David Croft was the first to rush over, lean into the car and start shaking Arnold's hand. Now, from a distance, as the rest of us walked over to join him, all we could see was the back of David, leaning towards Arnold, with his arm going up and down, so John turned to me and said: 'Look! Look! They're pumpin' him up! They're pumpin' him up again!' There really wasn't anything vindictive about it. He was just relishing the fact that he didn't require the same kind of treatment. It was another little victory for John.[19]

When it came to the most physical – and hazardous – routines, Croft had no choice but to rely heavily on the three most agile members of the cast: Clive Dunn, Ian Lavender and Bill Pertwee. It was down to Dunn, for example, to execute the kind of stunts – climbing up and hanging from trees, swinging over the side of bridges, tumbling into the hopper of a threshing machine – that required him to summon up all of the strength of a super-fit 50-year-old while still behaving like a vulnerable 70-year-old, and it was usually Lavender or Pertwee who was exposed to the worst of the mud, sludge and water. 'You could chuck anyone into a river, if you wanted to, in those days,' recalled Croft wistfully, 'and we chucked Bill into quite a few. He was terribly good-natured about it. Ian Lavender spent quite a bit of time in the water, too, and once had a large frog work its way up one of his trouser legs. Eventually, however, we had to put a stop to it, because there were rats in the rivers. Health and Safety weren't keen.'[20]

One feature of filming that never changed was the range of carefully-chosen period vehicles which helped lend the outside sequences such an authentic wartime feel. Hodges' greengrocer's lorry, for example, was a 1939 Bedford truck, owned originally by the Air Ministry, which was borrowed each year from a collector in Suffolk, and Jones' navy-and-white butcher's van – which served as the platoon's principal mode of transport – was a 1935 Ford box van that the BBC had found, restored and customised (complete with a line of lidded holes along each side through which the platoon's rifles could be poked) for use in a series of memorable set pieces. The odd elderly machine would sometimes misbehave – Bill Pertwee, Frank Williams and Edward Sinclair once overshot the set and ended up being thrown into a ditch when the throttle of their vintage motor-bike and sidecar became stuck – but most of the assorted staff cars, coaches, trucks, fire engines and steamrollers remained in excellent working order. The butcher's van, in particular, became a great favourite, and, according to Clive Dunn, there was never any short-age of volunteers to sit behind its steering-wheel when the vehicle was off-camera. On one occasion, he claimed, he and the other actors were on their way back to Thetford after a long day of filming when Arthur Lowe made his bid to assume control: 'He said, "Can *I* drive the van for a bit?" So I said, "Do you know how to drive it?" So he said, "Yes, 'course I do" . . . So he drove it round for a bit, and then we went near a farm and unfortunately he ran over a cockerel. Well, he was a perfect gent – stopped the van, knocked on the farmer's door and said, "I'm *awfully* sorry, my man, I'd like to replace your cockerel." And the farmer said, "Well, please yourself – the 'ens are round the back!"'[21]

The final daily ritual was the viewing of the rushes at The Palace, a little cinema in Thetford. Each evening at 10.30 p.m., the cast and crew would arrive outside the building and wait for the 'late' doors to open. Once inside, everyone would settle down and watch a few cartoons while the local projectionist spooled up the latest reel of newly-processed film – sent down by train from London – and readied it for screening. When the sequences were shown, Bill Pertwee remembered, they were often accompanied by such teasing remarks as, 'Look at the warden, overacting again', 'How many more faces is he going to pull?', or 'so and so could have done better then': 'A funny sequence would be greeted with spasmodic applause or laughter. Arthur Lowe would generally fall asleep but wake up at just the right moment to make a cryptic remark. We would then return to our respective hotels for a night-cap or two.'[22]

Armed with Croft and Perry's synopsis, Cohen proceeded to sound out a number of potential investors, and eventually, after suffering several setbacks, he managed (with the assistance of his agent, Greg Smith) to secure a deal with a US-based producer, John R. Sloan, and a Hollywood studio, Columbia Pictures.

Croft and Perry were delighted: now, freed from the kind of constraints that came with television's modest budgets and short spans of time, they could craft the sort of 90-minute screenplay that would allow them to tell a richer, more intricate story, at a more delicately modulated pace, against the backdrop of a fully-visible town peopled by innumerable extras. Cohen – who was duly set to direct – was similarly enthusiastic, announcing that he expected the movie to be 'clean, harmless fun', with 'a lot of visual humour' which he aimed to achieve without the use of 'gimmicks or tricksy camera work': 'The natural humour is in the playing, and it's in my job as director to bring it out and make it work on the big screen.'[4] His first encounter with the cast, however, was not a great success. 'He came to see us at Television Centre,' recalled Ian Lavender, 'and he admitted that he'd never seen a single episode. I don't know if he was winding us up or not, but we all thought, "*What?*"'[5] It was not long before news of Columbia's plans to 'improve' certain aspects of the production arrived to further dampen people's spirits.

The Americans decided, for example, to use the Buckinghamshire village of Chalfont St Giles, rather than the familiar surroundings of Thetford, for most of the scenes set in Walmington-on-Sea, to explore all of the ways in which Croft and Perry's screenplay (which had already been revised once by Norman Cohen) might be made a little more 'dynamic', and to cast Liz Fraser, rather than Janet Davies, in the role of Mrs Pike on the grounds that Fraser, fresh from the *Carry On* franchise, was a performer with a far higher profile.[6] 'Most of the changes struck us as arbitrary,' said Ian Lavender. 'I mean, why film in Chalfont St Giles instead of Thetford? Chalfont St Giles wasn't any nearer to the seaside! No explanation was given to *us*. And why was Jones' van changed for the film? Why was *that* necessary? They wanted another signature tune, too – not to replace "Who Do You Think You Are Kidding . . . ?", but for us to whistle and sing during the marching sequences and so on – and it was *awful*. [Columbia's] attitude seemed to be: "*We're* doing the film, *we'll* do it differently." The thought that went through *our* minds was: "What was wrong with how it was? Why do you want to make it different, if what you wanted to make was that?" '[7]

The shooting schedule said it all: Columbia expected the movie to be completed in six weeks – an almost risibly short period of time (seven weeks fewer, for example, than it took a disciplined director like Howard Hawks, back in the days when Hollywood studios were at their most efficient, to make *Bringing Up Baby*),[8] and a clear message to both the cast and the crew that they would not be encouraged to pause and polish. Like so many inexperienced directors before and after him, Cohen began to feel increasingly peripheral, and did what he could to claw back a little of what he took to be his original authority, but the only thing that he came close to achieving was the abrupt termination of his contract. 'Three weeks before they started filming,' David Croft recalled, 'I was told [by representatives of Columbia] that they'd had a lot of trouble with Norman Cohen and they asked me to take over. I said: "No, I won't do that, because, quite frankly, I don't really like the script now. It's been rewritten for him, to his specifications, and there are quite a lot of things which I think could have been done much, much better." I didn't actually think Cohen was competent as the director, but I was busy at the BBC, and it was really too late to become involved, so I turned them down.'[9] Jimmy Perry *was* still involved, as a 'technical adviser' (on £50 a day), yet he, too, felt disillusioned: 'I was fully prepared to stay on and fight a few battles, but it was obvious that the decision-making power had been taken out of our hands: they were going to do what they were going to do.'[10]

The first day of shooting began on 10 August 1970 at Shepperton Studios in Middlesex. Such was the depressed state of the British film industry at this time that *Dad's Army*, during the initial week or so of its production, was the only movie that was actually being made on the historic lot, and, as Clive Dunn was disappointed to discover, 'the vast studio restaurant was nearly always empty except for the Boulting brothers, who lunched there every day'.[11] John Le Mesurier, who over the course of a long film career had come to regard Shepperton as his own 'very much loved stamping ground',[12] had the greatest cause to feel saddened by the striking evidence of its decline, but he found some comfort in the fact that so many of his old friends – such as Bobby and Chuck, two of the most colourful and conscientious props men in the business – were still around and available to assist and reminisce.

Filming progressed, as expected, at a breathless pace, with the cast moving back and forth between the studio sets and a variety of outside locations (not only in Chalfont St Giles, but also in Chobham in Surrey and Seaford in Sussex), and Norman Cohen being badgered on a daily, and sometimes hourly, basis by John R. Sloan and an assortment of Columbia executives. 'They rather bullied him,' recalled Bill Pertwee. 'They used to keep coming up to him and saying: "How much have you got in the can today?" And he'd say: "I've got six minutes." So then they'd say: "That's not good enough! You should have *nine* minutes in the can each day! What's going wrong?"'[13] The principal actors, who had grown accustomed to working in Croft and Perry's warm and friendly atmosphere, suddenly found themselves being treated like mere employees. 'It was a lot of niggly little things,' remembered Ian Lavender. 'Like John R. Sloan coming over and saying, "Hey, guys, you shouldn't be sitting out here in the sun – you'll change colour!" We weren't wild about that.'[14] The regular members of the platoon's second row – the 'extra-specials' – suddenly found themselves being treated like mere extras. 'It wasn't an enjoyable time,' admitted Lavender, 'and the treatment of the so-called "extras" – lovely people like Colin Bean, Hugh Hastings, George Hancock and so on – upset us all. We'd keep hearing them being referred to as "extras", and we'd say, "*No*, they're part of *us*, actually," and we'd be told, "No, they're extras – same as all the rest." And they'd be shoved around, made to travel on public transport to locations and to the studios, and they were kept apart from us. Sloan once found me playing cards with some of them. "What are you doing with the *extras*?' he said. "We can't have that!" I said, "Look: they're my *friends*. We're playing threepenny poker here. Don't tell me I should not be playing cards with my friends!"'[15] Colin Bean, who played the discreetly eager Private Sponge, recalled an occasion early on when Arthur Lowe decided to intervene, in his inimitable manner, on the second row's behalf:

> To one rather officious crowd marshal (according to his very prominent armband) Arthur introduced us as 'an essential part

of this team which enables this show to retain its popularity'. He asked this man, in authoritative tones, if he'd be so kind as to remember this in future and when it came to catering and 'break' times we were part of the artists' cast. The said gentleman was, if no longer so officious, even less cordial towards us than before. He'd issue shouted orders to 'You extras!' and then equally loudly remember – 'Except, of course, these stars!'[16]

Lowe, it seems, concluded that if Columbia was going to be difficult, so, too, would he, and his subsequent behaviour drove Chuck the props man (who for some reason best known to himself had nicknamed the actor 'Kitty')[17] to complain that the fussy star was causing him more trouble in a few weeks than Gregory Peck had done during an entire year of filming *The Guns of Navarone*.[18] Lowe's most notorious gesture of rebellion was sparked off by what he judged to be the excessive heaviness of the .38 revolver that he was expected to use: he announced that, as it was never actually going to be fired, a lighter, plastic replica would surely suffice, and, when the props department failed to find one, he went off in search of one himself. He was still dressed in his Home Guard uniform when he ordered a unit car to take him out to the nearest branch of Woolworth's, where, to his great annoyance, he was advised that there was nothing in stock that was really suitable apart from a relatively pricey Roy Rogers Special. 'You could always buy a sixpenny pistol in Woolworth's when I was a lad,'[19] he grumbled as he made his way back to the studio (and to the cumbersome prop that from this moment on would be referred to, behind his back, as 'Kitty's revolver').[20]

The actors might have been more tolerant of the studio had they not felt so concerned about the screenplay. John Le Mesurier complained that it was 'little more than three half hour episodes joined together',[21] but it was actually far less coherent than that. Croft and Perry's original script had been 'opened out' by Cohen, who had looked to replace the intimacy of the television show with something more 'cinematic', and then Cohen's version had been 'pumped up' by Columbia executives who were looking for something with a stronger plot and a faster pace, and the finished product, unsurprisingly, was the kind of screenplay that tried to please everyone but failed to satisfy anyone.[22] The first two-thirds of the movie were basically a gently embellished reprise of the first television series, encompassing most of the key scenes and sequences from the formation of the LDV to the arrival of uniforms, weapons and a discernible Home Guard spirit. This was the section that still bore the distinctive fingerprints of Croft and Perry: the montage of authentic wartime images of the *Wehrmacht*, for example, recalled the title sequence that Croft had so wanted to use in the BBC shows, while the name of Mainwaring's bank – 'Martin's' rather than 'Swallow' – referred back to Perry's first draft of his 1967 pilot script (a short-lived copyright problem had prompted the original alteration), and the interaction between the central characters remained broadly true to the high television standards:

WILSON	The Germans have reached Holland.
MAINWARING	Good lord! How on earth did they manage to do that? I could've sworn that they'd never break through the Maginot Line.
WILSON	Quite right, sir – they didn't.
MAINWARING	Ah-ha! I thought not. I'm a pretty good judge of these matters, you know, Wilson.
WILSON	They went round the side.
MAINWARING	I see. (*he does a double-take*) They *what*?
WILSON	They went round the side.
MAINWARING	That's a typical shabby Nazi trick! You see the sort of people we're up against, Wilson?
WILSON	Most unreliable, sir.[23]

The final third of the movie, however, saw the familiar brand of character-driven comedy replaced by a clumsy kind of caper: three German pilots are forced to bail out over Walmington-on-Sea, where they stroll into the church hall during one of the mayor's meetings and hold all of those present as hostages; Mainwaring's men arrive just after Hodges has absconded through a back window and alerted the 'proper' authorities, and the subsequent intervention of the Regular Army leaves the platoon with no choice but to act on its own initiative.

The screenplay was shot through with a nervy spirit of compromise: it was a comedy in celebration of the amateur that was afraid to poke fun at the professional; a comedy about an invasion that never actually materialises, but with an actual mini-invasion thrown in for good measure. 'The big mistake,' said Ian Lavender, 'was that we saw the Germans. I know we had glimpses of them in the odd episode of the television series, but most of the time there was no real evidence of what Mainwaring and his platoon were really up against; the comedy was about these characters who were waiting to confront the enemy – it wasn't "about" the enemy at all. The film, however, *did* show the enemy, the German HQ, the hordes of bombers, tanks, the battalions of marching men – it showed it all – and I think, in doing so, much of the cosiness, the charm, of the television show was lost.'[24]

There were some nice touches – such as the series of cross-cuts that contrasted Nazi organisation ('All divisional commanders will be in touch with me by shortwave radio') with Home Guard improvisation ('All section leaders will be in touch with me by Boy Scout runners') – but there were also some clumsy, *Carry On*-style intrusions – such as the line (which deserved to be underscored by the sound of a trombone) that obliged Mainwaring to exclaim, 'I must ask you to take your hands off my privates.' There would have been far more errors both of detail and judgement had Jimmy Perry not been on hand to intervene. 'I don't think they were terribly fond of Jimmy,' remembered Bill Pertwee. 'He'd keep stopping and saying, "Look, I'm sorry, but this just isn't *right*, this scene, because that costume isn't right," or whatever, and they'd say, "Oh, it doesn't matter. People won't notice that sort of thing. Get on with it." But Jimmy was persistent, and he did manage to get one or two things changed.'[25]

Neither Perry nor Croft had much faith in Norman Cohen's eye for comedy: 'He missed the *reactions* to funny lines,' complained Croft. 'I ended up having to write a letter to Columbia, saying, "For God's sake, can you look through the out-takes to find some reaction shots from Arthur?" They did find a few, but not enough, in my view.'[26] The most glaring example of Cohen's comedic inexperience came with a scene early on in the movie, in which Mainwaring refused to cash the £10 cheque of an unfamiliar customer (played by Bernard Archard) on the grounds that he 'might be a German spy': instead of following the irate customer ('Damned bank clerk!')

back out on to the street, where it is revealed that he is actually Major General Fullard (one of Mainwaring's future superior officers and his most vehement critic), Cohen elected to end the scene at the counter. Perry, understandably, was horrified, pointing out that the only reason he and Croft had written the scene in the first place was to set up the later confrontation between the two pompous little men; the axiom 'Always let the audience in on the joke' was one of the 'golden rules' of *Dad's Army*, and he could not understand why Cohen felt entitled to depart from it.[27] Perry, eventually, won this particular battle, and the scene was allowed to reach its intended conclusion, but Cohen and Columbia would be the ones to win the war.

None of the actors felt much like fighting any more after filming a challenging sequence in Chobham. A white horse – 'borrowed' from a popular whisky commercial of the time – was supposed to carry first Major General Fullard, and then Lance Corporal Jones, downstream on a raft. 'After three weeks of practice,' recalled Clive Dunn, 'we were told that the stunt was no longer frightening, but nobody had bothered to tell the horse!':

> If I had been allowed to sit astride, I might have managed like Bernard Archard, but the action called for me to lie along the animal without gripping with my legs, merely clinging round its neck. On the shout 'Action!' the raft moved downstream and the frightened horse started bucking, rearing and stamping about. I thought this was the moment of truth and that the animal would rear backwards on top of me as we both fell into the river. Some of the more boring bits of my past life flashed before me and so did my lunch. All this, plus half an hour hanging perilously from a branch over the deep river, frightened the daylights out of me and the small round of applause, led by my family who were watching the filming, for these death-defying achievements hardly compensated. When the camera zoomed in to a close-up of me begging the horse to control itself, I wasn't acting.[28]

In a later section of the same sequence, Arthur Lowe, John Le Mesurier and John Laurie had to accompany the horse on the raft as it drifted down the river. The erratic movements of the hidden tow lines that were meant to be controlling the raft unbalanced the horse, causing it to slip and fall on John Laurie, badly bruising his ribs. It had been a fairly harrowing day, and, as John Le Mesurier would reflect, it was not over yet:

> As sun set at about seven o'clock, some clever publicity fellow thought it would be splendid if he could get a long shot of several of the platoon on the horse's back. We climbed on to this dear creature, someone shouted, 'Action!' and the horse, being tired after a long day, sank a few inches into the muddy banks of the Thames. She then reared up and threw us off. I landed in John Laurie's lap, which momentarily winded him. My wrist-watch disappeared into the Thames. Naturally, I put in for an over-extravagant sum in compensation. But next morning, someone had to go and retrieve it from the river. I could have killed him.[29]

Filming came to an end on Friday, 25 September, with the completion of a few minor inserts. Arthur Lowe congratulated himself on keeping his trousers up for the duration (John Le Mesurier had been left to lead the men in their underwear for Perry's 'passage of time' montage, while Lowe provided the rather smug voice-over: 'Jerry will never catch *us* with our trousers down!'), and everyone else congratulated themselves simply for having reached the end of an exhausting and sadly unrewarding month-and-a-half. The cast had grown rather fond of Norman Cohen – whom Le Mesurier described as 'a kind of pixie in the Irish/Jewish tradition'[30] – but his inadequacies as a director of comedy, coupled with his haste to meet his deadlines, had undermined some good performances. No one felt sorry to leave Shepperton and hurry back to London and the BBC: the first episode of the fourth television series was broadcast on the same day that work stopped on the movie, and several episodes still had to be shot. 'There wasn't really time for regrets,' said Ian Lavender. 'We just got on with the next thing.'[31]

Dad's Army: The Movie received its UK première on 12 March 1971 at the Columbia Theatre in London. The newspaper reviews that ensued were, on the whole, inclined to be charitable: the *Daily*

Mirror's Dick Richards, for example, reported that the movie 'produces no belly laughs but a lot of reminiscent smiles and enjoyment',[32] while Ian Christie commented in the *Daily Express* that the actors were in 'good form' even though the film lacked a 'good plot',[33] Derek Malcolm remarked in the *Guardian* that the 'rather clumsy but not utterly guileless attempt to translate a telly favourite into a movie money-spinner' was boosted by Arthur Lowe's 'supreme' performance,[34] and Alexander Walker of the *London Evening Standard* predicted that the movie, which encouraged 'easy and affectionate laughter', would 'appeal most to those who like to leave the box behind at home – and have an outing to the cinema to see the same thing'.[35] *Monthly Film Bulletin*'s Sylvia Millar, on the other hand, complained that the 'central joke' of *Dad's Army* – 'the perpetual non-appearance of the enemy against which Mainwaring's po-faced vigilance is eternally pitted' – had been betrayed by the decision to bring into view 'three quite lethal Germans' ('the spell is broken'), and she lamented the loss of the television show's 'intimacy and subtlety of characterisation', as well as 'the introduction of coarsening and inflating elements which overwhelm, almost to extinction, the fragile, nostalgic humour of the original'.[36]

In spite of the fact that the movie was, technically speaking, American, there was no serious attempt by Columbia to market the production on its own side of the Atlantic. The one significant US review – which appeared in the trade journal *Variety* – advised its readers (in its own peculiar patois) that non-British audiences 'may find some of the humor too parochial, but certain quick yocks and gag situations are all right in any lingo'. The critique concluded by declaring that '*Dad's Army* is not going to make a permanent mark in film history, but farcically it contributes a warm tribute to British war history. It will certainly please middle-agers and those who lately have been hooked on a tv idea that, at the time it was begat, must have seemed a most unlikely project.'[37]

The movie might have been a disappointment, but it was far from being a disaster. It had been inexpensive to make, it performed well at the domestic box office,[38] and it would go on to age much better than the majority of other big screen situation-comedies of the era: when it was shown for the first time on British television, on 5 May 1979, more than thirteen million viewers tuned in to watch.[39] David

Croft and Jimmy Perry, however, could not see it as anything other than a missed opportunity, and they resolved to try again – only the next time, they agreed, it would be done *their* way.

An outline, entitled 'Dad's Army and the Secret U-boat Base', was completed and distributed to a number of interested parties. The story was set in a small coastal town in North Wales: after several British warships sink in the Irish Sea, the War Office comes to suspect that the Germans have managed to establish a clandestine base somewhere along the coast; rather than draw attention to the investigation by sending in the Regular Army, the most innocuous-looking Home Guard unit the War Office can find, the Walmington-on-Sea platoon, is chosen to visit the area – ostensibly for manoeuvres – and sniff out the Nazis. Laurence Olivier, who was an avid admirer of the show, heard of the project, read the treatment, and subsequently expressed an interest in playing the key role of a Nazi leader who has taken over a country house and passed himself off as the lord of the manor. The funding, however, failed to materialise quickly enough, and Croft and Perry soon became distracted by their various television commitments; the moment was allowed to pass, and the project was consigned, for good, to the darkness of the bottom drawer.[40]

Dad's Army never would make it back on to the big screen. The move from one medium to the other had always been ill-conceived: the cinema framed the situation-comedy, it gave it a beginning, middle and end, whereas television allowed it to flow. There was no cause for regret: the show was still big – it was just the pictures that were small.

CHAPTER XII

Shaftesbury Avenue

Can we anywhere recapture the olden pleasure?
MAX BEERBOHM[1]

Stand by with your concertina.
GEORGE MAINWARING[2]

The cinema would not be the final digression for *Dad's Army*. In 1975, the decision was made to place the cast upon the stage. The show might not have been suited to the theatre, but Croft and Perry were, and, in a period before home video, the venture represented a good opportunity to exploit the programme's popularity with the public.

The plan was to use a fairly loose revue format as a showcase for both the actors and their characters: space would be found for special individual 'turns' as well as routines for the whole ensemble, and the situation-comedy's familiar features would be woven together with a range of real-life wartime themes. Details of the production had first been revealed to the cast during the previous summer's fortnight of filming in Thetford. Jimmy Perry got up one evening after dinner at the Bell Hotel, announced that he and his co-writer had been working on one or two ideas, and then, just like he used to do in his concert party days in India, he proceeded to act out every sketch and sing every song in the show, impersonating Churchill, Mainwaring, Max Miller, Pike, Robb Wilton, Wilson, a Nazi officer, the vicar, the verger and Hodges, jumping up and down, running from one side of the room to the other and even having a go at a one-man conga. 'Well,' he finally inquired, panting heavily, 'how does that sound?' Edward Sinclair, who had sat through it all in silence, replied: 'I'm tired out and the show hasn't even started yet!'[3]

Reactions to the proposal were mixed: Arthur Lowe, despite his snobbery about Variety, was fairly positive (particularly after it had been agreed that his wife, Joan, would also be appearing as Godfrey's sister, Dolly), whereas John Le Mesurier, as was his wont, remained unconvinced that it would work. John Laurie declined to take part, fearing that, at the age of 78, the slog might prove too much of a strain, but Arnold Ridley decided to brave it. Clive Dunn agreed to join in even though he felt there was a danger that the transfer from screen to stage would turn out to be 'diminishing',[4] and, with varying degrees of enthusiasm, the remaining members of the cast fell into line.

Croft and Perry enlisted the services of an old mutual friend, the eminently well-connected theatrical agent Richard Stone, to help them find a suitable producer. Stone duly found them two: 'We offered it to Duncan [Weldon], who was not yet rich enough to present what had emerged as quite a large revue-type musical without some financial help. Fortunately my old friend Bernie Delfont was happy to co-present and put up the money.'[5] Stone also found someone to stage it: Roger Redfarn, a promising young talent (and client of Stone's) who, in stark contrast to the likes of John R. Sloan or Norman Cohen, was quite prepared to work closely, and tactfully, with the two co-writers. A team was then put together: Ed Coleman, a vocal and energetic American, was brought in as the show's musical director; the well-regarded dancer Sheila O'Neill was installed as choreographer; the BBC's Mary Husband was handed the task of creating the costumes; and the experienced Terry Parsons was drafted in as the show's designer. Hamish Roughead,[6] a suitably mature Scottish actor, was chosen to play the part of Frazer, and John Bardon[7] was selected to play Walker, but neither role, in the absence of the original actor, was set to be much more than a cipher. 'I think Hamish Roughead, at least early on, was deeply upset at just how small the part of Frazer turned out to be,' recalled Ian Lavender. 'But Johnny Bardon was totally realistic about it from the start, saying, "We can't feature largely, obviously, because we're not the person they actually want to see." Which was right. That's one of the peculiarities of television: audiences will accept all kinds of actors playing Hamlet, but only one actor can play Sergeant Wilson, or Jones, or Walker, or Frazer.'[8] Redfarn also cast Jeffrey Holland[9] as an eccentric Nazi inventor, but he would also serve as the understudy to both John Bardon and Ian Lavender: 'Straightaway,' said Redfarn, 'Jimmy and David liked him so whenever any extra bits cropped up, he got them.'[10]

After three weeks of rehearsal at the Richmond Theatre in Surrey, the cast prepared to travel north to Billingham, in Cleveland, for the show's out-of-town try-out. 'Why do we have to go to this Billingham place, Billy?' John Le Mesurier moaned to Bill Pertwee. 'It's miles from anywhere, we shall all probably get lost.'[11] Le Mesurier's mood did not improve when he finally arrived at The Forum, the town's modern-looking theatre, and was greeted by a doorkeeper who said, 'Good morning, Sir, are you Arnold Lowe?'[12] It was, in the words of David Croft, 'quite a worrying time',[13] as the production team debated the best ways to knock the show into shape. Some scenes and songs were dropped and then reintroduced, various bits of business were added and subtracted, and the actors, as Bill Pertwee recalled, were driven increasingly hard:

> We were working long hours on some days and Roger Redfarn was becoming oblivious of the time of day as we went through songs, dance routines, dialogue and costume rehearsal. At two o'clock one morning I realised that the uncomplaining boys and girls had had no supper, not even a sandwich, and our strength was beginning to sag. I therefore walked on to the stage and quite out of turn, announced that everyone had obviously had enough for that night. There was a silence in which you could have heard a pin drop. Suddenly Arthur Lowe said, 'I quite agree' and that was the end of rehearsals for that night.[14]

The opening night of what by this time was billed as 'Dad's Army: A Nostalgic Music and Laughter Show of Britain's Finest Hour' arrived on Thursday, 4 September 1975, to warm applause, and the remainder of the performances during the fortnight-long stay elicited a similarly enthusiastic response. 'The jolly North Country audience had received us well,' Clive Dunn reflected, 'without looking for too many faults.'[15] Richard Stone, however, considered the production, as it stood, to be 'a mess',[16] and several changes were made before the show was allowed to commence its London run. 'Bernie [Delfont] and I sat at the back of the Shaftesbury Theatre for the first preview in London,' Stone recalled. 'It seemed to us that Clive Dunn, bless him, was singing innumerable songs. Bernie was back where he belonged in live theatre, "sorting it out".'[17] Dunn did not have to wait very long to discover just what Delfont had succeeded in sorting out:

> After the dress rehearsal, when Duncan Weldon, representing the management, came in to take my new agent, Peter Prichard, off for a little chat, I was highly suspicious. I had fluffed the patter a bit due to a few hitches in the staging, miscued lighting changes, and half expected to be told to polish up my lines, which I knew perfectly well. When my agent came back with the news that Delfont had cut [one of the songs] completely I should then and there have done the full demonstration and walked out of the theatre, threatening never to return. But that simply wasn't my scene, and after Peter Prichard had convinced me that his protestations had been of no avail I swallowed my deep disappointment. I had lost the number, but gained a reputation with the management as a non-wavemaker, and so Bernie Delfont later described me as a 'grand chap'.[18]

Further minor cuts were made, the running order was revised, ruffled thespian feathers were smoothed, and the show was pronounced ready.

The West End opening, on Thursday, 2 October, was later described by Stone as 'one of my happiest nights in the theatre'.[19] The show began with David Croft's cherished montage of Second World War news footage (he never would let it lie), followed by the familiar strains of 'Who Do You Think You Are Kidding, Mr Hitler?' and the appearance of the cast descending, rather gingerly, a steep flight of glittery stairs. Several of the sketches and routines that ensued had previously been seen, and enjoyed, on television. They reprised the increasingly aggressive morris dancing scene from 'The Godiva Affair' (JONES: 'I've faced whirling Dervishes, and I've faced charging Fuzzie Wuzzies, but I don't want to face Private Frazer when he's waving his whiffling stick. He's got a mad look in his eyes') and a tetchy rehearsal of the Cornish Floral Dance which had first been witnessed as a segment in the 1970 edition of BBC1's

Christmas Night With the Stars (MAINWARING: 'Wilson! Don't *anticipate* me. Watch my stick!'). A number of new and in some cases quite unlikely flights of fancy were added to the mix, such as the sight of Private Pike, in a dream sequence prompted by the rigours of rationing, performing a lavish Carmen Miranda-style production number while zipped up in a giant plastic banana. Most of the actors were allowed at least one party piece: John Le Mesurier, for example, gave a rather charming rendition of 'A Nightingale Sang In Berkeley Square' ('I didn't, of course, actually *sing*,' he would explain; 'it was a sort of half singing, half talking version, rather in the manner of a poor man's Rex Harrison');[20] Arthur Lowe delivered a splendid impersonation of Robb Wilton; Bill Pertwee contributed an equally impressive impersonation of Max Miller; and Arnold Ridley recited the poem 'Lords of the Air'. Lowe also teamed up with Le Mesurier to perform the old Flanagan and Allen number, 'Hometown', but, as an opening night surprise, he returned to sing it a second time with the surviving member of the double act, Chesney Allen: 'When Ches strolled on with Arthur Lowe for the encore,' Richard Stone recalled, 'the whole audience stood and cheered. It was a great moment.'[21] The two-and-a-half-hour show came to its conclusion with a short, poignant scene set on the beach at Walmington-on-Sea soon after the end of the war: 'The Home Guard never went into battle,' Mainwaring reflected, 'but the two million men – shop assistants, factory workers, doctors, lawyers, men from every walk of life – gave of their spare time and, in some cases, their lives, to defend their homeland. And if ever this island were in danger again, men like those would be there once more – standing ready.'[22] The speech was followed by an upbeat orchestral version of the *Dad's Army* theme song, and a succession of loudly applauded curtain calls.

The critics, on the whole, were kind. John Elsom, writing in *The Listener*, complained that the show was nothing more than 'a crude cartoon' with 'some appallingly jingoistic moments',[23] but a far more typical response came from Harold Hobson, the distinguished drama critic of the *Sunday Times*, who declared that Croft and Perry had 'produced something whose subtle simplicity is a total artistic success': '[The show] is funny and touching; it is satirical, and it has a great pride. It is remarkable what you can do if you wear your heart on your sleeve, but also have a brain in your head.'[24] The most measured appraisal was probably B. A. Young's account in the *Financial Times*: 'A kind of double nostalgia is seen to be working,' he remarked. 'Half the time the audience are nostalgic about the *Dad's Army* programmes themselves; the other half, they are nostalgic about the real wartime life.' Young doubted that 'these two kinds of nostalgia really blend', but acknowledged that 'this is an academic judgement'. The first appearance of the cast was greeted, he noted, with 'a standing ovation', and the audience 'were just as enthusiastic' during the subsequent sketches and solo spots, and when 'your actual Chesney Allen' made his unexpected entrance 'the cheers were deafening'. Young concluded: 'The impression I came away with was of enormous good nature on both sides of the footlights, friendliness and companionability and all those good qualities associated with wartime and the theatrical representation of wartime. Not such a bad thing, really, especially with Arthur Lowe at the head.'[25]

There was nothing truly exceptional about the show: it had no pretensions to bold theatrical ambition and it served its modest purpose. It enabled the audience to see a set of small screen stars fully sized and in the flesh, and it enabled the actors to see for themselves just how popular they, and the programme, had actually become. 'It was lovely,' said Ian Lavender. 'I don't think any of us, at the start, had known quite what to expect, and it had come as quite a bit of a surprise when it turned into a sort of musical, but, yes, it worked, it was very enjoyable, and it *was* a very warm, very affectionate kind of occasion.'[26] The demand, undeniably, was there: in addition to the actual West End run itself (which continued until February the following year), the cast also took part in a prestigious Royal Variety Performance at the London Palladium,[27] recorded an album based on the show[28] and made numerous personal appearances. John Le Mesurier also pondered an invitation from a kindred spirit, Derek Taylor (the former Beatles press officer who at that time was director of special projects at Warner Brothers), to make a suitably unorthodox solo album (it would eventually be released, two years later, under the title *What Is Going To Become Of Us All?*),[29] and Bill Pertwee, along with his fellow member of cast Norman MacLeod, was persuaded to release a novelty single called 'Hooligans!'[30]

Each actor was experienced enough to take it all in a steady stride. The production was disrupted on two separate occasions during the autumn by bomb scares – this was a period of intense terrorist activity in the English capital by the Irish Republican Army – but Arthur Lowe, as the self-appointed leader of the company, responded to both of these unhappy events by snapping into action and saying, 'Right, follow me, men',[31] and then leading his fellow performers straight out of the theatre and up the road to the nearest acceptable pub, where they would have a leisurely drink and relax until the message came that it was safe to return and resume the show. There was another brief interruption early on in the new year, but this time the reason was entirely welcome: Arnold Ridley, who had been coping remarkably well with a fairly draining schedule, reached the age of 80, and the occasion was celebrated on stage in the presence of both the press and the public. 'The more I work,' he declared, 'the better I feel.'[32]

After five well-attended months in the West End, the production went on tour: Manchester, Nottingham, Bradford, Birmingham, Bournemouth, Blackpool, Newcastle-upon-Tyne, Richmond, Brighton and Bath were all visited during the period from March through to September 1976. Clive Dunn had not been keen to continue, but, after receiving a firm assurance from Croft and Perry that his 'missing' epic song (about the demise of General Gordon at Khartoum) would be reinstated, he agreed to commit himself to half of the tour. David Croft replaced him for the remaining dates with the actor who, ironically, had been his first choice for the role of Jones back in 1968, Jack Haig.

Each enforced omission inspired a new commission: 'We had a marginally smaller cast,' Frank Williams remembered, 'and so Edward [Sinclair] and I were roped into one or two extra numbers, including the "banana" number, which was a great deal of fun.'[33] Colin Bean, who had declined to be involved in the show on the grounds that he feared it might become 'too "hyped up"', glamorised and far from the spirit of the TV show',[34] found this particular number to be slightly *too* odd when he attended a performance in Manchester: 'The sight of the "vicar" and the "verger" (still in flat cap) rumbaing away in a full-blown "Carmen Miranda"-style South American scene amid a bevy of clamorous dancers was not my idea of what *Dad's Army* was all about.'[35] The only occasions, however, when the routine failed to provoke the desired response were those when Jeffrey

Holland, rather than Ian Lavender, played the part of Private Pike. 'Poor Jeff,' Lavender recalled, 'went through the whole performance without getting a single laugh – except from some of the other members of the cast, who were sniggering at his discomfort. He told me: "Even when I went on dressed as a six-foot banana, dancing around, with all the '*Ay! Ay! Ays!*', I got no reaction. Nothing. Total silence. *I* knew it was a funny routine. *I* wasn't *that* bad doing it. But *I* wasn't *you*." That was the problem: he *was* funny, but he wasn't Pike.'[36]

The tour was punctuated by all kinds of extra-curricular adventures: The cast took part in a cricket match to raise money for the construction of a new pavilion at Hayfield Cricket Club (Arthur Lowe was its proud president), and Arnold Ridley, after executing one or two elegant cover drives and a surprisingly lusty square cut, became so excited that he forgot that he had been provided with a runner and started jogging down the wicket ('We all finished up in a heap at one end,' recalled his fellow batsman, Bill Pertwee, 'and it was deemed that I was out').[37] Arthur Lowe and John Le Mesurier agreed to fly to The Netherlands in order to appear on an irreverent television programme, dressed in their *Dad's Army* outfits, and, as Le Mesurier put it, 'say two rather rude words in Dutch' ('The live audience seemed to think that what we had said was the funniest happening that had ever come their way. Neither Arthur nor I knew what the real meaning of the words was, nor did we care very much. We took a bow and fled the building for the last plane out of Amsterdam').[38] When the show finally reached Bath, the last stop, the principal actors were invited to lunch at the home of Neville Chamberlain's daughter-in-law, where they had the opportunity to examine some of the letters written by the Prime Minister during the Munich crisis of 1938.[39] There was always some kind of novel experience to brighten the dull routine.

It all came to an end, after six generally enjoyable months, on Saturday, 4 September 1976. The production had not, in fact, been much of a money-spinner – 'the cast was large and pricey,' explained Clive Dunn, 'the sets enormous'[40] – but it had generated a great deal of good will. When the diversion was over, the attention turned back to television, the central attraction, and to those things that the makers of *Dad's Army* did best.

THE
CLASSIC

Wit lasts.
PENELOPE GILLIATT[1]

CHAPTER XIII

The Nation's Favourite

There is always a laugh in the utterly familiar.
JAMES THURBER[1]

Nothing would please me more than to have Dad's Army *on every week.*
HUW WHELDON[2]

'You'll undoubtedly go on for ever and ever with *Dad's Army*,'[3] Prince Philip opined, rather forcefully, when he encountered a crowd of BBC executives in the early 1970s, and none of them, on this particular occasion, felt inclined to disagree. *Dad's Army*, by this time, had indeed become something of a standard-bearer for the BBC's flourishing Light Entertainment department, providing visible proof of its continuing commitment to the principle Bill Cotton, its head, liked to define as 'the best possible entertainment by the best possible entertainers'.[4]

In June 1973, the programme, following five progressively successful series, was at its peak, and the next sequence of episodes that the team was set to record would contain some of the show's finest and funniest moments. Two months later, however, James Beck, at the age of just 44, would be dead, the cast and crew would be plunged into mourning, and nothing to do with *Dad's Army* would ever seem quite the same again.

Everyone had known that this particular summer was going to be extremely busy. There was not only a television series to record, but also, for the first time, a radio series,[5] and no one was looking forward to it all more keenly than Jimmy Beck. He had not always been the most disciplined of actors – 'he was sometimes quite naughty,' Clive Dunn recalled, 'and a few of his hangovers held up filming'[6] – but he had never lacked ambition, and his career now seemed at the start of a sharp ascent. During the first half of 1973 alone, he had recorded two series for London Weekend Television of a new starring vehicle called *Romany Jones*,[7] and co-starred alongside Arthur Lowe in the pilot of a new BBC1 situation-comedy entitled *Bunclarke With An 'E'* (adapted by Ray Galton and Alan Simpson from some of their old Tony Hancock scripts, featuring Lowe as the Hancock figure and Beck as the character associated with Sid James).[8] Once he had completed his *Dad's Army* duties, he was due to appear on Thames Television in a one-off play called *The Village Concert*. 'I think that Jimmy was one of those actors who wanted to explore further afield all the time,' reflected Bill Pertwee. 'I'm pretty sure that he would have stayed with *Dad's*, but he did have this drive, this quest, because he was a very good stage actor, and he wanted to keep proving himself.'[9]

His weakness, however, was alcohol. He had come to cherish the warm and relaxed domestic environment in East Sheen that he shared with his extremely supportive wife, Kay, and their three young children, but he continued to be fascinated by the night life, and susceptible to the drinking culture, of Soho, and his health, as a consequence, had started to suffer. It was obvious to the other members of the cast that something was wrong when, on Friday, 13 July, Beck joined them at the Playhouse Theatre in order to record a couple of episodes for the radio version of *Dad's Army*: 'It was a very hot night,' Ian Lavender remembered, 'and Jimmy was sweating profusely – far more than the rest of us were. He was wearing a short-sleeved summer shirt outside his trousers, and it looked as if he'd got a football under his shirt.'[10] This, it turned out, was the last time that Beck's fellow actors would see him alive. The following afternoon, shortly after opening a local school fête in aid of Guide Dogs for the Blind, he felt a sudden and excruciating pain in his stomach; his wife took him straight home, summoned a doctor, and within the hour he was rushed to the intensive care unit of Queen Mary's Hospital in Roehampton, Surrey, where he slipped into a coma. 'Doctors told me he has an organic disorder,' Kay Beck told reporters. 'The chemical balance of his body has been upset by something or other and the doctors have to try to put it right again. We have no idea what has caused it. The next 36 hours are vital. If he pulls through there will be hope again.'[11]

The news shook the *Dad's Army* team to its core. Another episode of the television series – 'Things That Go Bump in the Night' – was due to be recorded on Sunday in front of a studio audience, and, as Beck featured in those sequences that had already been shot outside on location, Croft and Perry were left with no option but to redistribute his remaining lines and then hope that a combination of brisk editing and clever lighting would distract from the fact that Walker had failed to join the others inside. The following week of rehearsal was punctuated by regular, but increasingly depressing, updates on Beck's condition, and then the time arrived to record 'The Recruit': the final episode in the current series, and the first without any footage of Beck. It featured a revised 'line-up' scene set in the church hall, which saw Mainwaring inspect Jones, and then Pike, and then the space where Walker ought to have been. A note, which is picked up from the floor, is sniffed by Wilson – 'Unusual perfume: petrol' – and then snatched by Mainwaring, who proceeds, in puzzled tones, to read it out:

Dear Cap,

Thanks for letting me off. Had to go up to the Smoke for a few days to do a deal. I think I can swing it for a grand, but I shall have to drop the geezer a pony. On the other hand, I may cop it for a bit under the odds, in which case I'll have to sweeten him with a monkey, and half a bar for his nippers.

PS Here's a couple of oncers for yourself![12]

Mainwaring, after slipping the pound notes into his pocket, is indignant: 'How *dare* he try to bribe me!' he exclaims. 'I'll see him in the office as soon as he comes back!'

Walker never would come back. On 6 August, three weeks after he first lost consciousness, Jimmy Beck died from what the coroner described as a combination of heart failure, renal failure and pancreatitis.[13] 'I'm shattered,' Arthur Lowe was quoted as saying. 'He was one of the greatest. He had great talent. All of us in *Dad's Army* were very fond of him. His contribution to the team was enormous.'[14] Clive Dunn would later confess that it felt not only as if he had lost a dear friend, but also, quite possibly, a much-loved job: 'It was awful for his wife and for all his friends,' he said. 'It was a shock, and, of course, from a selfish point of view, I thought, "My God! What's going to happen to the programme? Are we still going to be able to do it?" '[15]

When, three months later, the sixth series was actually broadcast, there was an obvious poignancy about the fact that Beck (and Walker) was still there, in five of the six episodes, a vivid presence that viewers knew was now absent. The opening episode, 'The Deadly Attachment', was broadcast by BBC1 on the evening of Wednesday, 31 October 1973, and, under normal circumstances, it would surely have been greeted with unqualified enthusiasm. It had everything: the confrontation with the German U-boat captain ('Face to face with the enemy at last, eh?'), the pertinent contribution from Pike ('Hitler is a twerp'), the swift intervention from Mainwaring ('Don't tell him, Pike!'), the order to supply the prisoners with a meal ('I'm afraid we've only got our own sandwiches, Colonel!'), the fussy fish and chip suppers ('Und I don't want any nasty, soggy chips. I want mine crisp und light brown'), the grenade down the trousers ('It was originally going to be down *Arthur's* trousers,' recalled David Croft, 'but, of course, he wasn't having any of it. He said he'd have it inside his tunic, but not down his trousers. So we handed that part of the business to Clive Dunn. It was much better that way, of course, and I think Arthur was a little jealous'),[16] and Wilson's very English brand of aggression ('Now, listen to me, you German fellows! Would you mind getting up against the wall and putting your hands up, please?'). The writing, the acting, the pace, the tone and the direction were all shrewdly judged, and it is hard to believe any series could have had a stronger start, but the reaction that it attracted was, by the programme's high standards, surprisingly subdued. The BBC's own audience research report noted that, while many viewers had expressed the opinion that *Dad's Army* was still 'one of the funniest situation-comedies on television', and that the latest episode had contained 'some remarkably fresh ideas', a significant number had commented on how sad it made them feel to see James Beck on the screen so soon after his death ('he provided so many laughs and one cannot forget he is no longer with us').[17]

Just under thirteen million people watched the show – a figure which, though by no means unimpressive, represented a loss of more than three million viewers from the previous season's average.[18] The feelings of discomfort engendered by the news of Beck's death may well have played a part in this relative decline, but so, too, did the new time-slot to which the programme had been assigned: 6.50 p.m. on Wednesdays. It now played against the final ten minutes of ITV's surprisingly popular soap opera, *Crossroads* (which regularly pulled in an audience of well over six, and sometimes seven million)[19] and the first twenty minutes of either *Whicker Way Out West* (a popular travel/'lifestyle' show that attracted some seven million viewers) or, later on in the run, *This Is Your Life* (which was normally watched by more than twelve million).[20] 'I never felt that [*Dad's Army*] was being well handled by the schedulers,' said David Croft. 'We never got good spots, *soft* spots, like opposite *World In Action*.'[21] There was no doubt that the programme was still extremely popular – BBC1's share of the general television audience rose by more than ten million viewers when each episode of *Dad's Army* began, and then fell by almost eleven million when the closing credits rolled[22] – but there was also no doubt that the show would have fared far better in the ratings if it had occupied a proper prime-time slot: 'The only regret of some,' noted the BBC's audience report, 'was that the programme was [on] so early in the evening that they missed the beginning ("on the way home" – "having a meal" – "clashed with *Crossroads*").'[23]

The irony was that, although neither the mood nor the time may have been quite right, this was actually a splendid series. 'The Deadly Attachment' was followed by such deftly entertaining episodes as 'My British Buddy' (which saw the first contingent of American troops arrive, belatedly, in Walmington-on-Sea, followed by several bungled photo-opportunities and one profoundly impolitic pub brawl); 'The Royal Train' (in which the mayor, the vicar, the verger and Hodges ended up on a pump truck, alternately pursuing, and being pursued by, an unruly steam engine); 'We Know Our Onions' (featuring a seemingly never-ending efficiency test); and 'The Honourable Man' (concerning the consequences of Wilson's elevation to an even loftier level of eminence). The critical response was positive – Peter Black praised the programme's 'innocent and sane comedy',[24] and Shaun Usher remarked that 'the characters are real enough to make us want to know more about them, even if the framework is familiar'[25] – but the disappointing dip in the ratings (the series ended up with an average audience of 12.3 million),[26] coupled with the sad loss of a key member of the cast, meant that the future of *Dad's Army* suddenly seemed a little less certain, and a little less bright, than it had done for some years.

'I don't think, at that stage, we considered stopping,' said Jimmy Perry, 'but it was obviously a very difficult time. Jimmy's death was pretty shattering. It was always a worry after that. You never knew what might happen.'[27] The character of Walker would be retained by the radio series – the role was passed first of all to Graham Stark and then later to Beck's close friend and neighbour, Larry Martyn – but there was never any attempt to recast the role for television. Croft and Perry did feel, however, that the front row of the platoon, for reasons of balance, ought to keep up its numbers, and so the decision was made to introduce a completely new regular character to fill, or at least obscure, the current gap in the line-up. The two co-writers thought back to one of their most recent episodes, 'My British Buddy', and the performance of Talfryn Thomas as the some-what gauche but very persistent photo-journalist from the *Eastbourne Gazette*, Mr Cheeseman. Thomas, a 52-year-old, Swansea-born actor whose top set of teeth stuck out like a row of high-kicking legs in a chorus line, had wrung every last laugh out of his modest little role, he had worked very well with Arthur Lowe, and, as one of the most notorious scene-stealers in the business, he had kept all of the other actors on their toes. 'I just thought he was amazingly funny,' recalled Jimmy Perry. 'And he was very different from Jimmy [Beck] – we didn't want a character that reminded the audience of Walker. And David and I were very fond of Welsh characters. So we built up the part of Cheeseman.'[28]

Work soon began on a seventh series, but, as Ian Lavender remembered, Beck's absence continued to be felt:

All kinds of silly little things used to set us off. There was the a cappella singing, for example. We had this habit, on location, of sitting around in the fields, while we were waiting to film something, and singing. It was never planned, it always just happened: someone would start singing – 'You'll never know just how much I love you' – and then someone else would join in – 'You'll never know just how much I care' – and it would just grow and grow, until all of us were together, singing, with Arthur, of course, conducting. It was one of those lovely little things. Well, the first time we went filming after Jimmy died, we were sitting around the van, waiting to begin filming, and somebody started it – 'You'll never know . . .' – and nobody took it up. We never did it again after Jimmy died. And that was how it was. Something had gone. No matter how good the things were that we went on to do without Jimmy, something was missing.[29]

The actual shooting, however, went well, and, when the time came for the new episodes to be recorded in the studio, the response from those who saw them seemed favourable, but, right up until the moment when the series reached the screen, the nagging doubts continued: 'We just didn't know what was going to happen,' said Ian Lavender. 'Would the viewers accept the show without Jimmy? Would they take to Talfryn Thomas? I honestly wasn't sure that we could actually survive.'[30]

The BBC gave the new series special support: it was scheduled on Fridays at 7.45 p.m. – a good day, traditionally, for situation-comedies and a great improvement on the previous slot – and it was thoughtfully promoted (with several well-positioned television trailers, and a tie-in exhibition at the Imperial War Museum).[31] The opening episode, 'Everybody's Trucking', went out on 15 November 1974, and, much to everyone's relief, was deemed a success: the faces were all familiar (Talfryn Thomas did not make an appearance), the plot (concerning an unmanned, stranded, steam engine) was simple but solid, the performances were strong and the viewing figures – 14,140,000[32] – represented a welcome step in the right direction. The reaction to the next episode, however, would be rather more significant, because it marked the introduction of the new character, Cheeseman.

'A Man of Action' provided further proof of just how accomplished Croft and Perry, as craftsmen, actually were: not only did they devise an effective way to draw Cheeseman into the platoon – Mainwaring agrees to enlist him as a temporary trainee recruit so that he can write a series of morale-boosting articles on the Home Guard – but they also employed American-style multiple plot strands in order to ensure that the audience would never have the time to over-analyse this unfamiliar figure. The show had seldom seemed so busy: Pike, in the course of reliving a childhood memory for the benefit of Lance Corporal Jones, gets his head stuck between the iron bars of a gate; Mainwaring is flattered into allowing Cheeseman to spend some time with the platoon ('"Captain Main-wearing: Man of Action!" I'm right behind you, boy! The power of the press, remember, the power of the press!'); a landmine hits the railway line and cuts off the town's gas and water supplies; the vicar, the verger, Hodges, a policeman, a fireman and the town clerk take over Main-waring's office; Mainwaring declares his intention to put Walming-ton-on-Sea under martial law; Mr Blewitt wanders into the church hall clad only in a flat-cap and pyjamas; and an officer from GHQ is sent over to relieve the power-hungry captain of command. All of this artful misdirection achieved its desired effect, and Cheeseman's potentially contentious arrival seemed more of a side-attraction than the main event. The closing credits – *sans* Beck – went by, the episode ended, and the show moved on.

Subsequent episodes saw the freshly enlisted Private Cheeseman become a little more involved in Home Guard activities – in 'Gorilla Warfare', for example, he arrives on parade sporting a home-made armband with the initials 'WC' ('That's so everyone knows what I do,' he tells Mainwaring. 'WC: War Correspondent!') – and a little more shamelessly sycophantic in his dealings with his leader ('Yes, indeed! There's no one more important than you, Captain Main-wearing! Yes, indeed!'), and, in general, a little more irritating ('Take that Welshman's name, Wilson'), but, in spite of the fact that he occupied a prominent position between Godfrey and Frazer in the front row of the platoon, he rarely seemed to interact with the other characters. The problem, perhaps, was that, although he was not remotely reminiscent of Private Walker, he *was* rather reminiscent not only of Frazer (another exotic Celt) but also of Jones (another enthusiastic flatterer of Captain Mainwaring), and the comic equilib-rium was disturbed. The show continued to be funny, and, indeed, popular – an average audience of 14.8 million[33] tuned in each week of the run – but, when the series came to an end, Croft and Perry decided, reluctantly, that their most recently-created character would have to go. 'It had been our mistake,' Croft reflected. 'It wasn't

John Laurie smiling off camera, on location at Winterton Beach, Norfolk.

Shooting at British Industrial Sands near King's Lynn.

The Bell Hotel,
Thetford (*top
left*): the oldest
members of the
cast preferred
those rooms
with another
view.

Nether Row,
Thetford (*centre
left*), which
doubled as a
street in wartime
Walmington-on-
Sea.

James Beck
(*bottom left*) as the
irreplaceable
Private Walker.

Talfryn Thomas
(*below*) drafted in
as new recruit,
Private
Cheeseman.

The Royal Gala Performance, BBC TV Centre, 1970 (*left to right*: the cast of *Dad's Army,* the Queen, Dudley Moore, Huw Wheldon, Dave Allen, Eddie Braben, Ernie Wise, Eric Morecambe, Vera Lynn).

The platoon push Jones's van past the Imperial War Museum at the launch of *The Real Dad's Army* Exhibition.

Dad's Army: The Movie (1971). No trousers, and, therefore, no Arthur Lowe.

Opposite: A final diversion for the television show.

SHAFTESBURY THEATRE
Shaftesbury Avenue, London WC2. Phone: 836 6596/7

LICENSEES: MARTIN GIBSON AND BRIAN RICHMOND-DODD FOR CHARTERGATE ESTATES LTD.
BERNARD DELFONT and RICHARD M. MILLS (for Bernard Delfont Organisation Ltd),
and DUNCAN C. WELDON and LOUIS I. MICHAELS (for Triumph Theatre Productions Ltd).

present

ARTHUR LOWE
JOHN LE MESURIER
CLIVE DUNN

in

DAD'S ARMY

by **JIMMY PERRY & DAVID CROFT**

BD 1975

A NOSTALGIC MUSIC & LAUGHTER SHOW OF BRITAIN'S FINEST HOUR

featuring

ARNOLD RIDLEY · IAN LAVENDER · BILL PERTWEE
FRANK WILLIAMS · EDWARD SINCLAIR
JOHN BARDON and HAMISH ROUGHEAD
JOAN COOPER · PAMELA CUNDELL and JANET DAVIES

Directed by
DAVID CROFT & JIMMY PERRY

Staged by
ROGER REDFARN

Designed by TERRY PARSONS
Choreography by SHEILA O'NEILL
Costumes by MARY HUSBAND

Musical Director ED COLEMAN
Lighting by ROBERT ORNBO
Sound by DAVID COLLISON

A FORUM THEATRE BILLINGHAM PRODUCTION

Jones's finest hour.

The cast put on a brave face for the final episode.

A medal at last:
a postprandial portrait taken at the dinner to mark the series' close.

'Come on Adolf: we're ready for you!'

Talfryn's fault – he was a good actor – but it had just been wrong to try to bring such a strong character into such a well-established show.'[34] One actor who was not particularly saddened by the news of Thomas's departure was John Laurie, who, as the series had progressed, had grown increasingly irritated by the Welshman's eagerness to steal the same scenes that *he* was intending to steal. 'John had come up to me to complain,' remembered Jimmy Perry. 'He said: "James, can I have a word, please? Is yon Welsh fellow going to be in the new series next year?" I said: "I don't know, John." So he said: "Well, make sure he isn't – he's getting *far* too many laughs!" Totally ruthless old pro! But that didn't influence our decision; we just came to the conclusion that the character wasn't quite right.'[35]

There would not, from this point on, be any new additions to the platoon. Croft and Perry decided simply to promote Private Sponge to the far end of the front row, and they also resolved to draw more than they had done before on some of the existing characters, such as the vicar, the verger and Hodges. One of the consequences of these changes would be an increase in competition among the actors for comic lines, but, as Clive Dunn acknowledged, the writers were actually rather good at keeping the cast contented – '[Croft and Perry] arranged laugh lines . . . as if giving out rations: so many laughs for the leading players, and then so many [fewer] for the "supports" '[36] – and, if anyone ever did feel moved to complain, a chart was available which demonstrated how fairly the lines had been distributed.[37]

Another subtle but significant change became evident soon after the cast started work on the next series: 'Have ye noticed the transmogrification of young Pike?'[38] remarked John Laurie to a colleague. It was true: the quality of Ian Lavender's recent performances had prompted the writers to push Pike a step or two further forward. 'I don't recall it being a conscious thing,' said David Croft. 'Pike was just a good, silly character, and Ian Lavender was getting some marvellous laughs with him, and the relationship that had developed between him and Mainwaring was very funny, so I think we just took advantage of that, really.'[39] Lavender's youthful energy, combined with his mature technique, would certainly prove to be increasingly valuable to an otherwise elderly cast. Arthur Lowe, for example, claimed not to care for most of what passed as the more 'physical' kind of comedy – 'I'm not doing that,' he would exclaim, somewhat haughtily, 'it's pantomime stuff'[40] – but he seemed perfectly happy to continue crumpling into Ian Lavender and then emerging with his cap askew, his glasses slanting across his cheeks and his face coloured cherry red. 'That was our favourite little bit of business,' Ian Lavender reflected. 'We'd worked out how we were going to do it – "I'll dive down there." "All right, and while you're down there, you do the glasses, because I can't, and I'll do the hat" – and, in the end, we got it down to a sort of shorthand. The reason it was me that he usually sprawled into was, of course, practical – he obviously couldn't have fallen into and been supported by Arnold or John Laurie, and so, particularly after Jimmy Beck died, it made sense for him to perform that sort of business with me – but it was so beautiful to play, because we trusted each other totally.'[41]

The show came back looking reassuringly refreshed. The eighth series began on Friday, 5 September 1975, with 'Ring Dem Bells' – an enjoyable episode in which the platoon was obliged to portray a group of Nazis in an Army training film (a task which encouraged Wilson to play up his supposed resemblance to the debonair Jack Buchanan, and Pike to don a monocle, a Hollywood-German accent and a cruelly arrogant manner). The BBC's audience research report noted that the vast majority of viewers had deemed the episode to be a 'splendid start' to the new series, with a script that was 'fresh and original' and 'as funny as ever'; the cast as a whole was judged to be 'impeccable', but many singled out the performance of Ian Lavender for special praise (he had 'surpassed himself' in a storyline that gave him 'his best chance to display his versatility and comedy talent', and his portrayal of the Germanic Pike was 'the highlight' of an 'hilarious' show).[42] These high standards were maintained in each one of the episodes that followed: 'When You've Got To Go' (in which Pike, much to his mother's horror, received his call-up papers); 'Is There Honey Still For Tea?' (a finely-crafted story about the imminent demolition of Godfrey's beloved Cherry Tree Cottage); 'Come In, Your Time Is Up' (concerning the platoon's attempts to come up with a harmless method – 'This is the penalty you pay for being a sporting nation and playing a straight bat' – for the retrieval of three German airmen stranded in a dinghy on a local lake); 'High Finance' (featuring Mainwaring's injudicious investigation, as bank manager, of a long chain of debtors); and 'The Face on the Poster' (in which the platoon voted in what Jones termed a 'secret ballet' in order to select someone to feature in a new recruitment campaign). The audience rose steadily to a peak of 15,503,500[43] for the final episode (the series average was 13.5 million),[44] and the praise – according to the BBC's audience reports – was gratifyingly high (with a number of viewers expressing their surprise at how the show 'seemed to have retained its original freshness').[45]

Croft and Perry's fine-tuning had paid off: most of the old stability, and charm, had been restored. They ended the year in style, with a special 40-minute episode for Christmas, entitled 'My Brother and I', which featured a glorious *tour de force* from Arthur Lowe as not only George Mainwaring but also his crude and crapulous travelling-salesman brother, Barry:

BARRY D'you want a drink?

GEORGE No, thank you.

BARRY Please yourself.

GEORGE I should have thought 5.30 in the afternoon was a bit early even for you.

BARRY Po-face! Look at you: rolled umbrella, striped trousers, pot hat! 'Course, you've 'got on', haven't you?

GEORGE I'm the Branch Manager.

BARRY Nice for you. Put your hand in the till when you get a bit short, do you?

GEORGE Don't be ridiculous![46]

'That episode was a real eye-opener for me,' recalled Ian Lavender, 'because it was just about the conflict between these two characters, Mainwaring and his awful brother, and the setting for it could have been just about anything. I thought: "Ah! Jimmy and David obviously feel, now, that they can write about things that have no reference at all to either the Home Guard or the war." That's when I realised: "Oh, I see – we've *really* made it. It's made it. This is something rather special." '[47]

Further proof of the fact that the programme was now firmly established as the nation's favourite situation-comedy was provided in time-honoured fashion by the nation's press, which seemed increasingly torn between taking its achievements for granted and searching for signs of decline. 'One was aware that *Dad's Army* was a great comedy show,' Peter Black would later confess, 'but did not go on to say: "What a fine institution the BBC must be, to be able to preserve such high quality in a comedy series aimed at the likes of us." One wrote a letter to say that much as one might have enjoyed the show one's pleasure was ruined by the fact that Capt. Mainwaring's form of reply to superior officers on the telephone was contrary to the correct procedure as practised daily by the writer for four years in the Home Guard at Wisbech, Cambs.'[48] 'The more successful the show became,' remembered Ian Lavender, 'the more convinced some journalists seemed to be that we were at each other's throats':

> They just wouldn't accept that we really did *like* each other. They'd always be at it, digging away – 'I hear that Arthur Lowe and John Le Mesurier don't talk to each other'; 'Arnold Ridley and John Laurie can't stand the sight of each other, can they?'; 'Is it true that David and Jimmy had a blazing row last week?' – and you'd answer, 'No. We all get on. Really. We're genuinely fond of each other', but they would not accept it. The sad thing was that it made us guarded, because, as friends, as mates, we'd play jokes on each other, and send each other up, so we had to be very careful about what we said to the press, or to people who might then talk to the press, or else some tongue-in-cheek remark would have been snapped up and used against us. It was extraordinary, really, that 'build 'em up and then knock 'em down' attitude. They really wanted us to hate each other.[49]

There had never been any shortage of backstage badinage, and it was certainly very much in evidence on the morning in 1975 when the award of an OBE to Clive Dunn was made public (Arthur Lowe chose to mark the occasion by announcing that 'when it comes to my turn I don't want any of that bargain basement stuff',[50] while John Laurie speculated that his politically active colleague had most probably secured the honour by 'climbing up Harold Wilson's arse').[51] There was also, by this stage, a deep-rooted sense of camaraderie, as well as a shared feeling of pride in what their programme had achieved (even the normally circumspect Arthur Lowe took to calling it 'a legend in its time').[52]

The show's remarkable reputation seemed set to be enhanced even further when an ambitious Los Angeles-based producer by the name of Herman Rush secured the exclusive rights to adapt *Dad's Army* for the American market. Rush was eager to follow in the footsteps of the illustrious Norman Lear, whose US versions of *Till Death Us Do Part* (*All in The Family*, launched in 1971)[53] and *Steptoe and Son* (*Sanford and Son*, 1972)[54] had soon established themselves as two of the most popular shows on network television. Rush's own first, and somewhat rash, attempt at a transatlantic adaptation, *Love Thy Neighbor*,[55] had been cancelled in 1973 after a single miserable season, but he believed that in *Dad's Army* he had found the kind of distinctive vehicle with which he could make his mark. Croft and Perry furnished him with their own 'Americanised' script – based on their 1968 opening BBC episode, but now set in 'Tulls Point', a small town on the coast of Maine, shortly after the bombing of Pearl Harbor – along with some advice concerning the casting of the characters: Mainwaring (whom they renamed 'Cornelius Bishop') should be, they said, a 'Gail Gordon type', Wilson was 'a Clifton Webb type' and Godfrey 'an Edward Everett Horton type'.[56] Rush, however, turned instead to an experienced American writer, Arthur Julian,[57] to restyle the show for the US audience.

Rush and Julian flew over to England, watched an episode of *Dad's Army* being made and studied a selection of tapes from past series. One episode, in particular, caught their eye: 'The Deadly Attachment'. Armed with a copy of Croft and Perry's original script, the two men travelled back to Los Angeles and put the process of 'Americanisation' into motion. There had been no wartime 'Home Guard', as such, in the US,[58] so the name of the force was changed to the 'Volunteer Civilian Defence Corps', and the setting switched from Walmington-on-Sea to Long Island, New York. Julian then transformed Captain George Mainwaring into 'Captain Nick Rosatti', a vain and somewhat garrulous Italian-American, and Sergeant Arthur Wilson into 'Sergeant Max Raskin', a wise-cracking Jew; he also renamed Pike 'Bobby Henderson', merged the personalities of Jones and Godfrey into 'Bert Wagner', an incontinent old soldier, and introduced a female character, Marsha Wilson, from the local aircraft plant. There was one other significant alteration: the title, *Dad's Army*, was deemed far too demographically specific for US television's taste, and so Julian renamed it *The Rear Guard*.

The actual storyline did not, in fact, stray too far from the BBC original – the volunteers have to guard a six-man German U-boat crew until the Regular Army is able to collect them – but most of the references were revised so as to match the new milieu. The 'fish and chip supper', for example, was transformed, for the US version, into a snack from 'Greenblatt's kosher delicatessen':

ROSATTI	All right, get six salami sandwiches.
U-BOAT CAPTAIN	I would like corned beef.
ROSATTI	All right. One corned beef . . .
U-BOAT CAPTAIN	Lean.
ROSATTI	. . . and five salami sandwiches.
U-BOAT CAPTAIN	Just a minute. (*he says something in German to his crew*) Make that three corned beef, two salamis and a tongue.
HENDERSON	Three corned beef, two salamis and a tongue.
U-BOAT CAPTAIN	Hold the mustard on the corned beef.
ROSATTI	Henderson, go back to the original order – six salami sandwiches.
RASKIN	On white bread, with mayonnaise . . . the hell with the Geneva Convention.[59]

The 'Don't tell him, Pike!' exchange underwent the same kind of cultural conversion:

U-BOAT CAPTAIN	I'm making a note of your insults, Sergeant. Your name will go on the list, and when we win the war, you will be brought to account.
RASKIN	You can put down whatever you want, but you're not going to win this war.
U-BOAT CAPTAIN	Oh yes we are . . .
RASKIN	Oh no you're not . . .
U-BOAT CAPTAIN	Oh yes we are . . .

RASKIN	Oh no . . .
HENDERSON	Adolf Hitler is a jerk
	He's nothing but a Nazi
	He thinks that he will win the war
	(*the U-boat Captain looks at him*)
	He's not so hotsy totsy.
U-BOAT CAPTAIN	Your name will also go on the list. What is it?
ROSATTI	Don't tell him, Henderson![60]

Hal Cooper – a seasoned situation–comedy specialist who had previously worked on such shows as *I Dream of Jeannie*, *The Odd Couple*, *The Mary Tyler Moore Show* and *Maude* – was brought in as director, and a cast was assembled that included such assured comic actors as Lou Jacobi (as Raskin), Cliff Norton (Rosatti) and Eddie Foy, Jr (Wagner). Rush and Julian also arranged for David Croft and Jimmy Perry to fly over and assist in the production. 'It started promisingly enough,' Perry remembered:

> We arrived at Los Angeles airport and were greeted by a stretch limo – 'You guys okay? Can I get you anything?' – and we were driven to the Beverly Wilshire Hotel. We then went down to the studio, did a week's rehearsal – I had the privilege of meeting Eddie Foy, Jr, a wonderful performer whose father was one of the great vaudevillians, and Lou Jacobi, a marvellous Jewish comedian – and then they recorded the show. I thought it was rather good.[61]

The Rear Guard was broadcast on ABC at 10 pm on 10 August 1976 as an edition of the 'Tuesday Night Pilot Film' series. Its fate, however, appears to have been more or less sealed prior to its transmission: a preview tape had met with a frosty reception from the network's overly-influential focus groups, and, as a consequence, the decision was made to drop it. 'They got cold feet,' said Jimmy Perry. 'They'd been very enthusiastic, and then they decided it didn't work. And David and I returned to Los Angeles airport in a yellow cab.'[62]

Back in Britain, meanwhile, *Dad's Army* was taking a break. The cast was on tour, the writers were tired, and, as Bill Cotton explained, the BBC was doing its best to be supportive:

> Success . . . demands a self-discipline by television companies. Somebody coined the phrase . . . that one was obliged to exert 'management of creativity'. The temptations of a hit show are to flog it into the ground . . . [but the BBC's] policy is to try to sustain the series. This entails a form of rationing so that the standards of production can be maintained over as long a period as possible. Showbusiness *is* a business. There is no reason why a series should not last for as long as 10 years if its exposure is handled in the right way.[63]

The result of this 'rationing' was that only one episode of the show – a low-key Christmas special entitled 'The Love of Three Oranges'[64] – reached the screen in 1976, but the BBC remained hopeful that it would not be long before the *Dad's Army* team – or 'my boys',[65] as Huw Wheldon had taken to calling them – was ready to return with another series.

There would not, however, be any more talk of *Dad's Army* going on 'for ever and ever'. The senior actors had always looked their age, but now they were starting to feel it. The writers had acquired other responsibilities, and a fresh set of challenges (both Croft and Perry's *It Ain't Half Hot Mum*[66] and Croft and Jeremy Lloyd's *Are You Being Served?*[67] were into their fourth series, and other projects were already in development).[68] The audience was still there, but, as all of the professionals involved in the programme were experienced enough to know, no audience – no matter how enthusiastic it was at present – could be relied on to stay there indefinitely. No one wanted it to stop, but no one wanted it to spoil. Croft and Perry did agree to go on, but not on how long. The clock could now be heard ticking.

CHAPTER XIV

Never Too Old?

*It is not so much that we care to be alive a hundred or a
thousand years hence, any more than to have been alive a
hundred or a thousand years ago: but the thing lies here, that we
would all of us wish the present moment to last for ever. We
would be as we are, and would have the world remain just as it
is, to please us.*[1]

WILLIAM HAZLITT

*There is a time – a right time – to stop any series, no matter how
much you'd like to keep going. You might not look out for it, but I
think you know when it's arrived.*

JIMMY PERRY[2]

Starting and stopping is not easy for a situation-comedy; it prefers
to stay in the middle, the moment, for as long as is possible. *Dad's
Army*, for example, progressed steadily, and with admirable historical
accuracy, from the summer of 1940 (in the first series) to the summer
of 1942 (in the sixth),[3] and then seemed disinclined to progress any
further. It came as no great surprise, therefore, when Croft and Perry
revealed that the ninth series would be set, yet again, in 1942. They
did not want it all to end, even though they knew it had to.

The decision had very nearly been taken out of their hands. Early
in 1977, John Le Mesurier had fallen seriously ill in Perth, Australia,
during rehearsals for a play. He was flown straight home and was
met at Heathrow by his wife, Joan. 'He was in a wheelchair looking
desperately ill,' she recalled. 'He seemed to have aged ten years in
the few weeks he had been away and I was hard pressed to hold
back the tears.'[4] He was taken to the hospital near his home in

Ramsgate, where he was diagnosed as suffering from cirrhosis of the liver and warned that if he continued consuming alcohol he would die. Joan consulted a naturopath, who prescribed a diet of raw fruit for one month, followed by raw vegetables and salads. 'John moaned,' she remembered, 'but I had the upper hand.'[5] His liver – much to the specialist's surprise – started to mend itself, although he remained seriously ill: 'He was out of danger, but so weak he could hardly walk unaided. He was as thin as a stick, and his eyes were great sunken hollows in his craggy face. People who came to visit were shocked at his appearance.'[6]

Le Mesurier was still in very poor health when, in June, the call came to join the rest of the *Dad's Army* team in Thetford for another fortnight of filming. He knew that he was not really well enough to work, and he also knew that this would almost certainly be the show's 'final parade',[7] and he could not bear to miss it. His colleagues had been forewarned about the fragility of his condition, but, when he arrived, they still found it hard to hide their distress at how frail and emaciated their friend had become. 'He was pathetic,' recalled David Croft:

> He looked so ill. I remember one day in particular, when the weather had turned rather cold, being so concerned about him that I ordered all the lights to be arranged around him in a sort of six-foot square area and then turning them all on to warm him up a bit. He was in such a bad way. It was very hard, very sad. And when we went on to do the last episode in the studio I remember thinking, 'Well, that's the last we shall see of John Le Mesurier.'[8]

Le Mesurier was not the only member of the cast to cause the team concern. Arthur Lowe, for example, had been suffering for some time from narcolepsy, a rare neurological disorder characterised by intermittent and uncontrollable episodes of drowsiness during the daytime, and, although he responded to this frustrating and sometimes frightening condition with disarming good humour – 'The mulligatawny's not as good as it was,'[9] he would observe as, upon waking, he raised his head from out of the soup bowl – it was starting to have a subtle but significant effect upon his acting. 'There'd be times when he'd seem sluggish,' said David Croft. 'And I don't think there can be much doubt that his timing wasn't quite what it was. We'd cover it up – we'd edit out some of the pauses, the "ums" and "ahs", and tighten scenes up – but he was slowing down.'[10] Some of the other actors were also beginning to struggle: Arnold Ridley's mobility was, at the age of 81, more restricted than ever, and John Laurie's emphysema was getting progressively worse. 'We realised that, well, none of them was getting any younger,' said Jimmy Perry. 'One day it just sort of hits you like that. They were the kind of tough old pros who wanted to go on till they dropped, but [David and I] knew that we'd have to finish it. "Leave the audience wanting more" – that was the motto.'[11]

Studio recording followed in July. David Croft had other commitments, and so all but one of the six episodes were directed by his new assistant, Bob Spiers.[12] It had been confirmed, by this stage,[13] that this series would indeed mark the end of the show's nine-year run (although, as Arthur Lowe revealed to reporters, there was still a possibility that the team would reunite for 'the occasional appearance in a Christmas special or something'),[14] and, as a consequence, the general mood on the set was quietly, but increasingly, emotional. John Le Mesurier likened the experience to that of 'an old boys' reunion, made all the more poignant by the knowledge that this was the final roll-call, the "last Post" as it were'.[15]

Any lingering doubts as to how 'final' this final series would turn out to be were dispelled one month later, on 29 August, with the death, at the age of 63, of Edward Sinclair.[16] 'That really did mark the end of it,' said Ian Lavender:

I remember all of us going back to Teddy's house after his funeral. It was a beautiful sunny day. We were standing by the french windows, looking out on to the little back garden, when David Croft suddenly said: 'Well, I think that's it, don't you?' And everyone went: 'Yeah. Yeah.' There might have been some value in us doing another hour-long special, at least, about, say, how we coped after the war when we had to settle back into civilian life, but I can see why David and Jimmy thought: 'Look, we went through Jimmy Beck's death, we're not going to go through all of that again for the sake of six more episodes, or even one special. So that's it. We've done it. We've done the last episode.'[17]

The newspapers duly alerted their readers to the imminent arrival of 'the last of the best long-running comedy series of them all',[18] and Peter Tinniswood previewed the series for the *Radio Times*:

> I could happily take up the whole of this issue . . . writing about this series. Sufficient to say that this is a flag-carrier for all that is finest in television comedy. The writers . . . have created a pageant of characters who are near-Dickensian in their richness and warmth.
>
> The splendid cast . . . has created a wholly believable world in which comedy of the highest order has been allowed to bloom and flourish. They are all irreplaceable.
>
> I believe the loss of this programme from television is tragic. Bring it back, Mr Producer, please.[19]

The opening episode, 'Wake-Up Walmington', went out on BBC1 at 8.10 p.m. on Sunday, 2 October 1977. It was a slightly shaky start: not all of the performances were up to their usual standards (Arthur Lowe, for example, acted at a postprandial pace, while John Le Mesurier both looked and sounded disturbingly weak), and the editing was also uncharacteristically clumsy, but the writing, reassuringly, was as apposite as ever. The close-knit world of Walmington-on-Sea is depicted as being in the process of unravelling: the townspeople have taken to calling the Home Guard 'the geriatric fusiliers', the platoon's morale has plummeted to rock bottom, and a rattled Mr Blewitt ('You wouldn't have done that to me if I was fifty-seven years younger!') stands up to Hodges ('I *hate* you!') and reduces the normally cocksure warden to tears ('See? He's got feet of clay!'). The old bully sits down and sobs:

HODGES   I can't take it any more, Napoleon! D'you know, I'm the most hated man in the town! Nobody's taking this war seriously!
MAINWARING I agree with you there.
WILSON   Well, you know, it's only human nature, sir.

> The Home Guard's been formed two years and there hasn't been an invasion yet. And people are beginning to think we're just wasting our time.
>
> MAINWARING   That's exactly what Germany wants, isn't it? Lull us into a false sense of security, and catch us when we're off guard. Something's got to be done about it![20]

Mainwaring's 'solution' – 'Operation Wake-Up' – has the platoon, and Hodges, dress up as a band of 'cut-throats and desperadoes' in order to shake the community out of its complacency (MAIN-WARING: 'Tell the men to march like a rabble in a shifty and furtive manner.' JONES: 'Very good, sir. Platoon: in a shifty and furtive manner, like a rabble, quick march!').

Subsequent episodes saw the show recover much of its old form. 'The Making of Private Pike', for example, featured a memorable little scene in which Wilson – who has jumped to quite the wrong conclusion after hearing that Pike was out all night with a young ATS woman in Mainwaring's new staff car – attempts, for the first time, to have an adult conversation with his 'nephew':

WILSON   Well, now, Frank. About last night . . .

PIKE   I know we shouldn't have taken it. But we didn't do the car no harm.

WILSON   Yes, well, I'm not talking about the car. I'm talking about the *girl*. A lot of people will know that you spent the night together. And a lot of people will tell you that what you did was wrong.

PIKE   (*defensively*) *I* was pushing – *she* was steering!

WILSON   Well . . . But, to *my* way of thinking, what you both did wasn't 'evil'. Do you follow me?

PIKE   (*sounding confused*) It was nine miles . . .

WILSON   You see, our sort of society has a rather rigid framework, and, er, if we don't stay within it, people point the finger at us.

PIKE   I had to work hard to get up Grant's Hill. Twenty yards at a time . . .

WILSON   Yes, well, just remember this, Frank: *I* understand. Now, we haven't been too close, I know, just recently, but now I feel we're sort of – d'you know what I mean? – kindred spirits. Sort of, you know, sort of 'men of the world'. Do you feel like that, too?

PIKE   (*still puzzled*) Y–Yeah. Kindred spirits. Men of the world.

WILSON   Good lad.[21]

'I'll never forget doing that scene with John,' said Ian Lavender. 'David and Jimmy had just come up with this new dialogue – two or three pages of it – and we didn't have time to learn it or rehearse it – we just got on and did it. And it felt like the most natural thing in the world – because the writing was so good, and because we knew each other so well. It was terrific. Absolutely terrific.'[22]

The series moved freely from style to style. 'Knights of Madness' was an elaborate and effective prop-based romp that featured a march by Mr Yeatman and his Sea Scouts, a keep-fit display by Mrs Yeatman and the ladies' netball team ('Come away from there, Frazer!'), a performance by the Eastgate Morris Dancers, and 'a spectacular medieval extravaganza' – inspired by England's patron saint – involving the Home Guard (WILSON: 'Have you decided who's going to play St George?' MAINWARING: 'I should have thought that was obvious') and the ARP wardens ('Right, Napoleon – you've asked for it!'). 'The Miser's Hoard' was a far more intimate, character-driven piece about Mainwaring's bid to persuade Frazer to exchange his stash of sovereigns for an annuity ('Cap'n Mainwaring, there's just one thing I want tae say t'ye: if you think you're goin' tae get your hands on my gold, you can think again. I don't trust banks, I don't trust burghers and I don't trust you! That's all I want tae say, thank ye!'). 'Number Engaged' – the penultimate episode – was a strong, simple story – shot mainly on location – about the platoon's attempts to dislodge a bomb that had become entangled in some telegraph wires ('Uncle Arthur – mum's going to hear all about this!').

An average of 10.5 million[23] tuned in each week, and, although John Le Mesurier's gaunt appearance continued to act as an unsettling distraction – 'He looked so ill,' said his wife, 'that the public thought he was on his last legs, and the press came down to Ramsgate to take photographs of him at home to prove that he was still alive and kicking'[24] – the general response, so far, had been extremely good. Dennis Potter, for example, commented in the *Sunday Times*:

> This ill-fitted platoon remains just about the last reliable example of the classic television comedies of a decade and more ago: that is, a show which provokes authentic laughs instead of uncomfortable sniggers, and one that grows out of the lasting eccentricities and memorable quirks of its acceptably imbecilic characters rather than the mostly salacious one-line gags which pass for dialogue in . . . later models . . .
>
> We shall miss these shambling warriors when they fade away as all old soldiers are supposed to do.[25]

The final episode, 'Never Too Old', was a real labour of love. Croft and Perry had wanted it to be funny but moving, and do justice to the show, the characters and the actors, and honour the spirit of the real-life Home Guard, and come to an elegant end rather than an awkward halt, and, thrillingly, it managed to do all of those things, within 30 minutes of consummate situation-comedy, with wit, good taste and compassion.

It went out on the evening of 13 November, Remembrance Sunday, and opened with an unexpected admission from Jones: 'I have fallen in love, Captain Mainwaring. With a woman.' Mainwaring is shaken by this news – 'I can't be expected to face a Nazi invasion with a woolly-headed corporal!' – and even more shaken when he is told that the woman in question is none other than Walmington-on-Sea's most flirtatious widow, Mrs Fox (whose relationship with the old soldier had previously been described as 'purely teutonic'). Once Mainwaring has established that this is not a passing fancy – 'Oh, no,' says Jones, 'it's definitely not a passing fancy – I've fancied her for seventeen years!' – and sat patiently through the butcher's bout of self-doubt – 'Does she love me for myself, or does she love me for my meat?' – he concludes that the union might actually work ('After all,' he confides to Wilson. 'They're both the same class'). Once Mrs Fox (played by Pamela Cundell with just the right air of innocent menace) has persuaded a distinctly ill-at-ease Mainwaring to act as her father (MRS FOX: 'You wouldn't give me away, would you?' MAINWARING: 'Wouldn't I?'), the wedding ceremony goes ahead (MRS FOX: 'Mr Mainwaring – I think I'm going to cry.' MAINWARING: 'Oh, do try not to'), and then, at the reception, Mainwaring offers the newly-married couple a toast: 'I wish you both the very best of luck, and may you be as happy as I have been with my own dear wife, who unfortunately can't be with us this afternoon.'

The atmosphere in the studio was made all the more special for the cast by the fact that the two writers had arranged for as many wives and partners who had Equity cards – such as Arthur Lowe's wife, Joan Cooper (who played Dolly Godfrey), and Arnold Ridley's wife, Althea Parker (who played an unnamed wedding guest) – to join the performers in front of the camera for the scene set at the reception. 'David [Croft] tends to hide a lot of his feelings,' observed Ian Lavender, 'but, deep down, he's a sentimental old bugger.'[26] Croft, who had returned to direct the final episode, acknowledged: 'It *was* a very emotional evening. The production gallery was unusually quiet throughout the recording, and, as the end drew near, there were plenty of people with lumps in their throats.'[27]

The fictional celebrations came to a sudden halt after a call from GHQ. Reports of barges moving around the North Sea coast led to the platoon being placed on immediate standby, and Jones found himself spending the night at the end of a cold pier with Pike instead of inside a warm hotel with his wife. While the two men stand on patrol, however, they are joined by Mainwaring, Wilson, Frazer and Godfrey, who have brought along a dusty bottle of champagne with which to drink their friend's health. Hodges, inevitably, arrives to disturb the mood, pausing only to point out that the invasion alert was a false alarm, and to mock the men who are still standing guard ('What good would *you* be against *real* soldiers? They'd walk straight through you!'), before departing back into the darkness. The champagne is then poured into mugs (or, in Godfrey's case, a medicine glass), the men begin to drink, and the final few beautifully-judged minutes are allowed to unfold:

PIKE   Mr Mainwaring? Warden wasn't right, was he, when he said the Nazis would walk straight through us?

MAINWARING   Of course he wasn't right!
JONES   I know one thing – they're not walking straight through me!
FRAZER   Nor me. I'll be beside you, Jonesie.
MAINWARING   We'll all be beside you, Jonesie. We'll stick together – you can rely on that. If anybody tries to take our homes or our freedom away from us they'll find out what we can do. We'll fight. And we're not alone – there are thousands of us all over England.
FRAZER   And Scotland.
MAINWARING   And Scotland. All over Great Britain, in fact. Men who'll stand together when their country needs them.
WILSON   Excuse me, sir – don't you think it might be a nice idea if we were to pay *our* tribute to *them*?
MAINWARING   For once, Wilson, I agree with you. (*raises mug*) To Britain's Home Guard!
ALL   (*turning to face the camera*) To Britain's Home Guard![28]

The studio audience applauded, the closing credits rolled, and then, after nine years, nine series, eighty episodes and forty-eight hours and ten minutes of great acting, fine writing and glorious television, it was all over. An estimated 12,524,000 people[29] had watched an era come to an end. The BBC's audience report was full of praise for the show and tinged with sadness at its passing: 'It was felt that all the characters had been beautifully portrayed ("superb performances from all") and special mention was made of Arthur Lowe as Captain Mainwaring and Ian Lavender as Private Pike. The production, too, was highly praised for bringing out a convincing sense of period and for paying great attention to detail. Altogether, it was generally agreed that the programme had always been magnificent, that the cast could not have been better chosen and it was sad to see the series come to an end.'[30] The critics, too, lined up to pay tribute to what the *Guardian*'s Peter Fiddick described as 'one of the jewels of TV comedy':

It is bound to be remembered for sentiment and nostalgia, and it's made the most of those, but that makes it all the more necessary to record, as the absolutely final credits roll, that it has given us finer farces, straighter faces, richer characterisation, and a deal more social observation, than most of the more pretentious dramas, and always kept us guessing which would turn up next . . .

It will be missed.[31]

The BBC, Bill Pertwee remembered, had failed to arrange a farewell celebration in time to mark the final studio recording: 'We'd all put our best bib and tuckers on, you know, thinking someone was probably going to surprise us with a bit of a party, but they just handed us the usual black dustbin bags for our stuff, turned off the lights and we all trudged off to the bar for a drink.'[32] The *Daily Mirror*,[33] sensing an opportunity to embarrass the Corporation, arranged for each member of the *Dad's Army* cast to receive a special medal – 'For services to television entertainment' – followed, on the night the final episode was transmitted, by a valedictory (and much-photographed) dinner at London's Café Royal. 'It was quite a jolly evening,'[34] recalled Clive Dunn, with a considerable amount of wine being consumed (John Le Mesurier, whose range of drinks was limited to orange juice or mineral water, would later confess that the 'only way I had of getting myself into the spirit' of the occasion was by smoking what he described, euphemistically, as 'extra strong cigarettes'),[35] and there were some memorable after-dinner speeches (which, Dunn pointed out, 'were not repeated in full, because some of the remarks we made were not necessarily conducive to selling more newspapers').[36] 'It was a good evening,' confirmed David Croft. 'A very funny evening. John Laurie got very abusive, as he was wont to do, but amusingly so, and I remember that Arthur's wife, Joan, who was inclined to get rather merry, got up to make a speech. She'd been going about three or four minutes when, all of a sudden, she slipped under the table – just like that – and Arthur, of course, took no notice and just carried on as if nothing had happened!'[37] Bill Pertwee thanked the hosts for their generosity, and then Arthur Lowe rose to second the sentiment (although he rather spoiled the effect by adding that, in spite of this, there was 'no way' he would allow 'such a rubbishy newspaper' as theirs inside his house).[38] 'This is a sad occasion for all of us,' Lowe went on to declare. 'I've never wanted the show to stop, but some of us,' he said, looking round at the others, 'are getting on a bit.'[39] John Le Mesurier observed that 'being in *Dad's Army* was like belonging to a gentleman's club';[40] Clive Dunn joked that 'Having a final dinner like this is a bit like going to your own funeral';[41] Ian Lavender remarked that he looked on the day when he was chosen for the part of Private Pike as 'the luckiest day of my life';[42] Arnold Ridley got unsteadily to his feet, smiled his usual crinkly smile, said 'Thank you very much',[43] and then sat straight back down again; and then John Laurie, Clive Dunn recalled, 'stood up and said in his wildest Scottish brogue that, although a lot of remarks had been made about the series and the participants, no one had so far mentioned that "Actors are a load of —ts!" Silence reigned for all of five seconds, and then the assembly fell apart. Marjorie Proops nearly fell off her chair.'[44]

Another function followed a short while later, when the team was summoned by the BBC's Board of Governors to an 'official' farewell luncheon party – a 'rather formal occasion,' sighed John Le Mesurier, 'which none of us enjoyed over much'[45] – and then Lowe, Le Mesurier and Laurie contributed one last cameo appearance, in character, to the Christmas edition of another much-loved and bona fide national institution, *The Morecambe & Wise Show* (Mainwaring glowered at Elton John and muttered, 'Stupid boy!').[46] The year came to an end, the reality sank in, and the cast and crew of *Dad's Army*, with some reluctance, 'stood down'.

CHAPTER XV

Revival

History books begin and end, but the events they describe do not.
R.G. COLLINGWOOD[1]

You know, this thing could run and run.
MICHAEL MILLS[2]

There was life, and work, after *Dad's Army*. Both David Croft and
Jimmy Perry were awarded the OBE (for services to television) in
1978, and the two men continued their writing partnership into the
1980s when they launched their third situation-comedy (inspired,
like the others, by personal experiences), entitled *Hi-de-Hi!*[3] The
actors, too, in spite of their advancing years, seemed determined to
keep their careers open and active.

Arthur Lowe, for example, continued to advertise everything from
Harvey's Bristol Cream to Cadbury's Hanky-Panky ('The man's got
no dignity,' John Laurie used to cry. 'Pay him a thousand pounds
and he'd dress up as a monkey')[4] and appear in plays (although his
range of choices, it seems, was limited artificially due to his insistence
that any offer had to include a part for his wife, Joan)[5] and movies
(the director Lindsay Anderson, with whom Lowe was reunited for
Britannia Hospital, commented that 'I never wanted to make a film
without Arthur in it'),[6] and he continued to serve as the narrator of
Roger Hargreaves' cartoon series for children, *Mister Men* (BBC1,
1974–82). He also showed no hesitation when the opportunity arose
to return to the genre of situation-comedy: *Bless Me, Father* (LWT,
1978–81) saw Lowe assume a smoky Irish brogue to portray, quite
delightfully, the mischievous Roman Catholic priest Father Charles
Duddleswell; he was superb in Roy Clarke's underrated (and under-

repeated) *Potter* (BBC1, 1979–80) as the pompous busybody Redvers Potter, the retired MD of Potter Mints ('The Hotter Mints'); and in *A. J. Wentworth, B.A.* (Thames, 1982), a gently funny series based on the stories of H. F. Ellis, Lowe appeared as the eponymous bumbling mathematics master.[7] 'I'll be an actor until I keel over and drop dead,'[8] he liked to declare.

Finding work was not so easy, however, for John Le Mesurier, whose well-publicised ill-health meant that he was now regarded as an insurance risk. 'I feel very lonely without you all sometimes,' he wrote to Arthur Lowe, 'and am sad not to be busy, as you are. But the slightest physical exertion puffs me out . . . Mind you, if we were all called on location to Thetford tomorrow, I'd be there!'[9] He missed his drink – his ex-wife Hattie Jacques sent him a crate of non-alcoholic wine, but he complained that it tasted like grape juice – and had found nothing that could act as a distraction (his wife tried to coax him into sharing her passion for gardening, a well-meaning attempt that was batted straight back: 'I'm sorry, darling,' he said with a shudder, 'but I think it's ghastly').[10] The money began to run out, and he was forced to sell his Barons Court flat. Old friends, such as Annie Ross, the jazz singer, Peter Campbell, the theatrical agent, and Derek Taylor, the casual *bon vivant*, and his two sons, Robin and Kim, often travelled down to Ramsgate to see him, but it was clear that he was growing increasingly morose.

His wife was saddened, if not entirely surprised, therefore, when she found out that he had started drinking again. A doctor was brought in to lecture him on the damage that he was doing to his liver, and his wife 'nagged, pleaded and wept', but, she would recall, 'John, for all his gentleness, was stubborn.'[11] Towards the end of 1978, Joan resolved, as the last resort, to call a family conference:

> I pleaded my case, then John pleaded his. He argued that it was, after all, *his* life, and without the normality of being able to have a drink when he fancied one, meet up with his mates in London from time to time and have a drink with them on an equal footing, then he would just as soon be dead. He said that he loved me and our life together, but for the past year and a half he had been unhappy. He preferred quality to quantity. He promised to drink nothing but beer, and that in moderation,

but he was incapable of giving up alcohol completely. I was out-voted. I gave up. All I could do was treasure each day with him from then on.[12]

The irony was that, as soon as the beer was added to his diet, he began to put on much of the weight that he had lost, the colour came back to his face, his mood brightened and, to his great relief and delight, fresh offers of work started to arrive. He toured the Far East in a production of Alan Ayckbourn's *Bedroom Farce*, took part in a revival of Noel Coward's *Hay Fever* at the Lyric, Hammersmith, recorded some lucrative voice-overs for a wide range of commercials, contributed to the Peter Sellers swansong movie *The Fiendish Plot of Dr Fu Manchu* (1980), and, on television, played the lead role in David Mercer's *Flint* (BBC1, 1978), portrayed a priest in *Brideshead Revisited* (Granada, 1981) and, at the request of David Croft, made a special guest appearance in an episode *of Hi-de-Hi!*[13] 'They were quality years of a good vintage,' his wife would reflect, 'during which he drank moderately. We were closer than ever, and happier.'[14]

The other ex-members of the cast were similarly industrious. Clive Dunn went on a cabaret tour of New Zealand, made his opera debut as the drunken gaoler Frosch in the ENO production of *Die Fledermaus*, appeared as Verges in the 1984 BBC2 production of *Much Ado About Nothing* and starred in four series of the children's television show *Grandad* (BBC1, 1979–84). Ian Lavender was active in the theatre as both a performer and a director, but also appeared on television in several more situation-comedies, including the revival of Frank Muir and Denis Norden's *The Glums* (LWT, 1978–9) and, as Tom the dentist, *Have I Got You . . . Where You Want Me?* (Granada, 1981). Bill Pertwee, in addition to his regular stage, television and radio work, began a second career as an author of popular showbusiness histories;[15] and Frank Williams continued to figure on the small screen, and, most memorably, in Croft and Perry comedies. John Laurie, meanwhile, resisted the chance to return to the theatre – 'At my time of life,' he explained, 'who wants to be commuting at midnight?'[16] – but, in spite of his fast-failing health, he still managed to summon up sufficient strength for one last spirited performance, in an edition of BBC2's nostalgic *The Old Boy Network* (1979),[17] before his death, at the age of eighty-three, on 23 June 1980. Arnold

Ridley, on the other hand, went straight from the last episode of *Dad's Army* into his very first pantomime,[18] collected an OBE in 1982, and, although physical infirmity prevented him from accepting most offers of work, he refused to contemplate an 'official' retirement ('When I die,' he liked to say, 'I want to break a contract').[19]

All of the actors took care to remain in touch with each other socially, but the nearest they came to a professional reunion[20] was at the start of the 1980s, when Harold Snoad and Michael Knowles – the two men who had been responsible for adapting the original scripts of *Dad's Army* for radio – came up with an idea for a post-war 'sequel'. The show, which they proposed to call *It Sticks Out Half a Mile*, would open in 1948 with the return to England of George Mainwaring after a two-year spell working as a supervisor in a cuckoo clock factory in Switzerland (the chilly Swiss air, it seems, did not suit Elizabeth's delicate chest); he settles in Frambourne – a few miles further down the coast from Walmington-on-Sea – and resolves to buy the town's dilapidated pier in order to save it from demolition. When, however, he visits the local branch of Swallow Bank, he is greatly distressed to discover that the manager with whom he must plead for a loan is none other than his old chief clerk and sergeant, Arthur Wilson.[21]

Once Croft and Perry had given their blessing to the project, a pilot script was written. Snoad gave it to Arthur Lowe, who liked it enough to recommend making it into a series for television.[22] No takers could be found, however, and so Snoad took it to BBC Radio 2, and a pilot programme – co-starring Lowe and Le Mesurier – was duly recorded in the summer of 1981 (although never broadcast).[23] A series was commissioned, but then, on 15 April 1982, before all of the scripts had been completed, Arthur Lowe – as he always said he would – 'keeled over' and died, from a stroke, in his dressing room at Birmingham's Alexandra Theatre.[24] 'Few can die and have it said about them that their passing caused as much grief as their living caused laughter,' declared the *Daily Mirror* in its leader. 'But it is true about Arthur Lowe.'[25] The surviving members of the *Dad's Army* cast mourned the loss of their friend and colleague – Clive Dunn put it simply and sincerely when he said, 'We'll miss him terribly'[26] – and Snoad and Knowles assumed that their project would now have to be shelved. It came as something of a surprise, therefore, when, following the memorial service that was held at St Martin-in-the-Fields, Lowe's widow, Joan, sought Snoad out and assured him that her late husband would have wanted the series, in some shape or form, to go ahead ('Arthur thought,' she said, 'it had so much potential').[27] The result was that the basic story was rewritten, with Wilson now being joined at Frambourne-on-Sea by Mavis and Frank Pike: their peacetime idyll is soon spoiled, however, by the arrival of Hodges, who has decided to sell his old greengrocer's business and persuade Wilson – via the still somewhat stupid Frank – to grant him a loan to purchase the pier. A new pilot episode, co-starring John Le Mesurier, Ian Lavender and Bill Pertwee, was recorded on 11 September 1982, and a thirteen-episode series would follow in November 1983.[28]

Before the ill-fated project could run for any longer, however, John Le Mesurier fell ill. Early one morning in the summer of 1983, he began to haemorrhage, and was rushed to hospital. He was discharged after a week, put on a strict salt-free diet, and told to rest as much as possible, but, a month or so later, he haemorrhaged again, and it was now clear that he was terminally ill. He lasted until the middle of November, when, in a bed in Ramsgate hospital, he squeezed his wife's hand, whispered, 'Darling, I'm fed up of it now and I think I'd like to die,' then squeezed again, mumbled, 'It's all been rather lovely,' and slipped into a coma.[29] After his death, his family honoured his wish by placing the following announcement in the obituary column of *The Times*: 'John Le Mesurier wishes it to be known that he "conked out" on November 15th. He sadly misses family and friends.'[30]

They were all there, at St Paul's in Covent Garden, for the memorial service for the sad-eyed, funny, gentle man who had always believed that the most important words in the English language were 'please' and 'thank you'.[31] 'Things did happen to him,' said Derek Taylor in his affectionate tribute. 'He told me once he had, that very week, seen a hen fall over as it walked down a lane. "Not an everyday sight," he said. He wrote to me from London in 1980: "At 3 a.m. the bell rang and there was someone breathing heavily through the letterbox saying that he had met me in Tregunter Road, Earls Court, in 1950 and had something to show me. We called the police and sent him merrily on his way." '[32] There were more stories, and jokes, and music (from 'Le Mez's' favourite movie, *Monsieur Hulot's Holiday*). 'He knew that life could be bloody,' Taylor remarked, 'knew that it *was*, but like those bad films among the good in which he appeared as that jobbing actor, there was always the shining Le Mesurier moment when things didn't seem quite so ghastly after all.'[33] After the service, on the steps outside, Ian Lavender and Bill Pertwee stopped to speak to Le Mesurier's widow, Joan. 'While we were talking,' Lavender recalled, 'a little man whom we recognised from a certain tabloid newspaper came up and literally interposed himself within the three of us and said: "Right, you can tell us now – Arthur and John really hated each other, didn't they?" And I had to hold Bill back – I just had to hold on to his arms – while he told this man what he could do with himself.'[34]

There was another loss early the following year, when Arnold Ridley died, aged 88, on 12 March 1984, and then Janet Davies – Mrs Pike – succumbed to cancer, at the age of 56, on 22 September 1986. Each new absence, however, seemed to revive old memories. Bill Pertwee thought back to the first time that he and Arthur Lowe dined out together in a high-class restaurant: 'The Warden will sort out the bill,'[35] Lowe had declared just loudly enough to catch the ears of the other customers. Ian Lavender reflected on the drive that he shared with John Laurie one warm summer evening after filming: 'He said, "Son, would you like me to recite something for you?" So I said, "Yes, please, John, I'd like that very much." He said, "D'you know *Tam O'Shanter*?" And I replied, "I read it once, yes." So he said, "Right, I'll recite *Tam O'Shanter*." And I had a one-to-one performance of *Tam O'Shanter* from John Laurie, on a wonderful summer's evening, all the way back to London. It was one of the great memories of my life.'[36] Jimmy Perry's mind returned to the untypically chilly morning back in April 1968 when the cast gathered in a field in Thetford for the very first day of filming: 'It started snowing – would you believe it? – and everyone was sitting inside David's Rolls Royce waiting for the first shot to be set up. I was *terribly* excited – this was the first day of filming of *my* first TV series! – and I went over to the car – the windows were completely steamed up – and pulled open one of the doors and said to them, "Er, we're ready in ten minutes!" And Arthur just looked at me and replied, "We'll come when we're ready." So I went back to David and said,

"We've got a right bunch of miserable old sods here!" But they didn't turn out badly, did they?'[37]

Life went on. Clive Dunn, along with his wife, Priscilla Morgan, drifted off into contented semi-retirement in the cool country hills above Vilamoura in Portugal. 'John Le Mesurier was probably right when he said actors are rogues and vagabonds and should be treated as such,' he reflected. 'All they really want is the odd round of applause and the occasional villa with a swimming pool!'[38] The other surviving members of the old team got on with other activities. There was even another Croft and Perry situation-comedy on television – *You Rang, M'Lord* (BBC1, 1988–93),[39] a costly period comedy featuring both Bill Pertwee and Frank Williams in regular roles – which David Croft professed himself to feel more proud of, at least in terms of its production values, than any of his previous projects.[40]

Dad's Army, however, failed to fade away. BBC1 began screening repeats in 1978, which regularly attracted audiences of more than seven million,[41] and by the late 1980's the reruns were being watched by as many as eleven million people;[42] BBC Worldwide began releasing three-episode video compilations at the start of the 1990s;[43] a 'Dad's Army Appreciation Society' was established in 1993;[44] and the programme continued to be broadcast overseas, via various means, in a vast number of countries ranging from Canada to Croatia.[45] A new generation started to watch, enjoy and, in time, treasure the old shows. 'Children keep discovering it,' said Frank Williams. 'There was this three-year-old girl whom I met when I was getting ready to do a reading for a service given by a vicar friend of mine. He said, "Oh, I'd like you to meet your youngest fan," and there she was. Apparently they'd recently shown an episode on television in which I'd had a bit of a row with Mainwaring about the use of the office, because this little thing turned to me and said: "Now, please tell me: that desk – is it *really* yours, or is it really Captain Mainwaring's?" I thought, well, not only is she watching it, she's taking the plot in, too! So that was really very gratifying.'[46]

The programme continued to be used – and, on occasion, mis-used[47] – throughout the 1990s and into the next millennium by ratings-conscious schedulers who knew that *Dad's Army*, unlike so many situation-comedies of more recent vintage, could always be relied on to bring in a broad range of viewers; more than two decades since the show came to a close, repeats of individual episodes were still being seen by audiences of well over six million.[48] When, in the year 2000, the British Film Institute published its list – compiled from a poll of 1,600 programme-makers, critics and executives – of the hundred best British television programmes, of any kind, from the past half-century, *Dad's Army* was placed thirteenth, and the only surprise was that it had not been rated even higher.[49] 'It's sad that the likes of Arthur [Lowe] and John [Le Mesurier] and the others didn't live to see the full extent of the show's fame,' said Jimmy Perry, 'because it's been quite something.'[50]

There have, over the years, been countless conventions, 'events' and tributes to the programme. A '*Dad's Army* Day' was held on 13 May 2000 in Thetford, during which most of the surviving members of the original cast and crew – including David Croft and Jimmy Perry, Harold Snoad, Clive Dunn, Bill Pertwee and Frank Williams – were driven in a procession of open-top Second World War-vintage vehicles through all of those areas of the town that used to double as Walmington-on-Sea. The following day, 'The *Dad's Army* Collection' – featuring many authentic artefacts from both the show and the era, as well as several specially-made walk-in shops and an accurate reconstruction of the church hall and its office – was opened at Bressingham Steam Museum, near Diss in Norfolk, in front of a crowd of more than two thousand.[51] 'It was unbelievable,' said Frank Williams. 'When we drove into the main square in Thetford the people were four or five deep, and then the next day, when we arrived in Bressingham, the crowds were just as large. And you could see fairly elderly pensioners, middle-aged men and women, and very small children, all smiling and cheering and waving as we went past. It was absolutely amazing.'[52]

'I can't believe I did it,' said Clive Dunn to Jimmy Perry as the two men sat in the back of a taxi and reminisced about the old days. 'It was all magic, like a fairytale.'[53] It is easy to see what he meant: there was – there is – something magical about it. *Dad's Army* was only a television programme, only a situation-comedy, but every single time that it comes on the screen, every time that the music begins and the lyrics start – 'Who do you think . . .' – we sit back, look forward, and, for the next thirty minutes, we *smile*.

EPILOGUE

If television is to take life seriously, and if we are to take television seriously, whether as practitioners or viewers, we have to recognise that the modern world makes many demands; it asks for laughter and reality and delight and stories and escape and insight and information and reassurance. Above all, it asks that as little of the coinage as possible be false. It asks for a true bill. That is what taking television seriously means.

HUW WHELDON[1]

It is glory – to have been tested, to have had our little quality and cast our little spell. The thing is to have made somebody care.

HENRY JAMES[2]

One day, some years after *Dad's Army* had ended, Ian Lavender, while on a tour of New Zealand, was interviewed about the old show:

INTERVIEWER Of course, there's not many of you left now, are there?

LAVENDER No, there aren't.

INTERVIEWER Because, well, Arthur Lowe is dead, isn't he?

LAVENDER Yes, Arthur's dead.

INTERVIEWER How did he die?

LAVENDER Arthur died in-between shows, in his dressing room, at the Alexandra Theatre, Birmingham.

INTERVIEWER Oh. And Jimmy Beck, the spiv, he was the first to go, wasn't he?

LAVENDER Yes. Appalling. He was so young.

INTERVIEWER Is the Scotsman still alive?

LAVENDER John Laurie?

INTERVIEWER Yes, John Laurie. Is *he* still alive?

LAVENDER No, sadly. John Laurie is dead. Very sadly, because he was godfather to one of my sons.

INTERVIEWER Oh. Of course, Arnold Ridley, he's dead, too, isn't he?

LAVENDER Yes. Arnold died.

INTERVIEWER Is your mother still alive?

LAVENDER	Pike's mother? Jan Davies? No, I'm afraid not.
INTERVIEWER	Ah. And didn't I read somewhere that the verger passed away?
LAVENDER	Yes, sadly, Teddy died just after the last series.
INTERVIEWER	And, of course, John Le Mes – how *do* you pronounce that name?
LAVENDER	'Le Mesurier'. Rhymes with 'treasurer'.
INTERVIEWER	Right, John Le Mesurier. He's dead. He had a very funny epitaph, didn't he?
LAVENDER	Yes. He wrote it himself: 'Conked out.'
	(*There is a short, thoughtful pause before the final question.*)
INTERVIEWER	Will you be making any more?[3]

'Will you be making any more?': it was yet another one of those 'Don't tell him, Pike!' moments, and, like the original, it sounded witless, but meant well. The programme might have stopped, but the need for it has not. We keep being told, in a tone that Captain Mainwaring might have reserved for a particularly stupid boy or girl, that television has changed, and that we have changed, and that the advent of satellite, cable and digital has at long last liberated the undernourished niche from the suffocating preoccupations of the nation, and that we are now too smart, or dumb, and too sophisticated, or shallow, to watch the same things, or enjoy the same things, or care about the same things, and yet, whenever an old episode of *Dad's Army* is shown, millions of us – in spite of our myriad individual differences – still manage to find it, and stay with it, and appreciate it. The enduring appeal of the show ought to *inspire* the programme-makers of today rather than merely embarrass them: it ought to reassure them that believable characters, in believable situations, can still hold the attention of a large, demographically-mixed audience, and that viewers still warm to shows that treat them like intelligent human beings rather than craven consumers, and that exceptional talent, exceptionally well-presented, will always stand out, and be applauded, and cherished, whether it exists in a world of two or three, or two or three hundred, channels.

'It is possible, on television, to serve a subject, to serve the audience, and to serve the craft of television itself, stinting none,' Huw

228

Wheldon used to insist. 'Indeed if a programme of any kind is to be any good, all this service, performed with zeal, is a first requirement. Television has never been a medium for mere self-expression.'[4] Both the cast and the crew of *Dad's Army*, clearly, believed wholeheartedly in this dictum: every little thing that they ever did, from Croft and Perry's much-deliberated decision, following the second series, to restrict Mainwaring to addressing the members of his platoon as 'men' rather than the more informal-sounding 'chaps',[5] to Arthur Lowe's choice and execution of each perfectly-paced, slow-burning response, carried a rare stamp of care. 'If ever a programme was written with love and compassion and respect,' Tom Sloan once said of the show, 'it was this.'[6] He was so right: it is the reason why *Dad's Army* was, and remains, such a privilege to watch, and such a pleasure to remember.

Episode Guide

Principal Cast

Arthur Lowe	: Captain George Mainwaring
John Le Mesurier	: Sergeant Arthur Wilson
Clive Dunn	: Lance Corporal Jack Jones
John Laurie	: Private James Frazer
Arnold Ridley	: Private Charles Godfrey
James Beck	: Private Joe Walker
Ian Lavender	: Private Frank Pike

Series One (BBC1, black and white)

1. THE MAN AND THE HOUR

It is Tuesday, 14 May 1940, and Anthony Eden has just announced the formation of the Local Defence Volunteers. In the sleepy little English town of Walmington-on-Sea, George Mainwaring, manager of Swallow Bank, wastes no time in appointing himself commander of the Invasion Committee, and Arthur Wilson, his chief clerk, as his second-in-command. Volunteers are enrolled at the church hall. 'Come on, Adolf,' cries their captain. 'We're ready for you!'

Cast: Janet Davies (Mrs Mavis Pike), Caroline Dowdeswell (Janet King), John Ringham (Bracewell), Bill Pertwee (ARP Warden Hodges) and Neville Hughes (soldier).

Recorded	15/4/1968
First broadcast	31/7/1968

2. MUSEUM PIECE

Mainwaring and Wilson come up with an idea for getting the platoon some much-needed weapons: Operation Gun-Grab. The plan is to requisition any firearms of use from the local Peabody Museum of Historic Army Weapons – but to do so the platoon must first find a way to outwit the wily 88-year-old caretaker who just happens to be the father of Lance Corporal Jones.

Cast: Janet Davies (Mrs Mavis Pike), Caroline Dowdeswell (Janet King), Eric Woodburn (museum caretaker), Leon Cortez (milkman) and Michael Osborne (boy scout).

Recorded	22/4/1968
First broadcast	7/8/1968

3. COMMAND DECISION

Leadership agrees with Captain Mainwaring – he has taken to quoting from Kipling – but the men, still without uniforms and weapons, are getting restless. The platoon's fortunes take an upward turn when the blustery old campaigner Colonel Square arrives with an offer of rifles and horses. There is, however, a catch: in order to secure their delivery, Mainwaring must hand over command to Square.

Cast: Caroline Dowdeswell (Janet King), Geoffrey Lumsden (Col. Square), Charles Hill (butler) and Gordon Peters (soldier).
Recorded   29/4/1968
First broadcast 14/8/1968

4. THE ENEMY WITHIN THE GATES

A stranger with a suspicious foreign accent convinces Mainwaring's men that he is a Polish officer serving with GHQ who has come merely to inform them of a 10 shilling reward for every Nazi arrested. While on night patrol, Jones' section capture two German pilots, but Private Godfrey complicates matters by allowing them to escape while he visits the lavatory.
Cast: Caroline Dowdeswell (Janet King), Carl Jaffe (Captain Winogrodzki), Denys Peek and Nigel Rideout (German pilots), Bill Pertwee (ARP Warden Hodges) and David Davenport (Military Police Sgt).
Recorded   6/5/1968
First broadcast 28/8/1968

5. THE SHOWING UP OF CORPORAL JONES

The brusque Major Regan pays the platoon a visit from Area HQ to assess its progress. All is well until he judges Jones to be a potential liability. In order to remain in the platoon, Jones must negotiate the divisional assault course in no more than 15 minutes. His comrades hatch a devious plan to save him.
Cast: Janet Davies (Mrs Pike), Martin Wyldeck (Major Regan), Patrick Waddington (brigadier), Edward Sinclair (caretaker) and Therese McMurray (girl at the window).
Recorded   13/5/1968
First broadcast 4/9/1968

6. SHOOTING PAINS

The platoon is selected to provide the guard of honour for the Prime Minister's impending visit, but a poor show at the shooting range prompts the irascible Major Regan to consider using the Eastgate platoon instead. A shooting contest between Walmington and Eastgate will settle the matter.
Cast: Barbara Windsor (Laura La Plaz), Janet Davies (Mrs Pike), Caroline Dowdeswell (Janet King), Martin Wyldeck (Major Regan), Jimmy Perry (Charlie Cheeseman) and Therese McMurray (girl at the window).
Recorded   20/5/1968
First broadcast 11/9/1968

Series Two (BBC1, black and white)

(Episodes marked * are missing, believed wiped, from the BBC Archives)

7. OPERATION KILT

Mainwaring has received an order from GHQ: there must be 15 minutes of PT before every parade. The platoon's first session is interrupted by the arrival of Captain Ogilvie from the Highland Regiment, who proceeds to brief the men on Saturday night's manoeuvres. A sergeant and nine others from Ogilvie's regiment will attempt to capture the Walmington-on-Sea HQ. Mainwaring's men should win comfortably: they have a numerical advantage. There is, however, a problem: Ogilvie's soldiers are 'one hundred percent fit'.
Cast: Janet Davies (Mrs Pike), James Copeland (Capt. Ogilvie) and Colin Bean (Pte Sponge).
Recorded   13/10/1968
First broadcast 1/3/1969

8. THE BATTLE OF GODFREY'S COTTAGE

In the event of an invasion, announces Mainwaring, the platoon will establish two command posts: Wilson will take one half of the platoon off to the crossroads, and he will take the other half off to Private Godfrey's cottage. When the church bells start ringing

their warning, however, one section of the platoon fails to realise where the other one has disappeared to, and each ends up attacking the other.
Cast: Janet Davies (Mrs Pike), Amy Dalby (Dolly Godfrey), Nan Braunton (Cissy Godfrey), Bill Pertwee (ARP Warden Hodges) and Colin Bean (Pte Sponge).
Recorded   20/10/1968
First broadcast   8/3/1969

9. THE LONELINESS OF THE LONG DISTANCE WALKER*
Private Walker is called up for National Service. The platoon is appalled: where will Mainwaring and Frazer get their whisky from, and Jones his gin, and Wilson his cigarettes, and Godfrey his boxes of fudge, if Walker walks? Mainwaring fights the War Office, but fails, and Walker joins the Army. There is only one thing that can save him now from his fate: a corned-beef fritter.
Cast: Anthony Sharp (brigadier, War Office), Diana King (chairwoman), Patrick Waddington (brigadier), Edward Evans (Mr Reed), Michael Knowles (Capt. Cutts), Gilda Perry (blonde), Larry Martyn (soldier), Robert Lankesheer (medical officer) and Colin Bean (Pte Sponge).
Recorded   27/10/1968
First broadcast   15/3/1969

10. SGT WILSON'S LITTLE SECRET
Mrs Pike tells Frank that the WVS has asked her to take in a little boy as an evacuee, and remarks that it will be 'funny being a mother again after all these years'. Sgt Wilson – who is on his way in for tea – overhears their conversation from outside the door and, jumping to completely the wrong conclusion, comes over all faint. Later that night, after a dazed Wilson has 'confessed' to his astonished superior officer – 'I thought you said you only went round there for meals!' – Mainwaring orders him to do the decent thing and marry the expectant mother – 'You can't go about behaving like Errol Flynn, you know.' The frantic wedding preparations are brought to a premature close, however, when Mrs Pike arrives with the boy – 'little Arthur'.
Cast: Janet Davies (Mrs Pike), Graham Harboard (Little Arthur) and Colin Bean (Pte Sponge).
Recorded   15/11/1968
First broadcast   22/3/1969

11. A STRIPE FOR FRAZER*
Mainwaring has the opportunity to promote one of his men to the rank of corporal. Rather than going straight ahead and handing Jones another stripe, he decides to appoint a second lance corporal and see which one shows the best potential. Mainwaring, rating himself 'a good judge of character', chooses Frazer: 'He's our man, mark my words.' The competition commences: Jones loses points for lagging behind, and Frazer for jumping the gun, but it is the volatile Scot who loses out after alienating the platoon with his increasingly dictatorial manner.
Cast: Geoffrey Lumsden (Capt.-Col. Square), John Ringham (Capt. Bailey), Gordon Peters (policeman), Edward Sinclair (caretaker) and Colin Bean (Pte Sponge).
Recorded   15/11/1968
First broadcast   29/3/1969

12. UNDER FIRE*
Hitler, Mainwaring announces, lacks the courage 'to come and scrap with us toe to toe', and so is now resorting to the cowardly strategy of aerial attack with fire bombs. The following night, while on guard, Frazer spots a flashing light on the corner of Mortimer Street and is convinced that a spy is signalling to the enemy planes overhead. Mainwaring and his men arrest a suspect, Sigmund Murphy – formerly Von Schickenhausen – who protests that he is a naturalised Englishman. An incendiary device lands on the church hall and the platoon struggles to control the fire that follows. Mrs Pike embarrasses the men by smothering the flames with a sand bag, and then the warden embarrasses them

further by confirming that not only is Mr Murphy a British subject but also that he is married to his Auntie Ethel.

Cast: Janet Davies (Mrs Pike), Geoffrey Lumsden (Capt.-Col. Square), John Ringham (Capt. Bailey), Queenie Watts (Mrs Keen), Gladys Dawson (Mrs Witt), Ernst Ulman (Sigmund Murphy), Bill Pertwee (ARP Warden Hodges), June Petersen (woman) and Colin Bean (Pte Sponge).

Recorded	27/11/1968
First broadcast	5/4/1969

Series Three (BBC1, colour)

13. THE ARMOURED MIGHT OF LANCE CORPORAL JONES

The Home Guard has been ordered to co-operate more closely with the ARP. The new Chief Warden, however, turns out to be 'that rather common fellow' Bill Hodges, who proceeds to 'co-operate' by bossing everyone around. When, however, he commandeers Jones' newly-converted delivery van as an ambulance for his air-raid practice, he comes to regret not walking to the 'flipping 'ospital'.

Cast: Janet Davies (Mrs Pike), Bill Pertwee (Chief Warden Hodges), Frank Williams (vicar), Pamela Cundell (Mrs Fox), Jean St Clair (Miss Meadows), Nigel Hawthorne (angry man), Queenie Watts (Mrs Peters), Olive Mercer (Mrs Casson), Harold Bennett (old man) and Dick Haydon (Raymond).

Recorded	25/5/1969
First broadcast	11/9/1969

14. BATTLE SCHOOL

The platoon set off by train for a 'perfectly straightforward' weekend course in guerrilla warfare. After arriving late, hungry and tired, and then oversleeping and missing breakfast, Mainwaring's men are determined to end up victorious.

Cast: Alan Tilvern (Capt. Rodrigues), Alan Haines (Maj. Smith) and Colin Bean (Pte Sponge).

Recorded	1/6/1969
First broadcast	18/9/1969

15. THE LION HAS PHONES

An enemy aircraft crashlands in the town reservoir. There is no sign of any Germans – until, that is, they start shooting in Mainwaring's direction. Jones goes off to call GHQ, but calls the local cinema by mistake. Private Walker, however, thinks he knows how to make the crew surrender.

Cast: Janet Davies (Mrs Pike), Bill Pertwee (Chief Warden Hodges), Avril Angers (telephone operator), Timothy Carlton (Lt Hope Bruce), Stanley McGeagh (Sgt Waller), Richard Jacques (Mr Cheesewright), Pamela Cundell, Olive Mercer and Bernadette Milnes (women in the queue), Gilda Perry (Doreen), Linda James (Betty), Colin Daniel and Carson Green (boys).

Recorded	8/6/1969
First broadcast	25/9/1969

16. THE BULLET IS NOT FOR FIRING

Captain Mainwaring is alarmed by the fact that the platoon has used up all of its ammunition firing at a solitary passing aircraft, and he feels obliged to insist that a Court of Inquiry be held. Constant interruptions, however, rapidly reduce the proceedings to farce.

Cast: Janet Davies (Mrs Pike), Frank Williams (vicar), Tim Barrett (Capt. Pringle), Michael Knowles (Capt. Cutts), Edward Sinclair (verger), Harold Bennett (Mr Blewitt), May Warden (Mrs Dowding), and Fred Tomlinson, Kate Forge, Eilidh McNab, Andrew Daye and Arthur Lews (choir).

Recorded	22/6/1969
First broadcast	2/10/1969

17. SOMETHING NASTY IN THE VAULT
The Swallow Bank takes a direct hit during an air raid. Mainwaring and Wilson end up in the strongroom holding an unexploded bomb. Captain Rogers arrives from Bomb Disposal, but, after discovering that they have a 'trembler' on their hands, he rushes off again in search of the right tools; in his absence, the anxious platoon takes matters into its own hands.
Cast: Janet Davies (Mrs Pike), Bill Pertwee (Chief Warden Hodges), Norman Mitchell (Capt. Rogers) and Robert Dorning (bank inspector).
Recorded   15/6/1969
First broadcast   9/10/1969

18. ROOM AT THE BOTTOM
The staff at GHQ have had a shock: Captain Mainwaring, they have discovered, has never, in fact, been commissioned as an officer, and, as a consequence, he is demoted to private. As a quietly gleeful Sgt Wilson assumes temporary charge of the platoon, Mainwaring does his best to toe the line.
Cast: Anthony Sagar (Drill Sgt Gregory), John Ringham (Capt. Bailey), Edward Sinclair (verger) and Colin Bean (Pte Sponge).
Recorded   29/6/1969
First broadcast   16/10/1969

19. BIG GUNS
Some good news: the platoon has been given a large and powerful naval gun. Some bad news: the town's bandstand is directly in its line of fire. Mainwaring demands that it be dismantled, but the town clerk insists that, as a rare example of Victorian ironwork, it must be preserved. A little demonstration of just what the gun can do, reasons Mainwaring, will win over any doubters.
Cast: Edward Evans (Mr Rees), Edward Sinclair (verger), Don Estelle (man from Pickfords) and Roy Denton (Mr Bennett).
Recorded   6/7/1969
First broadcast   23/10/1969

20. THE DAY THE BALLOON WENT UP
A stray barrage balloon has to be brought back down to earth, and so the platoon is called into action. One mistake leads to another, however, and eventually Captain Mainwaring finds himself embarking on an aerial sightseeing tour of the English countryside.
Cast: Bill Pertwee (Chief Warden Hodges), Frank Williams (vicar), Edward Sinclair (verger), Nan Braunton (Cissy Godfrey), Jennifer Browne (WAAF sgt), Andrew Carr (Operations Room officer), Therese McMurray (girl in the haystack), Kenneth Watson (RAF officer), Vicki Lane (girl on the tandem), Harold Bennett (Mr Blewitt) and Jack Haig (gardener).
Recorded   23/10/1969
First broadcast   30/10/1969

21. WAR DANCE
Captain Mainwaring decides a platoon dance is just the thing to lift morale. He is less than pleased, however, when Pike announces that his date for the evening will be none other than Violet Gibbons, whose mother used to clean for the Mainwarings. The more obvious it becomes that Pike is infatuated with this 'common' young woman, the more concerned his commanding officer grows.
Cast: Frank Williams (vicar), Edward Sinclair (verger), Janet Davies (Mrs Pike), Nan Braunton (Cissy Godfrey), Olive Mercer (Mrs Yeatman), Sally Douglas (Blodwen), the Graham twins (Doris and Dora), Hugh Hastings (pianist) and Eleanor Smale (Mrs Prosser).
Recorded   30/10/1969
First broadcast   6/11/1969

22. MENACE FROM THE DEEP

The platoon is manning the machine gun post at the end of the pier for four consecutive nights. Jones has brought some sausages, Godfrey some mustard, Pike some cake, Frazer some fruit, Walker some whisky and Wilson some acid drops: a 'gastronomic orgy' is keenly anticipated. Mainwaring and Wilson disagree about which one of them should sleep in the solitary hammock ('We shall take it in turns,' Mainwaring concludes. 'But I shall use it first'). Pike, however, loses both the boat and the food, and Frazer begins to hear the cries of ancient mariners. Worse is to come: a wandering sea mine threatens to blow the platoon up.

Cast: Bill Pertwee (Chief Warden Hodges), Stuart Sherwin (second ARP warden), Bill Treacher (1st sailor) and Larry Martyn (2nd sailor).

Recorded   7/11/1969
First broadcast   13/11/1969

23. BRANDED

Private Godfrey is revealed to have been a conscientious objector during the previous campaign. He is sent home in disgrace and ostracised by the rest of the platoon. During a subsequent exercise, however, the room fills with smoke, Mainwaring falls unconscious and one brave man saves him: 'that damned conchie', Godfrey.

Cast: Bill Pertwee (Chief Warden Hodges), Nan Braunton (Cissy Godfrey), Stuart Sherwin (2nd ARP warden) and Roger Avon (doctor).

Recorded   14/11/1969
First broadcast   20/11/1969

24. MAN HUNT

Private Walker introduces a tracking dog to the platoon. When a discarded parachute is discovered in the area, the new recruit is put to work in pursuit of the intruder.

Cast: Bill Pertwee (Chief Warden Hodges), Janet Davies (Mrs Pike), Patrick Tull (suspect), Robert Aldous (German pilot), Robert Moore (large man), Leon Cortez (small man), Olive Mercer (fierce woman), Miranda Hampton (sexy woman) and Bran the dog (as himself).

Recorded   21/11/1969
First broadcast   27/11/1969

25. NO SPRING FOR FRAZER

When Mainwaring inspects the Lewis gun with which Frazer has been entrusted, he discovers that the butterfly spring is missing. After searching Frazer's workshop it is surmised that the errant spring must have ended up inside the coffin of the recently deceased Horace Blewitt, brother of Sidney – in whose house he now lies in rest. How can it possibly be retrieved? Mainwaring has a plan.

Cast: Frank Williams (vicar), Edward Sinclair (verger), Harold Bennett (Mr Blewitt), Joan Cooper (Miss Baker) and Ronnie Brandon (Mr Drury).

Recorded   28/11/1969
First broadcast   4/12/1969

26. SONS OF THE SEA

'I have an idea,' Mainwaring tells a worried-looking Wilson. 'River patrols! Half a dozen determined men, armed to the teeth, with a boat. They could play havoc with the Nazis!' What Mainwaring thinks is wise, and what actually is wise, are often, as Wilson well knows, two entirely different things, and the platoon soon finds itself lost in thick fog, drifting helplessly across the English Channel.

Cast: Michael Bilton (Mr Maxwell), Ralph Ball (man on station), John Leeson (1st soldier) and Jonathan Holt (2nd soldier).

Recorded   5/12/1969
First broadcast   11/12/1969

Episode Guide

27. THE BIG PARADE

Spitfire Fund Week is coming up, and with it the prospect of a high-profile procession. Mainwaring hopes to head it with the Home Guard, Hodges with the ARP, the verger with his Sea Scouts. Mainwaring thinks he knows what will win that prime position for his platoon: a regimental mascot. Sponge volunteers one of his fiercest rams, and Walker comes up with a more expensive 'customised' model, but the burning question remains unresolved – who's on first?

Cast: Bill Pertwee (Chief Warden Hodges), Janet Davies (Mrs Pike), Edward Sinclair (verger), Colin Bean (Pte Sponge) and Pamela Cundell (Mrs Fox).

Recorded   17/7/1970
First broadcast   25/9/1970

28. DON'T FORGET THE DIVER

A major exercise takes place involving all of the Home Guard units, and the Walmington-on-Sea platoon has to plant a bomb in the windmill being occupied by their Eastgate rivals. Mainwaring's men rely on a variety of disguises to reach the building unnoticed, but then it is up to Jones to secrete the bomb inside.

Cast: Bill Pertwee (Chief Warden Hodges), Frank Williams (vicar), Edward Sinclair (verger), Geoffrey Lumsden (Capt. Square), Robert Raglan (Home Guard sergeant), Colin Bean (Pte Sponge), Don Estelle (2nd ARP warden) and Verne Morgan (landlord).

Recorded   24/7/1970
First broadcast   2/10/1970

29. BOOTS, BOOTS, BOOTS

The Walmington-on-Sea platoon receives instruction in the three Fs: fast, functional and fit feet. Mainwaring declares this a most excellent idea, and proceeds to march his men into an acute state of foot fatigue. When he then announces plans for a 20-mile route march, the exhausted platoon decides to teach him a lesson.

Cast: Bill Pertwee (Chief Warden Hodges), Janet Davies (Mrs Pike) and Eric Chitty (Mr Sedgewick).

Recorded   31/7/1970
First broadcast   9/10/1970

30. SERGEANT – SAVE MY BOY!

Pike – stupid boy – is caught on some barbed wire in the middle of a mine field. It gets worse: the minefield is on the beach, the tide is starting to come in, and poor Pike cannot swim. With the Engineers slow to arrive, and the rest of the platoon unsure of how to progress, it is left to Private Godfrey, of all people, to come up with a solution.

Cast: Bill Pertwee (Chief Warden Hodges), Janet Davies (Mrs Pike) and Michael Knowles (Engineer officer).

Recorded   27/6/1970
First broadcast   16/10/1970

31. DON'T FENCE ME IN

The men of Walmington-on-Sea have been sent over to guard the local Italian POW camp. Mainwaring, predictably, is most unimpressed by the prisoners' patent lack of discipline, but Walker's attitude towards them seems suspiciously *simpatico*. Could he possibly, Mainwaring wonders, be a 'fifth columnist'?

Cast: Edward Evans (General Monteverdi), John Ringham (Capt. Bailey) and Larry Martyn (Italian POW).

Recorded   10/7/1970
First broadcast   23/10/1970

32. ABSENT FRIENDS

Mainwaring – who has been delayed at another meeting – arrives at the church hall and is appalled by what Wilson has allowed the men to get up to in his absence: they have all gone down the pub to play against the ARP wardens at darts. Furious, he orders Wilson to bring all of them back immediately, but, as there are two free pints on offer to the victors of the match, the men are staying where they are. Mainwaring, as a consequence, finds himself short of help when reports come in of an armed IRA suspect at large in the area.

Cast: Bill Pertwee (Chief Warden Hodges), Janet Davies (Mrs Pike), Edward Sinclair (verger), J. G. Devlin (Regan), Arthur English (policeman), Patrick Connor (Shamus), Verne Morgan (landlord) and Michael Lomax (2nd ARP warden).

Recorded 7/8/1970
First broadcast 30/10/1970

33. PUT THAT LIGHT OUT

Mainwaring sets up an observation post in the local lighthouse. Jones' section is first on duty. By accident, the light is switched on – illuminating the entire town just as the sirens are signalling the imminent arrival of enemy bombers. Mainwaring must alert Jones to the problem – but the telephone is disconnected.

Cast: Bill Pertwee (Chief Warden Hodges), Stuart Sherwin (2nd ARP warden), Gordon Peters (lighthouse keeper) and Avril Rogers (telephone operator).

Recorded 30/10/1970
First broadcast 6/11/1970

34. THE TWO AND A HALF FEATHERS

Jack Jones: butcher, soldier, war-bore – and coward? Some of his friends and neighbours are forced to think the unthinkable after the arrival in town of George 'Nobby' Clarke, a former comrade who claims that Jones abandoned him in the desert to die when they fought together under General Kitchener in the Sudan. Jones, however, has still to tell his side of the story.

Cast: Bill Pertwee (Chief Warden Hodges), John Cater (Pte Clarke), Wendy Richard (Edith Parish), Queenie Watts (Edna), Gilda Perry (Doreen), Linda James (Betty), Parnell McGarry (Elizabeth) and John Ash (Raymond).

Recorded 6/11/1970
First broadcast 13/11/1970

35. MUM'S ARMY

Captain Mainwaring is recruiting Walmington women to join the fight against the common foe. The normally dour and aloof Captain, whose wife Elizabeth 'hasn't left the house since Munich', appears to take an instant shine to one woman in particular: the fragrant Fiona Gray, a new arrival in town from London. Brief though their encounter has been, it is not long before rumours start to circulate about how there is more to this relationship than meets the eye.

Cast: Carmen Silvera (Mrs Fiona Gray), Janet Davies (Mrs Pike), Wendy Richard (Edith Parish), Pamela Cundell (Mrs Fox), Julian Burberry (Miss Ironside), Rosemary Faith (Ivy Samways), Melita Manger (waitress), David Gilchrist (serviceman), Eleanor Smale (Mrs Prosser), Deirdre Costello (buffet attendant) and Jack Le White (porter).

Recorded 13/11/1970
First broadcast 20/11/1970

36. THE TEST

The ARP wardens have challenged the Home Guard to a cricket match. 'We're walking out here as free men to play a friendly British game,' Mainwaring assures Wilson. 'That's what we're fighting for, you know.' Hodges, however, has other ideas. He has a secret weapon in his team: the fiery cricket pro Ernie Egan. The wardens bat first and set an intimidating target of 152 for 4 declared. The run chase begins.

Cast: Bill Pertwee (Chief Warden Hodges), Frank Williams (vicar), Edward Sinclair

(verger), Don Estelle (Gerald), Harold Bennett (Mr Blewitt) and Freddie Trueman (Ernie Egan).
Recorded   20/11/1970
First broadcast   27/11/1970

37. A. WILSON (MANAGER)?
What a morning for Mainwaring: not only, he discovers, is Wilson about to be promoted by the Home Guard – his commission has come through – but he is also about to be promoted by the bank: he is set to be made manager of the Eastgate branch. This means that Mainwaring will have to make do with Pike as his chief clerk and Jones as his sergeant – unless, of course, Wilson's fortunes change suddenly for the worse.
Cast: Frank Williams (vicar), Edward Sinclair (verger), Janet Davies (Mrs Pike), Blake Butler (Mr West), Robert Raglan (Capt. Pritchard), Arthur Brough (Mr Boyle), Colin Bean (Pte Sponge) and Hugh Hastings (Pte Hastings).
Recorded   27/11/1970
First broadcast   4/12/1970

38. UNINVITED GUESTS
Following the bombing of the ARP HQ, Hodges moves his wardens into the church hall alongside the Home Guard. Mainwaring, appalled by this development, protests to the vicar, Area HQ, the Civil Defence people and a fellow Rotarian, and eventually Hodges' mob are ordered to leave, but not for another week.
Cast: Bill Pertwee (Chief Warden Hodges), Frank Williams (vicar), Edward Sinclair (verger), Rose Hill (Mrs Cole) and Don Estelle (Gerald).
Recorded   4/12/1970
First broadcast   11/12/1970

39. FALLEN IDOL
Mainwaring has always epitomised the principle of military sobriety to his men, but, after Captain Square leads him astray one day in the officers' mess, he ends up inebriated. Only something genuinely heroic now can restore his damaged reputation in the eyes of his men.
Cast: Geoffrey Lumsden (Captain Square), Rex Garner (Capt. Ashley-Jones), Michael Knowles (Capt. Reed), Anthony Sagar (sgt major), Tom Mennard (mess orderly) and Robert Raglan (Capt. Pritchard).
Recorded   11/12/1970
First broadcast   18/12/1970

Special Episode for Christmas (BBC1, colour)

40. BATTLE OF THE GIANTS
Captain Square provokes Captain Mainwaring into accepting the challenge of an initiative test between Walmington-on-Sea's Home Guard and its Eastgate rivals, with Hodges, the vicar and the verger as judges. The contest, to begin with, goes well for Mainwaring's platoon, but then Jones gets a bad attack of malaria, and defeat seems set to be snatched from the jaws of victory.
Cast: Bill Pertwee (Chief Warden Hodges), Geoffrey Lumsden (Capt. Square), Frank Williams (vicar), Edward Sinclair (verger), Robert Raglan (colonel), Charles Hill (sergeant), Colin Bean (Pte Sponge) and Rosemary Faith (barmaid).
Recorded   19/10/1971
First broadcast   27/12/1971

Series Five (BBC1, colour)

41. ASLEEP IN THE DEEP
A bomb falls on the local pumping station where Walker and Godfrey have the misfortune to be on patrol. Efforts at freeing them result in the rest of the platoon – and Hodges – being trapped alongside them. When a pipe bursts and the room fills rapidly up with water, Frazer is moved to mouth his favourite words of comfort: 'We're doomed!'
Cast: Bill Pertwee (Chief Warden Hodges) and Colin Bean (Pte Sponge).
Recorded   26/5/1972
First broadcast   6/10/1972

42. KEEP YOUNG AND BEAUTIFUL
The government has decided to call for an injection of youth into the Home Guard, along with the syphoning-off of the more elderly of its current members into the ARP. When an exchange of personnel is mooted, the platoon decides to take drastic action: some dye their hair, others enrich their skin, the sergeant dons an 'abdominal corset' and the captain a toupee. 'It's awful!' laughs Wilson. 'No, no, no: awfully good.' 'Watch it, Wilson', mutters Mainwaring, 'You might snap your girdle.'
Cast: Bill Pertwee (Chief Warden Hodges), Derek Bond (minister), Robert Raglan (colonel), James Ottaway (1st MP) and Charles Morgan (2nd MP).
Recorded   9/6/1972
First broadcast   13/10/1972

43. A SOLDIER'S FAREWELL
Mainwaring is depressed: his men are falling far short of his expectations, his leadership is underappreciated, and now – following a rich cheese supper – his dreams are filled with Frenchmen.
Cast: Bill Pertwee (Chief Warden Hodges), Frank Williams (vicar), Robert Gillespie (Charles Boyer), Joan Savage (Greta Garbo), Joy Allen (clippie) and Colin Bean (Pte Sponge).
Recorded   2/6/1972
First broadcast   20/10/1972

44. GETTING THE BIRD
Wilson is missing from the platoon. Frazer – 'I'm not one for tittle-tattle or gossip of any kind' – fears there has been some kind of 'r-r-rift', and Godfrey has spotted their sergeant with his arm around an attractive – and much younger – woman. Jones, meanwhile, is looking not so much for something 'on the side' as 'off the ration', and Walker thinks he can help . . .
Cast: Bill Pertwee (Chief Warden Hodges), Frank Williams (vicar), Edward Sinclair (verger), Pamela Cundell (Mrs Fox), Olive Mercer (Mrs Yeatman), Seretta Wilson (Wren) and Alvar Lidell (newsreader).
Recorded   19/5/1972
First broadcast   27/10/1972

45. THE DESPERATE DRIVE OF CORPORAL JONES
The platoon, during the course of a weekend exercise, occupies a deserted barn which turns out to be the target for some 25-pounders. Back at HQ, Jones and Godfrey try phoning to stop the firing, but Godfrey has cut the telephone wire by mistake. There is only one solution: Jones will have to reach the barn before it is blown to bits.
Cast: Bill Pertwee (Chief Warden Hodges), Frank Williams (vicar), Edward Sinclair (verger), Robert Raglan (colonel), Larry Martyn (signals private) and James Taylor (artillery officer).
Recorded   16/6/1972
First broadcast   3/11/1972

46. IF THE CAP FITS . . .

Mainwaring is giving a slide show, and Frazer is far from happy. It is a fine summer's evening, moans the Scot, and this pompous fool is wasting everyone's time with his irrelevant lectures. One way to deal with a grumbler is to let him take over, so, for a few days, Mainwaring decides to swap roles with Frazer.

Cast: Bill Pertwee (Chief Warden Hodges), Campbell Singer (Major General Menzies), Robert Raglan (colonel), Edward Sinclair (verger), Alex McAvoy (sergeant) and Dennis Blanch (2nd lieutenant).

Recorded   30/6/1972
First broadcast   10/11/1972

47. THE KING WAS IN HIS COUNTING HOUSE

Mainwaring, sensing 'the last twitchings of the wounded Nazi beast', has invited the platoon into his home to socialise in 'a happy, carefree, relaxed atmosphere'. Then disaster strikes: a bomb lands on the strong room of Swallow Bank. There is £96,478 1s to be counted, guarded and then taken by Mainwaring – on a horse and cart – to the Eastgate branch.

Cast: Bill Pertwee (Chief Warden Hodges), Frank Williams (vicar), Edward Sinclair (verger), Wendy Richard (Shirley) and Colin Bean (Pte Sponge).

Recorded   23/6/1972
First broadcast   17/11/1972

48. ALL IS SAFELY GATHERED IN

It is time for Mrs Prentice – a widowed lady friend of Godfrey's – to gather in the harvest on her 100-acre farm, and the very gallant Godfrey requests three days' leave from the platoon in order to assist her. Realising the importance of this task, Mainwaring puts the rest of his men at her disposal, too. All goes well – until, that is, the home-made potato wine is served.

Cast: Bill Pertwee (Chief Warden Hodges), Brenda Cowling (Mrs Prentice), Frank Williams (vicar), Edward Sinclair (verger), Colin Bean (Pte Sponge), April Walker (Judy) and Tina Cornioli (Olive).

Recorded   3/11/1972
First broadcast   24/11/1972

49. WHEN DID YOU LAST SEE YOUR MONEY?

Jones arrives at the bank to deposit a donation by local shopkeepers of £500 for the servicemen's canteen, but the packet that he hands over contains sausages, not money. He has, it goes without saying, permission to panic.

Cast: Bill Pertwee (Chief Warden Hodges), Frank Williams (vicar), Edward Sinclair (verger), Harold Bennett (Mr Blewitt) and Tony Hughes (Mr Billings).

Recorded   10/11/1972
First broadcast   1/12/1972

50. BRAIN VERSUS BRAWN

Mainwaring's men have been challenged to prove that brain is better than brawn. The exercise involves placing a dummy bomb in the OC's office. Mainwaring devises a cunning plan to spirit his platoon past the guards: everyone will disguise themselves as firemen, and travel to the building in a fully equipped fire engine. They encounter one tiny snag: Hodges has spotted a house fire.

Cast: Bill Pertwee (Chief Warden Hodges), Robert Raglan (colonel), Edward Sinclair (verger), Anthony Roye (Mr Fairbrother), Maggie Don (waitress), Geoffrey Hughes (bridge corporal) and David Rose (dump corporal).

Recorded   17/11/1972
First broadcast   8/12/1972

51. A BRUSH WITH THE LAW

A 60 watt light bulb is left burning in the church hall's office, and a vengeful Hodges responds by prosecuting the supposed culprit – Captain Mainwaring. When the verger informs the warden that he has the wrong man, the unscrupulous Hodges blackmails him into remaining silent. Things look bleak for poor Mainwaring, but then the wily Walker takes to the stand.

Cast: Bill Pertwee (Chief Warden Hodges), Frank Williams (vicar), Edward Sinclair (verger), Geoffrey Lumsden (Capt. Square), Jeffrey Gardiner (Mr Wintergreen), Stuart Sherwin (2nd ARP warden), Marjorie Wilde (lady magistrate), Chris Gannon (clerk of the court) and Toby Perkins (usher).

Recorded   26/11/1972
First broadcast   15/12/1972

52. ROUND AND ROUND WENT THE GREAT BIG WHEEL

Operation Catherine Wheel has been set up in order to test the War Office's latest weapon: a large, radio-controlled, high explosive-carrying wheel. The Walmington-on-Sea platoon is chosen for fatigues. When Pike and Walker sneak off to listen to the wireless, they cause interference to the wheel, which rolls promptly out of control.

Cast: Bill Pertwee (Chief Warden Hodges), Geoffrey Chater (Colonel Pierce), Edward Underdown (Major General Sir Charles Holland), Michael Knowles (Capt. Stewart), Jeffrey Segal (minister) and John Clegg (wireless operator).

Recorded   1/12/1972
First broadcast   22/12/1972

53. TIME ON MY HANDS

A German pilot has bailed out and is now tangled up on the town hall's clock tower. Mainwaring's men are obliged to retrieve him. Getting up is not a problem – they can climb a makeshift ladder. Getting back down again proves more difficult – Jones has broken the ladder.

Cast: Bill Pertwee (Chief Warden Hodges), Frank Williams (vicar), Edward Sinclair (verger), Harold Bennett (Mr Blewitt), Colin Bean (Pte Sponge), Joan Cooper (Miss Fortescue), Eric Longworth (Mr Gordon) and Christopher Sandford (German pilot).

Recorded   8/12/1972
First broadcast   29/12/1972

Series Six (BBC1, colour)

54. THE DEADLY ATTACHMENT

Mainwaring's men – 'Face to face with the enemy at last, eh?' – have been detailed to guard a captive U-boat crew until an armed escort arrives. When the escort is delayed, however, the platoon has to guard them all night. It turns out to be the most trying of times: not only do the unrepentant Germans expect to be fed the finest and freshest fish and chips, but they also have a defiant leader who lets it be known that he is noting down enemy names ('Don't tell him, Pike!').

Cast: Philip Madoc (U-boat captain), Bill Pertwee (Chief Warden Hodges), Edward Sinclair (verger), Robert Raglan (colonel) and Colin Bean (Pte Sponge).

Recorded   22/6/1973
First broadcast   31/10/1973

55. MY BRITISH BUDDY

The Americans have, at long last, deigned to join in the fight against fascism, and the first modest contingent of troops arrives in Walmington-on-Sea. Mainwaring tells them to make themselves at home, so they do – particularly with his men's girlfriends. When the British are told that they do not know the right temperature to serve beer, and the Americans are told that they do not know the right time to enter a war, a fight breaks out. A photographer from the local paper is on hand to record the flowering of this special relationship.

Cast: Bill Pertwee (Chief Warden Hodges), Alan Tilvern (Colonel Shultz), Frank Williams (vicar), Edward Sinclair (verger), Janet Davies (Mrs Pike), Wendy Richard (Shirley), Pamela Cundell (Mrs Fox), Verne Morgan (landlord), Talfryn Thomas (Mr Cheeseman), Suzanne Kerchiss (Ivy), Robert Raglan (colonel) and Blain Fairman (US sergeant).

Recorded   8/6/1973
First broadcast   7/11/1973

56. THE ROYAL TRAIN

'Very exciting news': King George VI is set to pass through Walmington-on-Sea by train, and the platoon is readying itself to provide the guard of honour. A train duly arrives, but it is the wrong train, and its drivers fall fast asleep after stopping off for a quick cup of tea 'sweetened' by the wrong kind of sugar. Now the platoon has to move the train in order to clear the line for the King.

Cast: Bill Pertwee (Chief Warden Hodges), Frank Williams (vicar), Edward Sinclair (verger), William Moore (station master), Freddie Earlle (Henry), Ronnie Brody (Bob), Fred McNaughton (mayor), Sue Bishop (ticket collector) and Bob Hornery (city gent).

Recorded   29/6/1973
First broadcast   14/11/1973

57. WE KNOW OUR ONIONS

The platoon takes part in a Home Guard efficiency test. If the men pass with flying colours they will be graded a 12-star platoon. Travelling with their Smith gun in the back of Jones' van, they notice a huge mass of onions – Walker's order for Hodges – and decide to use them as a novel form of ammunition.

Cast: Fulton Mackay (Capt. Ramsey), Bill Pertwee (Chief Warden Hodges), Edward Sinclair (verger), Alex McAvoy (sergeant), Pamela Manson (NAAFI girl) and Cy Town (mess steward).

Recorded   15/6/1973
First broadcast   21/11/1973

58. THE HONOURABLE MAN

When Wilson allows it to be known that his family has 'moved up one place' and that he is now entitled to style himself 'The Honourable', he finds himself being courted by the grandees at the golf club and being proposed as the right man to welcome a visiting Russian VIP. Mainwaring, of course, is furious.

Cast: Bill Pertwee (Chief Warden Hodges), Frank Williams (vicar), Edward Sinclair (verger), Eric Longworth (town clerk), Janet Davies (Mrs Pike), Gabor Vernon (Russian), Hana-Maria Pravda (interpreter), Robert Raglan (colonel), Pamela Cundell (Mrs Fox) and Fred McNaughton (mayor).

Recorded   8/7/1973
First broadcast   28/11/1973

59. THINGS THAT GO BUMP IN THE NIGHT

The night is dark and stormy. The platoon is lost. Jones' van has only half a gallon of petrol left in the tank. Tired, cold and miserable, the men decide to spend the night in a nearby house. It appears to be deserted – but is it?

Cast: Jonathan Cecil (Capt. Cadbury) and Colin Bean (Pte Sponge).

Recorded   15/7/1973
First broadcast   5/12/1973

60. THE RECRUIT

Mainwaring is indisposed due to an ingrowing toenail, so Wilson takes charge temporarily of the platoon. When, however, he allows the vicar and the verger to join the ranks, the rest of the men are far from happy.

Cast: Bill Pertwee (Chief Warden Hodges), Frank Williams (vicar), Edward Sinclair (verger), Susan Majolier (nurse) and Lindsey Dunn (small boy).
Recorded   22/7/1973
First broadcast   12/12/1973

Series Seven (BBC1, colour)

61. EVERYBODY'S TRUCKING

Nothing is ever easy. The platoon has to signpost the route for a divisional scheme, but this simple task is complicated by the fact that an abandoned steam engine is blocking the road ahead. There is nothing for it but to set up a diversion.
Cast: Bill Pertwee (Chief Warden Hodges), Frank Williams (vicar), Edward Sinclair (verger), Pamela Cundell (Mrs Fox), Harold Bennett (Mr Blewitt), Olive Mercer (Mrs Yeatman), Felix Bowness (driver) and Colin Bean (Pte Sponge).
Recorded   27/10/1974
First broadcast   15/11/1974

62. A MAN OF ACTION

There may be trouble ahead: a landmine has ripped up 100 yards of railway track; gas and water supplies have been cut out; the telephone wires are down; and Pike has got his head stuck between the bars of a gate. Cometh the hour, cometh the Mainwaring: he declares martial law.
Cast: Bill Pertwee (Chief Warden Hodges), Talfryn Thomas (Mr Cheeseman), Frank Williams (vicar), Edward Sinclair (verger), Eric Longworth (town clerk), Harold Bennett (Mr Blewitt), Arnold Peters (Fire Officer Dale), Jay Denyer (Inspector Baker), Robert Mill (Capt. Swan) and Colin Bean (Pte Sponge).
Recorded   7/5/1974
First broadcast   22/11/1974

63. GORILLA WARFARE

During an exercise, Mainwaring casts himself as a highly important secret agent whom his platoon must escort to a clandestine destination. GHQ has put out counter-agents to catch him, so the platoon decides to trust no one – not the two stranded nuns, nor the woman with a pram, and certainly not the distressed-looking doctor who appears with some story about an escaped gorilla who is roaming the woods. It is all 'sheer r-r-rubbish,' scoffs Frazer, and Mainwaring agrees, but then Hodges arrives with news of 'an 'orrible 'airy monster' that is on the loose, and they have cause to think again.
Cast: Bill Pertwee (Chief Warden Hodges), Talfryn Thomas (Pte Cheeseman), Edward Sinclair (verger), Robert Raglan (colonel), Robin Parkinson (Lieutenant Wood), Erik Chitty (Mr Clerk), Rachel Thomas (mother superior), Michael Sharvell-Martin (lieutenant), Verne Morgan (farmer) and Joy Allen (woman with pram).
Recorded   27/10/1974
First broadcast   29/11/1974

64. THE GODIVA AFFAIR

As the town is still £2,000 short of the sum it requires for the purchase of a Spitfire, the platoon decides to drum up support by performing a morris dance at the fund-raising carnival. It is the identity of the Lady Godiva figure, however, that ends up grabbing most people's attention.
Cast: Bill Pertwee (Chief Warden Hodges), Talfryn Thomas (Pte Cheeseman), Frank Williams (vicar), Edward Sinclair (verger), Janet Davies (Mrs Pike), Pamela Cundell (Mrs Fox), Eric Longworth (town clerk), Peter Honri (Pte Day), Rosemary Faith (waitress), Colin Bean (Pte Sponge) and George Hancock (Pte Hancock).
Recorded   3/11/1974
First broadcast   6/12/1974

65. THE CAPTAIN'S CAR

The mayor has a Rolls-Royce, and now, thanks to Lady Maltby's generous donation to the war effort, so too does Mainwaring. The mayor is due to greet a visiting French general, and Mainwaring's platoon is due to provide a guard of honour. The mayor's Rolls does not need to be camouflaged, but is, whereas Mainwaring's Rolls does, but is not. Someone needs to find some black paint, and quickly.

Cast: Bill Pertwee (Chief Warden Hodges), Talfryn Thomas (Pte Cheeseman), Frank Williams (vicar), Edward Sinclair (verger), Robert Raglan (colonel), Eric Longworth (town clerk), Fred McNaughton (mayor), Mavis Pugh (Lady Maltby), John Hart Dyke (French general) and Donald Morley (Glossip).

Recorded   17/11/1974
First broadcast   13/12/1974

66. TURKEY DINNER

It was a night-watch. There was a prodigious amount of alcohol. Corporal Jones ended up with a dead turkey on his hands. Mainwaring decides to put things right by treating the town's senior citizens to a rare and welcome feast, but, he adds ominously, 'it must be organised properly'.

Cast: Bill Pertwee (Chief Warden Hodges), Talfryn Thomas (Pte Cheeseman), Frank Williams (vicar), Edward Sinclair (verger), Harold Bennett (Mr Blewitt), Pamela Cundell (Mrs Fox), Janet Davies (Mrs Pike), Olive Mercer (Mrs Yeatman) and Dave Butler (farmhand).

Recorded   10/11/1974
First broadcast   23/12/1974

Series Eight (BBC1, colour)

67. RING DEM BELLS

Mainwaring is not best pleased when his platoon is chosen to play Nazis in an Army training film. He is more than a little peeved when Pike is selected to play a German officer. He is positively livid when the men pop in to the pub for a pint, while still dressed in Nazi uniforms.

Cast: Bill Pertwee (Chief Warden Hodges), Frank Williams (vicar), Edward Sinclair (verger), Jack Haig (landlord), Robert Raglan (colonel), Felix Bowness (special constable), John Bardon (Harold Forster), Hilda Fenemore (Queenie Beal), Janet Mahoney (barmaid) and Adele Strong (woman with umbrella).

Recorded   3/7/1975
First broadcast   5/9/1975

68. WHEN YOU'VE GOT TO GO

In spite of his chronically bad chest, his painful sinuses, his weak ankles and his recently acquired nervous twitch, Private Pike has been passed A1 on his call-up medical and is set to become 'the second of the few'. Before the platoon can hold a farewell fish-and-chip supper, however, Mainwaring must compete with Hodges in a blood donor drive.

Cast: Bill Pertwee (Chief Warden Hodges), Frank Williams (vicar), Edward Sinclair (verger), Janet Davies (Mrs Pike), Eric Longworth (town clerk), Freddie Earle (Italian sergeant), Tim Barrett (doctor), Colin Bean (Pte Sponge) and Frankie Holmes (fish-fryer).

Recorded   6/6/1975
First broadcast   12/9/1975

69. IS THERE HONEY STILL FOR TEA?

Private Godfrey's beloved Cherry Tree Cottage is set to be flattened in order to make way for a new aerodrome. Frazer, however, champions his cause: he knows the minister responsible for the plan, and he knows his father on the Isle of Barra, and he also knows all about a certain little incident in the draper's shop. 'Blackmail' is an ugly word . . .

Cast: Bill Pertwee (Chief Warden Hodges), Gordon Peters (man with the door), Robert

Episode Guide

Raglan (colonel), Campbell Singer (Sir Charles McAllister), Joan Cooper (Dolly) and Kathleen Sainsbury (Cissy).
Recorded 26/6/1975
First broadcast 19/9/1975

70. COME IN, YOUR TIME IS UP

Mainwaring's platoon discovers a German aircraft crew in an inflatable dinghy on a lake. 'I've never seen such surly-looking brutes,' moans Mainwaring. 'If there's one thing I can't stand it's sulking Nazis!' Pike suggests that they shoot through the dinghy and sink them, but his captain reminds him about 'being a sporting nation and playing with a straight bat'. Wilson comes up with a rather more civilised strategy, but Pike remains poised, with his gun, just in case.
Cast: Bill Pertwee (Chief Warden Hodges), Frank Williams (vicar), Edward Sinclair (verger), Harold Bennett (Mr Blewitt) and Colin Bean (Pte Sponge).
Recorded 10/7/1975
First broadcast 26/9/1975

71. HIGH FINANCE

Mainwaring decides that Jones' bank account has been in the red for far too long. 'You're rapidly becoming insolvent,' he warns him, and a shaken Jones goes home 'to have a little bit of a think'. An investigation into the elderly butcher's affairs, however, reveals an intriguing chain of debtors, and it also transpires that Mr Swann, the grocer, has some news that he is keen to impart.
Cast: Bill Pertwee (Chief Warden Hodges), Frank Williams (vicar), Edward Sinclair (verger), Janet Davies (Mrs Pike), Ronnie Brody (Mr Swann), Colin Bean (Pte Sponge) and Natalie Kent (Miss Twelvetrees).
Recorded 30/5/1975
First broadcast 3/10/1975

72. THE FACE ON THE POSTER

Mainwaring wants his platoon to become a company. He wants to become a major, too, but, most of all, he wants his platoon to become a company. To help him achieve his goal he launches a recruitment drive with a newly designed poster. Jones, of all people, wins the right to be the face featured on the poster, but, in the event, this turns out to be one honour he could well have done without.
Cast: Bill Pertwee (Chief Warden Hodges), Frank Williams (vicar), Edward Sinclair (verger), Peter Butterworth (Mr Bugden), Harold Bennett (Mr Blewitt), Gabor Vernon (Polish officer), Colin Bean (Pte Sponge), Bill Tasker (Fred) and Michael Bevis (police sergeant).
Recorded 17/7/1975
First broadcast 10/10/1975

Special Episode for Christmas (BBC1, colour)

73. MY BROTHER AND I

Frazer encounters a very rum fellow on the train back to Walmington-on-Sea: short, round, cherry-nosed Barry Mainwaring, purveyor of carnival novelties. This cheerfully indiscreet little man is surely, inquires Frazer, no relation of that paragon of lower-middle-class sobriety, George Mainwaring, nor of his equally respectable father, who was a master tailor in Eastbourne? Barry – 'Tell the truth and shame the devil, that's me!' – is happy to confirm the connection, and settles down to reveal all about 'old Po-Face'. Frazer delivers his gleeful judgment: 'They're boozers, the lot of 'em! Boooozers!'
Cast: Bill Pertwee (Chief Warden Hodges), Frank Williams (vicar), Edward Sinclair (verger), Arnold Diamond (major general), Penny Irving (chambermaid) and Colin Bean (Pte Sponge).
Recorded 23/5/1975
First broadcast 26/12/1975

Episode Guide

Special Episode for Christmas (BBC1, colour)

74. THE LOVE OF THREE ORANGES
The entire platoon joins forces with the rest of the town for a comforts-for-the-troops bazaar: Godfrey pledges some of his sister Dolly's chutney, along with three pots of honey and 'quite a lot' of her elderberry wine; Jones donates a 'monster brawn'; Frazer deigns to fashion a few silhouettes; Mainwaring promises some of the lampshades that his lady wife has created out of 'odds and ends'; and Hodges has 'a rather wonderful surprise' – three oranges. Mrs Mainwaring, however, fails to show up – due to a bizarre enamelling accident – and there is no sign either of her 'rather unusual' lampshades. Mainwaring himself has only one chance of redemption: he must get his hands on one of Hodges' oranges.
Cast: Bill Pertwee (Chief Warden Hodges), Frank Williams (vicar), Edward Sinclair (verger), Pamela Cundell (Mrs Fox), Janet Davies (Mrs Pike), Joan Cooper (Dolly), Eric Longworth (town clerk), Olive Mercer (Mrs Yeatman) and Colin Bean (Pte Sponge).
Recorded 10/10/1976
First broadcast 26/12/1976

Series Nine (BBC1, colour)

75. WAKE UP WALMINGTON
Complacency is setting in among the townsfolk, so Mainwaring devises 'Operation Wake-Up'. He gets his platoon to masquerade as fifth columnists – 'cut-throats and desperadoes' in 'very sinister' clothes – in order to shake everyone up. At first, it seems, the plan is not working, but then it starts to work rather too well.
Cast: Bill Pertwee (Chief Warden Hodges), Frank Williams (vicar), Edward Sinclair (verger), Geoffrey Lumsden (Capt. Square), Sam Kydd (yokel), Harold Bennett (Mr Blewitt), Robert Raglan (colonel), Charles Hill (butler), Jeffrey Holland (soldier), Barry Linehan (van driver), Colin Bean (Pte Sponge), Alister Williamson (Bert) and Michael Stainton (Frenchy).
Recorded 8/7/1977
First broadcast 2/10/1977

76. THE MAKING OF PRIVATE PIKE
At long last, Mainwaring has his own staff car. Pike – still heady from drinking raspberryade – 'borrows' it to drive his new girlfriend, who thinks he has 'smashing eyebrows', to the cinema at Eastgate; on the way back, however, and nine long miles from home, the car runs out of petrol, and it takes Pike all night to push it back. It is time for Wilson to have a serious word with the stupid boy.
Cast: Bill Pertwee (Chief Warden Hodges), Frank Williams (vicar), Edward Sinclair (verger), Jean Gilpin (Sylvia), Anthony Sharp (colonel), Jeffrey Segal (brigadier), Pamela Cundell (Mrs Fox), Janet Davies (Mrs Pike) and Melita Manger (Nora).
Recorded 1/7/1977
First broadcast 9/10/1977

77. KNIGHTS OF MADNESS
To support the 'Wings for Victory' week, the platoon restages the battle of St George and the Dragon. This does not go down well with Hodges and his ARP wardens, however, because they have been planning to stage precisely the same thing.
Cast: Bill Pertwee (Chief Warden Hodges), Frank Williams (vicar), Edward Sinclair (verger), Colin Bean (Pte Sponge), Janet Davies (Mrs Pike), Olive Mercer (Mrs Yeatman), Eric Longworth (town clerk) and Fred McNaughton (mayor).
Recorded 22/7/1977
First broadcast 16/10/1977

78. THE MISER'S HOARD

Frazer keeps his savings in the form of gold sovereigns. Mainwaring thinks the money should be kept in a bank – his bank. Rumours start to spread around town about the Scotsman's hoard, and Frazer is spotted setting off with a box to the graveyard. The platoon prepares to investigate.

Cast: Fulton Mackay (Dr McCeavedy), Bill Pertwee (Chief Warden Hodges), Frank Williams (vicar), Edward Sinclair (verger) and Colin Bean (Pte Sponge).

Recorded   24/6/1977
First broadcast   23/10/1977

79. NUMBER ENGAGED

A 'highly secret invasion warning device' – or, as Hodges prefers to put it, 'some silly telephone wires' – has been set up along the coast, and the platoon is to guard it. When the vicar arrives to give an open-air service, Mainwaring 'raises his face to heaven' and notices an unexploded bomb caught up in the wires. Wilson, however, has a bright idea.

Cast: Bill Pertwee (Chief Warden Hodges), Frank Williams (vicar), Edward Sinclair (verger), Ronnie Brody (GPO man), Robert Mill (Army captain), Kenneth MacDonald (Army sergeant), Felix Bowness (van driver), Colin Bean (Pte Sponge), Stuart McGugan (Scottish sergeant) and Bernice Adams (ATS girl).

Recorded   15/7/1977
First broadcast   6/11/1977

80. NEVER TOO OLD

A wedding is announced, an invasion is threatened, and an institution is celebrated. At the end, Mainwaring, Wilson and all of the platoon raise their glasses for a toast: 'To Britain's Home Guard.'

Cast: Bill Pertwee (Chief Warden Hodges), Frank Williams (vicar), Edward Sinclair (verger), Pamela Cundell (Mrs Fox), Janet Davies (Mrs Pike), Colin Bean (Pte Sponge), Joan Cooper (Dolly) and Robert Raglan (colonel).

Recorded   29/7/1977
First broadcast   13/11/1977

Notes

1 Opening epigraph: Huw Wheldon, *The Achievement of Television* (London: BBC, 1975), p. 16.

PROLOGUE

1.   Randy Newman, 'My Country', from the album *Bad Love* (Dreamworks, 1999), published by Randy Newman Music.

2.   Ludwig Wittgenstein, *Culture and Value*, ed. G. H. von Wright with Heikki Nyman (Oxford: Basil Blackwell, 1980), p. 78.

3.   J. B. Priestley, *English Humour* (London: Longmans, Green & Co., 1929), p. 4.

4.   In a survey of 600 viewers conducted by *Classic Television* magazine for its June 1999 issue, the top three funniest moments in the history of British television were: (1) the 'Don't tell him, Pike!' scene from the *Dad's Army* episode 'The Deadly Attachment' (first broadcast on BBC1 on 31 October 1973); (2) the scene featuring Del Boy's unexpected fall in the wine bar from the *Only Fools and Horses* episode 'Yuppy Love' (first broadcast on BBC1 on 8 January 1989); (3) the 'Don't mention the war' exchange from the *Fawlty Towers* episode 'The Germans' (first broadcast on BBC1 on 24 October 1975). Other, similar, surveys confirm that the scene is rated highly by the majority of television viewers and critics: the *Observer* 'TV 1,000' readers' poll concerning 'TV's greatest moments' (both comic and serious) rated the 'Don't tell him, Pike!' scene at number 34, just behind the Sex Pistols' live, expletive-laden clash with Bill Grundy and just ahead of the coverage of Churchill's funeral (see *Observer*, 'TV 1,000' booklet, 12 September 1999, p. 18), while the *Radio Times* list of the '50 funniest sitcom moments' (compiled by a panel of actors, writers and producers) placed the scene at number 4 (see the *Radio Times*, 19–25 August 2000, pp. 18–22).

5.   Apart from all of the celebratory books – such as Bill Pertwee's *Dad's Army: The Making of a Television Legend* (London: Pavilion, 1998) – and the positive critical summaries – such as the entry included in Mark Lewisohn's splendid *Radio Times Guide to TV Comedy* (London: BBC, 1998, pp. 176–7) – the programme has also figured prominently in a succession of polls, including one from 1993 which rated it the most popular television comedy show of the past two decades (see the *Daily Mail*, 21 August 1993, p. 9), and one from 2000, compiled by the British Film Institute, which rated it thirteenth in a list of the hundred best British television programmes from 1955 to 2000 (see *Guardian*, p. 3, and *Daily Mail*, pp. 8–9 – both 6 September 2000 – and *Financial Times*, 13 September 2000, p. 29).

6.   These viewing figures are based on the percentages of the viewing public recorded in the BBC's internal Daily Viewing Barometers for the following dates: 31 October 1973, 25 April 1974, 24 June 1978 and 21 November 1989. (For an account of the BBC's method of measuring viewing figures, see Roger Silvey, *The Measurement of Audiences*, London: BBC, 1966, pp. 7–15.)

7.   Everyone, some claim – except for those independently-minded souls who write about it – is drawn to the programme for reasons of nostalgia. Stuart Jeffries, for example, argues in his *Mrs Slocombe's Pussy* (London: Flamingo, 2000, p. 36) that *Dad's Army* 'was part of the nostalgia industry that held this country by the throat', but there is no real empirical evidence to justify such critical claims. (For a more sympathetic consideration of this aspect of the programme's appeal, see Jeffrey Richards' '*Dad's Army* and the politics of nostalgia' in his *Films and British National Identity* (Manchester: Manchester University Press, 1997).)

8.   Priestley, *English Humour*, p. 18.

9.   J. B. Priestley, *The English Comic Characters* (New York: Phaeton Press, 1972), p. 242.

10.   The 'Englishness' of *Dad's Army* has been commented on before, most notably by Jeffrey Richards in his '*Dad's Army* and the politics of nostalgia'. Richards argues that the programme embodies the six common characteristics of Englishness defined and summarised by Sir Ernest Barker in his *The Character of England* (London: Oxford University Press, 1950, pp. 563–70): (1) a tendency to social homogeneity qualified by a preoccupation with 'position'; (2) a love of amateurism and a concomitant distrust of professionalism; (3) a gentlemanly code; (4) a voluntary habit; (5) eccentricity; and (6) youthfulness. Richards is a little rash, however, in forcing what Barker offered as 'examples' rather than 'a complete list' into such a formulaic construction; *Dad's Army* could be said to epitomise such qualities, but, then again, it could be said to epitomise several others as well.

11.   Dennis Potter, 'Where comedy is king', *Sunday Times* (weekly review section), 16 October 1977, p. 37.

12.   Transcribed from the episode 'Never Too Old' (first broadcast 13 November 1977, written by David Croft and Jimmy Perry, reproduced here with their permission). As readers will be more familiar with the programmes than with the scripts, I will quote the dialogue in the form that it was actually performed rather than as it was written in the original script.

13.   George Orwell, 'The lion and the unicorn' (1940), in *The Penguin Essays of George Orwell* (Harmondsworth: Penguin, 1984), p. 156. Orwell signed up as a member of the Local Defence Volunteers – as the Home Guard was originally called – on 10 May 1940. He eventually became a sergeant in 'C' company of the 5th County of London Home Guard Battalion in St John's Wood. He left, on medical grounds, on 23 November 1943. Some of his writings on the Home Guard are included in *The Collected Essays, Journalism and Letters Vol. 2* (London: Penguin, 1970).

14.   Orwell, 'The lion and the unicorn', p. 156.

15.   George Santayana, *Soliloquies in England* (New York: Charles Scribner's Sons, 1922), p. 30.

16.   Ralph Waldo Emerson, *English Traits* (Cambridge, Mass.: The Riverside Press, 1903), p. 313.

17.   Arnold Bennett, *The Old Wives' Tale* (Harmondsworth: Penguin, 1983), p. 512.

18.   Orwell, 'The lion and the unicorn', p. 149.

19.   Huw Wheldon, 'A reply to charges of trivia in BBC-TV programmes', published originally in the *Sunday Times*, 8 November 1970, and reproduced in Charles Curran *et al.*, *In The Public Interest* (London: BBC, 1971), p. 16.

THE SITUATION

1.   Robb Wilton, 'The Home Guard' (1944), *Music Hall to Variety*, Vol. 3 (World Records SH 150).

Notes to Chapter I

Chapter I

1. J. B. Priestley, BBC radio broadcast, 20 October 1940; reproduced in *Postscripts* (London: Heinemann, 1940), p. 99.

2. *Dad's Army*: 'The Deadly Attachment', first broadcast on BBC1, 31 October 1973, script by David Croft and Jimmy Perry

3. Anthony Eden, *Freedom and Order: Selected Speeches 1939–1946* (London: Faber, 1947), pp. 71–3.

4. It is beyond the scope of a book such as this to provide a detailed historical account of the Home Guard. Interested readers might wish to consult the following specialised studies: Charles Graves, *The Home Guard of Britain* (London: Hutchinson, 1943); John Brophy, *Britain's Home Guard: A Character Study* (London: George G. Harrap & Co., 1945); Norman Longmate, *The Real Dad's Army* (London: Arrow, 1974); A. G. Street, *From Dusk Till Dawn* (London: Blandford Press, 1945); Frank and Joan Shaw (eds), *We Remember the Home Guard* (Hinckley: Echo Press, 1983); S. P. Mackenzie's excellent paper, 'Citizens in arms: the Home Guard and the internal security of the United Kingdom, 1940–41', *Intelligence and National Security*, vol. 6, no. 3 (July 1991) pp. 548–72; and Ian Beckett's broader and equally well-researched history of volunteer forces, *The Amateur Military Tradition 1558–1945* (Manchester: Manchester University Press, 1991). Policy papers relating to the Home Guard are kept in the Public Records Office among the following classes: Cabinet Office – Historical Section Files (CAB 106), Ministry of Defence Secretariat Files (CAB 120); Ministry of Home Security – Air Raid Precautions Registered Files 1931–57 (HO 186), Intelligence Branch Registered Files 1939–50 (HO 199); Prime Minister's Office – Operational Papers (PREM 3); and the War Office – Registered Papers (WO 32 Code 66), Reports/Miscellaneous Papers (WO 33), War Diaries Home Forces 1939–45 (WO 166), Military Headquarters Papers, Home Forces 1939–45 (WO 199).

5. Quoted by Martin Gilbert in *Finest Hour: Winston S. Churchill*, Vol. 6 (London: Heinemann, 1983), pp. 59–60. (See also Graves, *The Home Guard of Britain*, Appendix C, pp. 177–8.)

6. The so-called 'Phoney War' lasted from the fall of Poland in September 1939 to the German invasion of Norway in April 1940.

7. Public Record Office (PRO): INF 1/264: 'Public Opinion on the Present Crisis', 30 May 1940. See also *The Times*, 18 May 1940, p. 3, column 1.

8. Imperial War Museum (IWM): HR V. Jordan, 'Military Security', p. 24.

9. *The Times*, 11 May 1940, p. 7.

10. See, for example, the proposal Lord Mottistone made to the House of Lords on 8 May 1940, which involved 'local levies armed with rifles . . . to guard isolated places of importance' (*Hansard*, vol. 116, HL (DEB) 5s, col. 329), and also the opinions expressed in such newspapers as the *Sunday Express* (12 May 1940, p. 6), the *Sunday Pictorial* (12 May 1940, p. 11) and the *Daily Mail* (17 May 1940, p. 4).

11. IWM: Hawes Papers, 'Formation of the L.D.V.', encl. Anderson to Hawes, 26 June 1941.

12. Brophy, *Britain's Home Guard*, p. 16. Two plans, in fact, were debated during the second week of May 1940: one – originating in GHQ Home Forces – had been proposed by General Sir Walter Kirke, the Commander-in-Chief of the Home Forces; the other – originating in the War Office – was put forward by Major General Sir Robert Gordon-Finlayson, the Adjutant General. Kirke's plan envisioned a loosely organised volunteer force raised in towns and villages, and led at county level by the lords lieutenant, for the defence of the immediate locality. Gordon-Finlayson's plan, which, as the more cautious of the two, sought to ensure that the new force be kept as controllable as possible, proposed utilising small groups of British Legion volunteers attached to searchlight companies; the volunteers, upon sighting an invader, would enable the regulars to report the landing area to a higher authority. On 12 May, after a lengthy and intensive period of debate (it seems that neither party, to begin with, had been aware of the other's proposals), it was eventually

agreed within the War Office that Kirke's plan should be the one to go forward. (See IWM: Brigadier William Carden Roe Papers, 77/165/1, 'Birth Pangs of the Home Guard'; PRO: WO 199/3236, 'Home Guard [Local Defence Volunteers] Origins', memo by Major J. Maxse; Graves, *The Home Guard of Britain*, pp. 10–13, 18–20; and Mackenzie, 'Citizens in Arms', p. 553.)

13. See Sir Anthony Eden, *The Reckoning* (London: Cassell, 1965), p. 103.

14. Quoted by Longmate, *The Real Dad's Army*, pp. 9–10.

15. See Graves, *The Home Guard of Britain*, p. 21.

16. Ernest Raymond, quoted by Longmate, *The Real Dad's Army*, pp. 8–9.

17. See *The Times*, 27 May 1940, p. 3; Central Statistical Office, *Statistical Digest of the War* (London: HMSO, 1951), p. 13, table 15; PRO: T 162/864/E1628/1, Humphreys-Davies to Crombie, 14 May 1940.

18. It is not practicable, in a book such as this, to discuss in detail the evolution of the LDV/Home Guard administrative structure. To put it briefly: the LDV was, to begin with, organised by Areas (like the Regular Army's Military Commands); each Area was subdivided into Zones; each Zone was broken down into Groups; each Group was then subdivided into Battalions; each Battalion consisted of several Companies; each Company was composed of several Platoons; and each Platoon was made up of several Sections. There was a regular chain of command all the way down from the Area to the Section. See the explanatory speeches made in the House of Commons by Sir Edward Grigg on 22 May 1940 (*Hansard*, vol. 361 HC (DEB) 5s, col. 239) and by Anthony Eden on 23 July 1940 (*Hansard*, vol. 363 HC (DEB) 5s, col. 577).

19. Sir Edward Grigg, 22 May 1940: *Hansard*, vol. 361 HC (DEB) 5s, col. 241.

20. *Ibid.*, col. 242.

21. See *The Times*, 16 May 1940, p. 3, and Graves, *The Home Guard of Britain*, p. 17.

22. See B. G. Holloway (ed.), *The Northamptonshire Home Guard, 1940–1945* (Northampton: n.p., 1949), p. 59; Graves, *The Home Guard of Britain*, pp. 15–16, 85; and Brophy, *Britain's Home Guard*, p. 19. The Germans, in a propaganda broadcast, had warned the British public that: 'Civilians who take up arms against German soldiers are, under international law, no better than murderers, whether they are priests or bank clerks' (quoted by Graves, *The Home Guard of Britain*, p. 16).

23. The wait was longer for some: according to Captain F. W. Simkiss, it was not until mid-September 1940 that a supply of uniforms began to 'trickle in' to the unit based at Broadcasting House (Graves, *The Home Guard of Britain*, p. 183).

24. Lt Col. L. W. Kendish, DSO, *Records and Reminiscences of the 4th Buckinghamshire Battalion Home Guard* (London: Vernon Lock, 1946), p. 19.

25. Street, *From Dusk Till Dawn*, p. 62.

26. See Longmate, *The Real Dad's Army*, Chapter 4; Graves, *The Home Guard of Britain*, p. 32.

27. General Edmund Ironside (the successor to General Kirke as Commander-in-Chief Home Forces), 5 June 1940; quoted by Graves, *The Home Guard of Britain*, p. 70.

28. See PRO: INF 1/264, 'Public Opinion on the Present Crisis', 15 June 1940. In the national newspapers of the time one or two military critics described the LDV as 'a complete failure', and began calling for it to be scrapped and replaced by a more organised force (see Graves, *The Home Guard of Britain*, p. 83).

29. See *Hansard*, vol. 362 HC (DEB) 5s, col. 62.

30. Pownall, Diary entry, 20 June 1940, reproduced in *Chief of Staff: The Diaries of Lieutenant-General Sir Henry Pownall*, vol. 2, ed. Brian Bond (London: Leo Cooper, 1974), p. 5.

31. PRO: PREM 3/223/3, Churchill to Eden, 22 June 1940.

32. *Ibid.*, 26 June 1940.

33.   See Graves, *The Home Guard of Britain*, p. 57; letter from Lt Col. C. P. Hawkes to *The Times*, 18 May 1940, p. 7.

34.   See Longmate, *The Real Dad's Army*, p. 28.

35.   PRO: PREM 3/223/3, Churchill to Eden, 26 June 1940. See also Herbert Morrison, *An Autobiography* (London: Odhams, 1960, p. 185), and Gilbert, *Finest Hour*, p. 600.

36.   PRO: PREM 3/223/3, Eden to Churchill, 28 June 1940.

37.   *Ibid.*, Cooper to Churchill, 3 July 1940.

38.   Cited by Norman Longmate, *How We Lived Then: A History of Everyday Life during the Second World War* (London: Arrow Books, 1973), p. 103.

39.   As the journalist W. F. Deedes ('With pikes and pitchforks, they waited for Hitler', *Sunday Telegraph*, 16 July 2000, p. 22) has recalled: 'Nobody argued much with Churchill in those days.'

40.   PRO: PREM 3/223/3, Churchill to Cooper, 6 July 1940.

41.   Liddell Hart Centre, King's College, London: Pownall Diary (unpublished entry), 29 July 1940.

42.   Churchill, BBC Home Service, 14 July 1940. Quoted by Graves, *The Home Guard of Britain*, p. 84.

43.   The Woolton Papers (Bodleian Library, Oxford): Diary, Box 2, 30 November 1940.

44.   The Avon Papers (Birmingham University Library): AP/20/1/20A, diary entry, 22 July 1940.

45.   Anthony Eden confirmed the name change in the House of Commons when asked by a fellow MP: *Hansard*, vol. 363 HC (DEB) 5s, col. 576.

46.   The phrases, of course, come from Winston Churchill's first speech in the House of Commons as Prime Minister on 13 May 1940, reproduced in Winston Churchill, *The Speeches of Winston Churchill* ed. David Cannadine (Harmondsworth: Penguin, 1990), p. 149.

47.   C. D. Lewis, quoted by Longmate, *The Real Dad's Army*, p. 33.

48.   J. B. Priestley, BBC Home Service, 16 June 1940; the transcript is included in *Postscripts*, pp. 10–11.

49.   John Lehmann, quoted by Longmate, *The Real Dad's Army*, p. 32.

50.   On the occasion of Taylor's 80th birthday, he was presented, in a unique military ceremony, with an ornamental clock, and the officer who made the presentation declared that Taylor 'carried an illuminated history of the British Empire on his left breast' (see Graves, *The Home Guard of Britain*, pp. 38–9).

51.   Orwell, letter to *Partisan Review*, 15 April 1941; reproduced in *The Collected Essays, Journalism and Letters*, vol. 2, p. 141.

52.   The character of Colonel Horatio Blimp was created by the left-wing cartoonist David Low in 1934, appearing in the *London Evening Standard* and later in both the *Daily Herald* and the *Manchester Guardian* (see Colin Seymour-Ure and Jim Schoff, *David Low*, London: Secker, 1985). The Michael Powell and Emeric Pressburger movie, *The Life and Death of Colonel Blimp* (1943), though inspired by Low's cartoons, softened the satire significantly, but still managed to anger the War Office.

53.   See Peter Lewis, *A People's War* (London: Methuen, 1986), p. 31; Leonard Mosley, *Backs to the Wall: London Under Fire 1939–45* (London: Weidenfeld, 1971), p. 55; and Rex Harrison, *Rex: An Autobiography* (London: Macmillan, 1974), p. 67.

54.   Liddell Hart Centre: Pownall Diary (unpublished extract), 20 June 1940.

55.   See Longmate, *The Real Dad's Army*, p. 21.

56.   Street, *From Dusk Till Dawn*, pp. 118–19.

57.   Sir Edward Grigg, speech to the House of Commons, 6 November 1940: *Hansard*, vol. 365 HC (DEB) 5s, cols. 1347–8.

58.   *Ibid.*, cols. 1352–3.

59.   Grigg, speech to the House of Commons, 19 November 1940: *Hansard*, vol. 365 HC (DEB) 5s, cols. 1886–97.

60.   Liddell Hart Centre: Pownall Diary, 29 September 1940.

61.   Brophy, *Britain's Home Guard*, p. 35.

62.   Liddell Hart Centre: Pownall Diary (unpublished entry), 12 August 1940.

63.   Pownall had applied successfully for a transfer to Northern Ireland. Eastwood – described by the War Office as 'one of the foremost young generals in the British Army' (WM J. K. Howard and H. W. Endicott, *Summary Report, British Home Guard*, 1941, p. 12) – was not formally appointed by Churchill himself, but Eden acknowledged that he had been the choice of the Prime Minister (PRO: PREM 3/223/4, Eden to Churchill, 16 November 1940). Eastwood, in turn, gave way to Major General Lord Bridgeman in the summer of 1941.

64.   See Sir Edward Grigg, speech to the House of Commons, 6 November 1940: *Hansard*, vol. 365 HC (DEB) 5s, cols. 1349–50.

65.   See Graves, *The Home Guard of Britain*, p. 254.

66.   Winston Churchill confirmed the details in the House of Commons on 2 December 1941: *Hansard*, vol. 376 HC (DEB) 5s, col. 1032.

67.   See Longmate, *The Real Dad's Army*, p. 60.

68.   The phrase is Herbert Morrison's (PRO: CAB 123/204, Morrison to Sir John Anderson, 10 October 1942).

69.   Gloucestershire Record Office: D2095/1, Bn Order 3, paragraph 6, 24 June 1940. The decision was backed up by Home Guard Director-General Eastwood, who wrote in December 1940: 'Under no circumstances should women be enrolled in the Home Guard', adding that 'it is undesirable for women to bear arms' (PRO: WO 32/9423, J. R. Eastwood, 27 December 1940).

70.   P. J. Grigg, PRO: CAB 123/204, Grigg to Herbert Morrison, 22 December 1942.

71.   PRO: WO 166/173, Minute to the PM on the future of the HG. Churchill had confirmed his support for Summerskill on 31 October 1941: PRO: WO 32/9423. (See also *Hansard*, vol. 365 HC (DEB) 5s, cols. 1887, 1897, 1928–32 and vol. 376 HC (DEB) 5s, cols. 1033–8; and Penny Summerfield and Corinna Peniston-Bird, 'Women in the firing line: the Home Guard and the defence of gender boundaries in Britain in the Second World War', *Women's History Review*, vol. 9, no. 2 (2000), pp. 231–55.)

72.   Kentish, *Records and Reminiscences of the 4th Buckinghamshire Battalion Home Guard*, p. 34.

73.   *The Story of No. 2 Company of the 7th Battn. Somerset Home Guard* (1944), p. 29.

74.   E. D. Barclay, *The History of the 45th Warwickshire (B'Ham) Battalion Home Guard* (Birmingham: n.p., 1945), p. 94.

75.   Brophy, *Britain's Home Guard*, p. 34.

76.   Longmate, *The Real Dad's Army*, p. 79.

77.   *The Times*, 12 February 1942, p. 2.

78.   Captain Godfrey Nicholson, Conservative MP for Farnham, 11 March 1942; *Hansard*, vol. 378 HC (DEB) 5s, col. 1129.

79.   Brophy, *Britain's Home Guard*, p. 36.

80.   Orwell, Diary entry, 21 June 1942; reproduced in *The Collected Essays*, p. 490.

81.   Longmate, *The Real Dad's Army*, pp. 85 and 106.

82.   See, for example, the first-hand accounts in Frank and Joan Shaw, *We Remember the Home Guard*.

83.   Supplementary Report by the 10th Bucks Battalion Home Guard, included in Graves, *The Home Guard of Britain*, p. 191.

84. *The Times*, 15 May 1942, p. 2.

85. *Ibid.*, 13 May 1942, p. 2.

86. *Ibid.*, 14 May 1942, p. 4.

87. James Grigg wrote to Churchill on 8 September 1942 informing him of the forthcoming film's focus 'on an imaginary type of Army officer who has become an object of ridicule to the general public', and warning him that its release would give the 'Blimp conception' a 'new lease of life'. Churchill, prompted by Grigg's over-reaction, attempted, unsuccessfully, to have the film banned. (See the 'Colonel Blimp File', PRO: PREM 4 14/15, reproduced in Ian Christie, ed., *Powell, Pressburger and Others* (London: BFI, 1978), pp. 106–11; and James Chapman, '*The Life and Death of Colonel Blimp* (1943) reconsidered', *Historical Journal of Film, Radio and Television*, no. 15 (1995), pp. 19–54.)

88. Winston Churchill, *The Second World War*, Vol. 3: *The Grand Alliance* (London: Cassell, 1950), p. 840.

89. *Ibid.*

90. *The Times*, 14 May 1943, p. 4.

91. *Ibid.*

92. See, for example, *The Times*, 8 July 1943, p. 2 and 21 December 1943, p. 2.

93. See *The Times*, 7 September 1944, p. 2.

94. Letter to *The Times*, 27 October 1944, p. 2.

95. PRO: PREM 3/223/12, Churchill to Grigg, 19 September 1944.

96. Quoted by Longmate, *The Real Dad's Army*, p. 122.

97. King George VI, quoted by J. W. Wheeler-Bennett, *King George VI: His Life and Reign* (London: Macmillan, 1958), p. 615.

98. Pownall, Diary entry, 29 September 1940, *Chief of Staff*, vol. 2, p. 6.

99. Edmund Burke, 'Thoughts on the cause of the present discontents' (1770), in *Pre-Revolutionary Writings*, ed. Ian Harris (Cambridge: Cambridge University Press, 1993), p. 184.

100. Measured in March 1943 (see Longmate, *The Real Dad's Army*, p. 120), although Graves, in *The Home Guard of Britain* (p. 168), put the figure at approximately 'two million'.

101. See Deedes, 'With pikes and pitchforks', p. 22; Longmate, *The Real Dad's Army*, p. 121; and Vt. Bridgeman, 'When we had 1,700,000 Home Guards', *Home Guards News*, May 1954, p. 14.

Chapter II

1. Phil Silvers, *The Man Who Was Bilko* (London: W. H. Allen, 1974), p. 203.

2. Larry Gelbart, quoted by Vince Waldron, *Classic Sitcoms*, 2nd edn (Los Angeles: Silman-James Press, 1997), p. 248.

3. Jimmy Perry, interview with the author, 27 August 2000.

4. *Ibid.*

5. *Ibid.*

6. *Ibid.*

7. Jimmy Perry, quoted by Pertwee, *Dad's Army*, p. 13.

8. Jimmy Perry and David Croft, *Dad's Army: The Lost Episodes* (London: Virgin, 1998), p. 9.

9. Jimmy Perry, interview with the author, 27 August 2000.

10. *Ibid.*

11. *Ibid.*

12. *Ibid.*

13. *Ibid.*

14. *Ibid.*

15. *Beggar My Neighbour* (written by Ken Hoare and David Croft's nephew Mike Sharland) ran on BBC1 for three series (the first two produced-directed by David Croft) between March 1967 and March 1968. It featured two married sisters who lived next door to each other with their respective husbands and it starred Peter Jones (replaced by Desmond Walter-Ellis after the first series), June Whitfield, Reg Varney and Pat Coombs.

16. See Chapters 3–7 of Bill Cotton's *Double Bill* (London: Fourth Estate, 2000), for a vivid account of this era at the BBC.

17. David Croft, interview with the author, 23 May 2000.

18. Jimmy Perry, interview with the author, 27 August 2000.

19. David Croft, interview with the author, 23 May 2000.

20. Jimmy Perry, interview with the author, 27 August 2000.

21. David Croft, interview with the author, 23 May 2000.

22. Jimmy Perry, interview with the author, 27 August 2000.

23. David Croft, interview with the author, 23 May 2000.

24. *Ibid.*

25. Bill Cotton, interview with the author, 6 June 2000.

26. *Ibid.*

27. Barry Took, interview with the author, 17 May 2000.

28. Michael Mills, in Denis Norden *et. al.*, *Coming To You Live!* (London: Methuen, 1985), p. 9.

29. Bill Cotton, interview with the author, 6 June 2000.

30. David Croft, interview with the author, 23 May 2000.

31. Tom Sloan, quoted by Paul Ferris, *Sir Huge: The Life of Huw Wheldon* (London: Michael Joseph, 1990), p. 172.

32. Donald Baverstock, quoted in *ibid.*

33. Paul Fox, interview with the author, 2 May 2000.

34. Barry Took, interview with the author, 17 May 2000.

35. Tom Sloan, in a BBC lunch-time lecture delivered on 11 December 1969 and published in pamphlet form as *Television Light Entertainment* (London: BBC, 1969), p. 4.

36. *Ibid.*, p. 5.

37. *Ibid.*, p. 20.

38. *Ibid.*, pp. 17–18.

39. *Ibid.*, p. 17.

40. *Ibid.*, pp. 12–13.

41. *Ibid.*, p. 9.

42. David Croft, interview with the author, 23 May 2000.

43. Hugh Carleton Greene, quoted by Sloan, *Television Light Entertainment*, p. 18. (See also Hugh Greene, *The Third Floor Front* (London: Bodley Head, 1969), pp. 13 and 122–42).

44. Mary Whitehouse, quoted by Michael Tracey in *A Variety of Lives* (London: Bodley Head, 1983), p. 231. (See also Mary Whitehouse, *A Most Dangerous Woman?* (London: Lion, 1982).)

45.   Richard Crossman, *The Diaries of a Cabinet Minister*, Vol. 2 (London: Hamish Hamilton, 1976), p. 445.

46.   *The Phil Silvers Show* – originally titled *You'll Never Get Rich*, and more often referred to informally as *Bilko* – was broadcast in the US on the CBS network from 20 September 1955 to 19 June 1959; it ran on BBC TV from 20 April 1957 to 2 June 1960, and has continued, of course, to be repeated ever since.

47.   *The Army Game*, made by Granada for ITV, ran for five series from 19 June 1957 to 20 June 1961.

48.   *Hogan's Heroes* (whose slogan was: 'If you liked World War II, you'll love *Hogan's Heroes*') ran in the US on CBS from 17 September 1965 to 4 July 1971; it was shown in the UK by some ITV regional companies from 6 January 1967 to 20 February 1971.

49.   Sloan, *Television Light Entertainment*, p. 12.

50.   Mills' basic response has been preserved in the BBC's Written Archive Centre (WAC) at Caversham; the rest of his remarks, including his views on the need for a co-writer, were discussed in interviews with both David Croft (23 May 2000) and Jimmy Perry (27 August 2000).

51.   Croft and Perry, *Dad's Army: The Lost Episodes*, p. 8.

52.   *Ibid.*

53.   Perry renamed the bank 'Swallow' after it was discovered that his original choice, 'Martin's', was the copyright of an existing bank. The real Martin's Bank was absorbed into Barclays Bank a year after *Dad's Army* began its run, and the name was used in the 1971 movie version of the show.

54.   BBC WAC: *Dad's Army* File T12/881/1: 'The Man and the Hour': Michael Mills, memo to script editor, Light Entertainment, 4 October 1967. (According to a letter dated 25 October 1967 from Heather Dean of the BBC's Copyright Department to Ann Callender, Jimmy Perry was paid £200 for co-writing the pilot script; David Croft's fee, as a BBC employee, was dealt with internally, and came to £250.)

55.   BBC WAC: James Perry File.

Chapter III

1.   F. Scott Fitzgerald, 'The Rich Boy' (1922), in *The Rich Boy and Other Stories* (London: Phoenix, 1998), p. 119.

2.   *Dad's Army*, 'Shooting Pains', first broadcast 11 September 1968.

3.   David Croft, interview with the author, 23 May 2000.

4.   *Ibid.*

5.   Reiner's pilot episode, *Head of the Family*, was broadcast by CBS on 19 July 1960. After the producer Sheldon Leonard told Reiner that he was 'just not the type to play himself', Dick Van Dyke was brought in and the retitled show ran for six extremely successful seasons from October 1961 to June 1966. (See Waldron, *Classic Sitcoms*, pp. 77–82.)

6.   Jimmy Perry, interview with the author, 27 August 2000.

7.   *The Life and Death of Colonel Blimp* (1943), screenplay by Powell and Pressburger ('Colonel Mannering' appears in the dinner party scene set in Cadogan Place).

8.   Jimmy Perry, interview with the author, 22 November 2000.

9.   Quoted by Jimmy Perry, interview with the author, 27 August 2000.

10.   Jimmy Perry, interview with the author, 27 August 2000.

11.   *Ibid.*

12.   *Ibid.*

13.   Michael Mills, quoted by David Croft, interview with the author, 23 May 2000.

14. David Croft, interview with the author, 23 May 2000.

15. The cockney Chief Petty Officer Pertwee; the stuttering Commander Wetherby; the self-echoing Admiral Buttonshaw; the audibly introspective Vice Admiral 'Burbly' Burwasher; Commander High Price; and camp criminal The Master.

16. Broadcast 20 March 1967.

17. David Croft, interview with the author, 23 May 2000.

18. BBC WAC: *Dad's Army* File T12/881/1: 'The Man and the Hour': memo from Michael Mills to E. K. Wilson, 13 November 1967.

19. There is no record in the BBC archive concerning the sum that Pertwee was offered, but what is clear is that none of the actual cast received more than £262.10 per episode for the first series of *Dad's Army* (BBC WAC: File T12/890/1).

20. Jimmy Perry, interview with the author, 27 August 2000.

21. David Croft, interview with the author, 23 May 2000.

22. Jimmy Perry, interview with the author, 22 November 2000. Richard Webber, in both his *Dad's Army: A Celebration*, p. 19, and *The Complete A–Z of Dad's Army* (London: Orion, 2000), p. 91, claims that 'Jimmy [Perry] initially saw Arthur Lowe playing Sergeant Wilson and Robert Dorning . . . as Captain Mainwaring.' Perry told me: 'That's wrong. It's sort of wrong. It *is* easy to misunderstand. This is the truth: I never said, "Let's cast Robert Dorning as the Captain." I just liked them both, liked the way they worked together as actors, and I just knew I wanted to get them both. Then once I'd settled on Arthur as Mainwaring, I tried to get Robert Dorning as Wilson.'

23. Michael Mills, quoted by David Croft, interview with the author, 23 May 2000.

24. John Le Mesurier, *A Jobbing Actor* (London: Elm Tree Books, 1984), p. 113.

25. *Ibid.*, p. 117.

26. *Ibid.*, pp. 117–18.

27. Michael Mills, in his memo (13 November 1967) to E. K. Wilson (BBC WAC: *Dad's Army* File T12/881/1: 'The Man and the Hour'), had asked the bookings department to 'engage' Jack Haig for the first series of *Dad's Army*. David Croft (interview with the author, 23 May 2000) believes that Tom Sloan advised Haig that he did 'not suppose that they'll have more than three series', and therefore Haig concluded that 'Wacky Jacky' was the better bet.

28. See Clive Dunn, *Permission to Speak* (London: Century, 1986), p. 196.

29. *Ibid.*, p. 197.

30. *Ibid.*

31. Clive Dunn, quoted by John Le Mesurier, *A Jobbing Actor*, p. 118.

32. *Ibid.*

33. David Croft, interview with the author, 23 May 2000. (Jason had also appeared in an episode of *Hugh and I*, broadcast on BBC1, 3 June 1967.)

34. Dunn, *Permission to Speak*, p. 198.

35. David Jason, correspondence with the author, 1 June 2000.

36. Dunn, *Permission to Speak*, p. 198.

37. BBC WAC: *Dad's Army* File T12/890/1: the cast was paid, per episode, the following sums for the first series: John Le Mesurier, £262.10; Arthur Lowe, £210; Clive Dunn, £210; John Laurie, £105; James Beck, £78.15s; Arnold Ridley, £63; Bill Pertwee, £57.15s; and Ian Lavender, £52.10s.

38. David Croft, interview with the author, 23 May 2000.

39. Broadcast on BBC1, 3 January 1965.

40. David Croft, interview with the author, 23 May 2000.

41. BBC WAC: James Beck TV Artists File 1963–70: letter to Bush Bailey, 22

December 1963. Bailey replied on 30 December, and interviewed him on 14 January 1964.

42. The police constable featured in *Beggar My Neighbour* (broadcast on BBC1, 13 March 1967) and the customs officer in *Hugh and I Spy* (BBC1, 22 January 1968).

43. David Croft, interview with the author, 23 May 2000. (Arthur English, ten years Beck's senior, had been briefly considered for the role before the decision was made to opt for a slightly more 'youthful' spiv.)

44. *Ibid.*

45. *Ibid.*

46. Ian Lavender, interview with the author, 29 May 2000.

47. *Ibid.*

48. Quoted by Webber, *The Complete A–Z of Dad's Army*, p. 35. (Ringham had recently appeared in an episode of *Hugh and I Spy* broadcast on BBC1, 29 January 1968).

49. Davies – a part-time typist at Richard Stone's agency – appears as a typist in an episode broadcast on 16 July 1967.

50. Recalled by David Croft, interview with the author, 23 May 2000.

51. The Boswell of the back row, Colin Bean (Private Sponge), published a memoir entitled *Who Do You Think You Are Kidding!* (London: Minerva, 1998). Other actors who appeared in the back row at some stage during the show's nine year run were: Freddie Wiles, Freddie White, Leslie Noyes, Michael Moore, Evan Ross, Roger Bourne, Alec Coleman, William Gossling, Peter Whitaker, Martin Dunn, Chris Franks, Ken Wade, Emmett Hennessy, Arthur McGuire, David Chaffer and Lindsay Hooper.

52. Bill Pertwee, interview with the author, 27 May 2000.

53. *Ibid.*

54. David Croft, interview with the author, 23 May 2000.

55. *Ibid.*

THE COMEDY

1. Frank Muir, quoted by David Nathan, *The Laughtermakers* (London: Peter Owen, 1971), p. 36.

Chapter IV

1. Duncan Wood, quoted by Nathan, *The Laughtermakers*, p. 118.

2. James Frazer (*Dad's Army*): 'Asleep in the Deep', broadcast on BBC1, 6 October 1972/'If the Cap Fits . . .', broadcast on BBC1, 10 November 1972.

3. Jimmy Perry, interview with the author, 27 August 2000.

4. *Ibid.*

5. *Ibid.*

6. David Croft, interview with the author, 23 May 2000.

7. John Laurie, quoted in Ted Hart, *Dad's Army* (London: Peter Way, 1972), p. 33.

8. Jimmy Perry, interview with the author, 27 August 2000.

9. 'Who Do You Think You Are Kidding, Mr Hitler', words by Jimmy Perry, music by Jimmy Perry and Derek Taverner (Veronica Music Ltd). Before the song was edited for television it ended as follows: 'So watch out Mr Hitler/You have met your match in us./If you think you can crush us/We're afraid you've missed the bus./'Cause who do you think you are kidding Mr Hitler/If you think old England's done?'

10.   Jimmy Perry, interview with the author, 27 August 2000.

11.   *Ibid*.

12.   Ian Lavender, interview with the author, 29 May 2000.

13.   *Ibid*.

14.   Clive Dunn, *Permission to Speak*, p. 198.

15.   Ian Lavender, interview with the author, 29 May 2000.

16.   Jimmy Perry, interview with the author, 22 November 2000.

17.   John Le Mesurier, *A Jobbing Actor*, p. 118.

18.   James Beck, quoted in Hart, *Dad's Army*, p. 40.

19.   David Croft, interview with the author, 23 May 2000.

20.   Croft and Perry, *Dad's Army: The Lost Episodes*, p. 110.

21.   Wheldon, *The Achievement of Television*, p. 11.

22.   *Ibid*.

23.   *Ibid*. Wheldon also discussed this experience in his 1976 Richard Dimbleby Lecture, *The British Experience in Television* (London: BBC, 1976), p. 6.

24.   John Le Mesurier, quoted in Hart, *Dad's Army*, p. 19.

25.   Barry Took, interview with the author, 17 May 2000.

26.   Paul Fox, interview with the author, 2 May 2000.

27.   David Croft, interview with the author, 23 May 2000.

28.   Bill Cotton, interview with the author, 6 June 2000.

29.   Paul Fox, interview with the author, 2 May 2000.

30.   David Croft, interview with the author, 23 May 2000.

31.   Bill Cotton, interview with the author, 6 June 2000.

32.   BBC WAC: *Dad's Army* File T12/880/1: memo from Michael Mills to Paul Fox, 23 May 1968.

33.   BBC WAC: *Dad's Army* File T12/880/1: memo from Paul Fox to Michael Mills, 27 May 1968.

34.   The first episode of *Monty Python* was broadcast on BBC1 on 5 October 1969; the pilot episode of *Up Pompeii!* was broadcast on BBC1 on 17 September 1969.

35.   BBC WAC: *Dad's Army* File T12/880/1: Fox to Mills, 27 May 1968.

36.   *Ibid*.

37.   The original title sequence is missing, believed wiped (although the stock wartime footage is preserved at the Imperial War Museum and in the BBC's film library), and therefore it has not been possible to compare the two versions as they were actually screened to preview audiences. My impression of the original sequence is based on the descriptions given to me by David Croft, Jimmy Perry, Paul Fox and Bill Cotton Jr, as well as the various references to it in the BBC's written archives.

38.   David Croft, interview with the author, 23 May 2000.

39.   Jimmy Perry, interview with the author, 27 August 2000.

40.   David Croft, interview with the author, 23 May 2000.

41.   Jimmy Perry, interview with the author, 27 August 2000.

42.   David Croft, interview with the author, 23 May 2000. (There is no trace of the report in the BBC's written archives.)

43.   Bill Cotton, interview with the author, 6 June 2000.

44.   Russell Twisk, 'Dad's Army', *Radio Times*, 25 July 1968, p. 32.

45.   A new set of ITV companies – including Thames (the result of a merger between

Rediffusion and ABC), London Weekend, HTV and Yorkshire – came into existence on 30 July 1968. The change necessitated a renegotiation of the working agreement between ITV and the ACTT: formerly, ACTT members worked a 40 hour week, receiving salaries ranging from £19 per week for trainees to £70 for producers and directors; the ACTT's new demand was for a reduction of the working week to 35 hours, 4 weeks annual holiday and a 7 per cent pay rise. The new ITV companies complained that this would cost them more than £1,000,000 per year, and offered instead to increase pay by 42 per cent and grant 4 weeks annual holiday to some, but not all, grades. The ACTT rejected this offer on 23 July, and the stoppages began. The industrial action lasted three weeks, ending on 19 August after both sides had compromised. See *Daily Mail*, 31 July 1968, p. 1; *Daily Express*, 1 August 1968, p. 1; *Daily Mirror*, 2 August 1968, p. 11; and *London Evening Standard*, 5 August 1968, p. 16, 7 August 1968, p. 7 and 13 August 1968, p. 16. (In 1991, the ACTT was absorbed into a new union: BECTU, the Broadcasting Entertainment, Cinematograph and Theatre Union.)

46.   *London Evening Standard*, 5 August 1968, p. 16.

47.   *Ibid*.

48.   Jimmy Perry, interview with the author, 27 August 2000.

49.   'The Man and the Hour', written by David Croft and Jimmy Perry, first broadcast on BBC1, 31 July 1968.

50.   The BBC Daily Viewing Barometer for 31 July 1968 put the size of audience at 14.2 per cent of the UK population (50,500,000 at the time); programmes on BBC2 and ITV during this 8.20–8.50 period attracted audiences of 0.5 per cent and 19.4 per cent respectively.

51.   David Croft, interview with the author, 23 May 2000.

52.   Sir Tom Stoppard, correspondence with the author, 31 May 2000.

53.   Peter Black, 'Can one person criticise the full range of television?', *Journal of the Society of Film and Television Arts*, vol. 2, no. 7 (1973), pp. 4–5.

54.   Nancy Banks-Smith, *Sun*, 1 August 1968, p. 12.

55.   Sean Day-Lewis, *Daily Telegraph*, 1 August 1968, p. 19.

56.   Michael Billington, *The Times*, 1 August 1968, p. 7.

57.   Mary Malone, *Daily Mirror*, 1 August 1968, p. 14.

58.   Philip Purser, *Sunday Telegraph*, 4 August 1968, p. 13.

59.   Tom Stoppard, *Observer*, 4 August 1968, p. 20.

60.   Ron Boyle, *Daily Express*, 1 August 1968, p. 10. (As often happened with television and theatre reviews, this piece arrived too late to appear in early editions of the paper, although some of them did carry another review of the programme – also positive – by Robin Turner; Boyle's review first appeared in the *fourth* edition of that day's *Express*.)

61.   BBC WAC: Audience Research Report (VR/68/461, 16 August 1968) on *Dad's Army*, 'The Man and the Hour'.

62.   See Freddie Hancock and David Nathan, *Hancock* (London: BBC, 1986), p. 59.

Chapter V

1.   Huw Wheldon, *The British Experience in Television*, p. 11.

2.   Nat Hiken, quoted by Mickey Freeman and Sholem Rubinstein, *Bilko: Behind the Lines With Phil Silvers* (London: Virgin, 2000), p. 13.

3.   Ian Lavender, interview with the author, 29 May 2000.

4.   David Croft, interview with the author, 23 May 2000.

5.   Bill Cotton, interview with the author, 6 June 2000.

6.   Viewing figures calculated from the percentages recorded in the BBC's Daily Viewing Barometer for 7 August 1968.

7.   Richard Last, *Sun*, 8 August 1968, p. 12.

8.   BBC WAC: *Dad's Army* File T12/880/1 (General and External Correspondence): letter from H. Gregory, 16 August 1968.

9.   *Ibid.*, letter from J. Board, 7 September 1968.

10.   *Ibid.*, letter from Barry Took to David Croft, 15 August 1968.

11.   BBC WAC: *Dad's Army* File T12/880/1 (General and External Correspondence). (Mr G. Watson, 1 August 1968, complained that his enjoyment had been 'completely spoiled by the repeated gales of inane laughter from the unseen audience', and Mr J. W. Camp, 3 August, was similarly irritated by the 'idiotic laughter'.)

12.   *Ibid.* (Mr Michael Sheppard, for example, wrote on 3 September 1968 offering the loan of his three wartime period GPO vans; Sonia Thurley, on 8 August, offered to donate her grandfather's old Home Guard uniform and Mr R. Fortescue-Foulkes, on 9 August, proposed passing on his old overcoat and battledress. None of the scripts, or script suggestions, were taken up.)

13.   David Croft, interview with the author, 23 May 2000.

14.   Ian Lavender, interview with the author, 29 May 2000.

15.   Michael Mills, quoted in Croft and Perry, *Dad's Army: The Lost Episodes*, p. 86.

16.   Michael Colbert, *Yorkshire Post*, 15 August 1968, p. 6.

17.   Mary Malone, *Daily Mirror*, 16 August 1968, p. 16.

18.   Stewart Lane, *Morning Star*, 24 August 1968, p. 2. (As there was no edition of *Dad's Army* on 21 August, it seems likely that Lane was referring to the most recent episode, on 14 August.)

19.   Viewing figures calculated from the percentages recorded in the BBC's Daily Viewing Barometers for 14 and 28 August. The Reaction Index rating for episode 2 was 60.

20.   The ACTT industrial action ended on 19 August 1968.

21.   Such big-budget shows as *The Avengers*, *Man in a Suitcase*, *The Champions* and *Department S* were usually scheduled opposite *Dad's Army* at this time in most ITV regions.

22.   BBC WAC: Audience Research Report, VR/68/540, 'The Showing Up of Corporal Jones', 10 October 1968.

23.   Stanley Reynolds, *Guardian*, 5 September 1968, p. 9.

24.   Maurice Wiggin, *Sunday Times* (Weekly Review section), 4 August 1968, p. 44.

25.   Wiggin, *Sunday Times* (Weekly Review section), 8 September 1968, p. 51.

26.   David Croft, interview with the author, 23 May 2000.

27.   BBC Daily Viewing Barometer, 11 September 1968. The Reaction Index was 64.

28.   Richard Last, *Sun*, 12 September 1968, p. 12.

29.   BBC WAC: *Dad's Army* File T12/880/1: memorandum from Keith Smith to David Croft, 16 September 1968.

Chapter VI

1.   Dennis Main Wilson, quoted in Nathan, *The Laughtermakers*, p. 119.

2.   Jerry Seinfeld, *SeinOff* (London: Boxtree, 1999), p. 66.

3.   John Laurie, quoted by Pertwee, *Dad's Army: The Making of a Television Legend*, p. 22.

4.   Averages calculated from percentages recorded in the BBC Daily Viewing Barometers.

5.   In 1971, when David Croft received the award, it was still known as SFTA (Society of Film and Television Arts); it was renamed BAFTA (British Academy of Film and Television Arts) in 1975.

6.   BBC1's Christmas-time compendium featured specially-written *Dad's Army* sketches on 25 December 1968, 1969, 1970 and 1972.

Notes to Chapter VI

7.   *The Royal Television Gala Performance*, which also featured Morecambe and Wise and Dave Allen, was recorded at Television Centre in the presence of Queen Elizabeth and Prince Philip, and was broadcast on BBC1 on 24 May 1970.

8.   The 'Monty on the Bonty' sketch (written by Eddie Braben) was featured in the 22 April 1971 edition of *The Morecambe & Wise Show*, broadcast on BBC1.

9.   See Chapter 11.

10.   The *Look In* comic strip ran from 1970 to 1980; a *Dad's Army* colouring and dot-to-dot book was published by World Distributors in 1971; the *Dad's Army Activity Book* was published by World Books in 1973; Ovaltine produced a board game in 1971; Denys Fisher produced another in 1974; Lever Brothers marketed a *Dad's Army* bubble bath in 1972; Primrose Confectionery produced a set of 25 sweet cigarette cards in 1971; Peter Way published an 'official souvenir' magazine, *Dad's Army*, in 1972; and a series of six *Dad's Army Annuals* was published by World Distributors between 1973 and 1978.

11.   BCNZ (the Broadcasting Corporation of New Zealand) began showing episodes from Series 3 (the first to be filmed in colour) on 20 March 1970. The other countries followed soon after, each one starting from Series 3 (source: BBC Worldwide).

12.   *Parsley Sidings* was set in a backwater railway station. Lowe was the stationmaster, Lavender his son and Pertwee his rival. The show ran for two series between December 1971 and December 1973.

13.   Lowe appeared on *Desert Island Discs* on 12 December 1970. The movies he made with Lindsay Anderson during this period were *If . . .* (1969) and *O Lucky Man!* (1973); he also appeared in Anderson's *Britannia Hospital* in 1982.

14.   Le Mesurier appeared on *Desert Island Discs* on 17 February 1973. *Traitor* was broadcast on BBC1 on 14 October 1971; it won him the 'Best Actor' award that year.

15.   Dunn appeared on *Desert Island Discs* on 19 June 1971. *This Is Your Life* was broadcast on ITV on 24 March 1971. *An Hour With Clive Dunn* (comprising a repeat of 'The Armoured Might of Lance Corporal Jones' and a half-hour *Parkinson* interview) was broadcast on BBC1 on 18 August 1971. 'Grandad' entered the charts in December 1970, reaching number one at the start of January 1971, and remained in the top 40 for 14 weeks.

16.   Dunn, *Permission to Speak*, p. 207.

17.   *The Gnomes of Dulwich* (a play on Harold Wilson's description of Swiss bankers as 'gnomes of Zurich') was about the British (stone) garden gnomes of 25 Telegraph Road and their recently arrived (plastic) European counterparts. The show, starring Terry Scott and Hugh Lloyd, ran for one series, from 12 May–16 June 1969. *Lollipop Loves Mr Mole* starred Peggy Mount and Hugh Lloyd as a lovey-dovey couple whose domestic bliss is disrupted by the arrival of a pair of sponging relatives (played by Rex Garner and Pat Coombs); the show ran for two series (25 October–29 November 1971 and 17 July–4 September 1972) on ATV/ITV.

18.   The first series of *Up Pompeii!* ran from 30 March–11 May 1970. *Born Every Minute*, a 'Comedy Playhouse' pilot written by Jack Popplewell about two con men, was broadcast on 28 January 1972. The short-lived Not Now Films was set up in 1973; its first movie – directed by Croft – was *Not Now Darling* (1973). The pilot edition of *Are You Being Served?* was broadcast on 8 September 1972; the first series began on 21 March 1973, and the tenth and final one ended on 1 April 1985.

19.   David Croft, interview with the author, 23 May 2000.

20.   Jimmy Perry, interview with the author, 27 August 2000.

21.   David Croft, interview with the author, 23 May 2000.

22.   Jimmy Perry, interview with the author, 27 August 2000.

23.   *Ibid.*

24.   David Croft, interview with the author, 23 May 2000.

25. Denis Norden, interviewed by David Bradbury and Joe McGrath in *Now That's Funny!* (London: Methuen, 1998), p. 4.

26. Jimmy Perry, interview with the author, 27 August 2000.

27. *Ibid.*

28. *Ibid.*

29. David Croft, interview with the author, 23 May 2000.

30. Jimmy Perry, interview with the author, 27 August 2000.

31. Arthur Lowe, quoted by Terence Pettigrew, *Photoplay*, August 1978, pp. 54–5.

32. David Croft, interview with the author, 23 May 2000.

33. Ian Lavender, interview with the author, 29 May 2000.

34. Arthur Lowe, quoted by Dunn in *Permission to Speak*, p. 204.

35. Arthur Lowe, quoted by Stephen Lowe, *Arthur Lowe* (London: Virgin, 1997), p. 121.

36. 'The Test', first broadcast on BBC1, 27 November 1970.

37. David Croft, interview with the author, 23 May 2000.

38. Croft and Perry, in *Dad's Army: The Lost Episodes*, p. 36.

39. Ian Lavender, interview with the author, 29 May 2000.

40. Arthur Lowe, quoted by David Croft, interview with the author, 23 May 2000.

41. Ian Lavender, interview with the author, 29 May 2000.

42. David Croft, interview with the author, 23 May 2000.

43. *Ibid.* (Studio 8 was the preferred studio.)

44. *Ibid.*

45. Bill Pertwee, interview with the author, 27 May 2000.

46. Dunn, *Permission to Speak*, p. 200.

47. BBC WAC: *Dad's Army* File T12/880/1: Michael Mills, memorandum to David Croft, 1 November 1968.

48. Croft and Perry, *Dad's Army: The Lost Episodes*, p. 6. (All six scripts from Series 2 are included in this book.)

49. The episodes, 'Operation Kilt' and 'The Battle of Godfrey's Cottage', were recovered from a skip at Elstree Studio in the early 1970s, then stored at the home of a private collector until the summer of 2001, when they were handed back to the BBC (see *Guardian*, 2 June 2001, p. 18).

50. According to the figure in the BBC's Daily Viewing Barometer, ITV regional companies, who screened such programmes as *Mission: Impossible* and *The Avengers*, attracted an average audience of 7,322,500.

51. BBC WAC: Audience Report (VR/69/142, 17 April 1969), on *Dad's Army*, 'Operation Kilt'.

52. The sequence of Reaction Index figures for the series was as follows: 68, 64, 66, 67, 66 and 71.

53. BBC WAC: Audience Research Report (VR/69/220, 5 June 1969) on *Dad's Army*, 'Under Fire'.

54. Bill Cotton, interview with the author, 6 June 2000.

55. Frank Williams, interview with the author, 4 October 2000.

56. *Ibid.*

57. Paul Fox, interview with the author, 2 May 2000.

58. Figures and comparisons based on the percentages of the viewing public recorded in the BBC's Daily Viewing Barometers for the period in question.

59. BBC WAC: Audience Research Report (VR/69/664, 2 February 1970) on *Dad's Army*, 'Sons of the Sea'. (The average Reaction Index for the series was 67.)

60. See, for example, his congratulatory note to David Croft on the show's 'tremendous achievement' in attracting twelve million viewers early on in its third series (BBC WAC: File T12/880/1: *Dad's Army*: Sloan to Croft, 30 September 1969).

61. BBC WAC: *Dad's Army* File T12/880/1: Paul Fox to David Croft, 13 January 1970.

62. The fourth series ran on Fridays from 25 September to 18 December 1970.

63. 'Mum's Army', first broadcast on BBC1, 20 November 1970.

64. 'A. Wilson (Manager)?', first broadcast on BBC1, 4 December 1970.

65. David Croft, interview with the author, 23 May 2000.

66. Figure calculated from the percentage of the UK viewing public recorded in the BBC's Daily Viewing Barometer for 27 December 1971.

67. BBC WAC: Audience Report (VR/72/585, 25 October 1972) on *Dad's Army*, 'Asleep in the Deep'.

68. David Croft, interview with the author, 23 May 2000.

69. Figures calculated from the percentages recorded in the relevant BBC Daily Viewing Barometers.

70. See Chapter 13.

THE CHARACTERS

1. Robb Wilton, 'The Home Guard'.

2. William Shakespeare, *Henry V* (London: Penguin, 1968), line spoken by Bates, IV.1.215.

Chapter VII

1. Ralph Waldo Emerson, *Representative Men* (Cambridge, Mass.: Belknap Press, 1996), p. 4.

2. Walter Bagehot, *The Best of Bagehot*, ed. Ruth Dudley Edwards (London: Hamish Hamilton, 1993), p. 136.

3. Jimmy Perry and David Croft, *Dad's Army* (London: Elm Tree, 1975).

4. Compiled from references in the following episodes: 'The Man and the Hour', 'Mum's Army', 'A. Wilson (Manager)?', 'If the Cap Fits . . .', 'The King Was In His Counting House', 'The Godiva Affair' and 'My Brother And I'. (See also the summary in Perry and Croft, *Dad's Army*, pp. 28–9.)

5. Compiled from references in the following episodes: 'The Man and the Hour', 'War Dance', 'A. Wilson (Manager)?', 'Getting the Bird' and 'The Honourable Man'. (See also Perry and Croft, *Dad's Army*, p. 49.)

6. Benny Green, *Punch*, 23 November 1977, p. 1017.

7. Quoted by John Craven Hughes, *The Greasepaint War* (London: New English Library, 1976), p. 138.

8. John Le Mesurier, *A Jobbing Actor*, pp. 18–19.

9. Alec Guinness, *Blessings in Disguise* (London: Hamish Hamilton, 1985), p. 57.

10. John Le Mesurier, quoted by Hart, *Dad's Army*, p. 21.

11. Details included in Roy Plomley (ed.), *Desert Island Lists* (London: Hutchinson, 1984), pp. 178 and 198.

12. Recalled by Barry Took, interview with the author, 17 May 2000.

13. See John Le Mesurier, *A Jobbing Actor*, pp. 38–44, 61–3.

14. *Ibid.*, pp. 64–73, 85–100.

15. See Joan Le Mesurier, *Lady Don't Fall Backwards* (London: Sidgwick, 1988), pp. 53–192.

16. John Le Mesurier, *A Jobbing Actor*, p. 111.

17. See Pertwee, *Dad's Army*, p. 30, and Dunn, *Permission to Speak*, p. 205.

18. Recalled by Pertwee, *The Story of Dad's Army*, Speaking Volumes audiotape (Polygram, 1995).

19. John Le Mesurier, *A Jobbing Actor*, p. 114. (See Joan Le Mesurier, *Lady Don't Fall Backwards*, for a first-hand account of this period.)

20. John Le Mesurier, quoted by Joan Le Mesurier, *Lady Don't Fall Backwards*, p. 176.

21. See Pertwee, *Dad's Army*, p. 38.

22. Ian Lavender, interview with the author, 29 May 2000.

23. John Le Mesurier, *A Jobbing Actor*, p. 119.

24. Arthur Lowe, quoted by Hart, *Dad's Army*, p. 18.

25. *Ibid.*

26. George and Weedon Grossmith, *The Diary of a Nobody* (London: The Folio Society, 1969), p. 19.

27. *Ibid.*

28. *Ibid.*, p. 44.

29. *Ibid.*, p. 71.

30. *Ibid.*, p. 29.

31. *Ibid.*, p. 40.

32. *Ibid.*, p. 34.

33. *Ibid.*

34. *Ibid.*

35. *Ibid.*, p. 14.

36. See the *Dad's Army* episodes 'War Dance', 'Mum's Army', 'A Soldier's Farewell' and 'The Royal Train'.

37. 'Absent Friends', first broadcast on BBC1, 30 October 1970.

38. 'When Did You Last See Your Money?', first broadcast on BBC1, 1 December 1972.

39. 'No Spring For Frazer', first broadcast on BBC1, 4 December 1969.

40. John Le Mesurier, *A Jobbing Actor*, p. 119.

41. 'Wake Up Walmington', first broadcast on BBC1, 2 October 1977.

42. 'We Know Our Onions', first broadcast on BBC1, 21 November 1973.

43. 'Menace from the Deep', first broadcast on BBC1, 13 November 1969.

44. 'High Finance', first broadcast on BBC1, 3 October 1975.

Chapter VIII

1. Edmund Burke, *Reflections on the Revolution in France* (Oxford: Oxford University Press, 1993), pp. 46–7.

2. Thomas Paine, *Rights of Man* (Harmondsworth: Penguin, 1985), p. 236.

3. See Perry and Croft, *Dad's Army*, p. 89.

4.   No entry on Walker was included in Perry and Croft's book, *Dad's Army*, because James Beck, by this time, had died, but details about the character can be gleaned from such episodes as 'The Loneliness of the Long Distance Walker', 'Don't Fence Me In' and 'Getting the Bird'.

5.   See Perry and Croft, *Dad's Army*, p. 89, and the episodes 'The Deadly Attachment', 'When You've Got To Go' and 'The Making of Private Pike'.

6.   John Laurie, quoted by John Le Mesurier, *A Jobbing Actor*, p. 120.

7.   'Asleep in the Deep', first broadcast on BBC1, 6 October 1972.

8.   'If The Cap Fits . . .', first broadcast on BBC1, 10 November 1972.

9.   'Brain Versus Brawn', first broadcast on BBC1, 8 December 1972.

10.   'Is There Honey Still For Tea?', first broadcast on BBC1, 19 September 1975.

Chapter IX

1.   Goethe, 'Prelude in the Theatre', part 1 of *Faust*, translated by Philip Wayne (London: Penguin, 1949), p. 36.

2.   Philip Larkin: 'The old fools', *Collected Poems* (London: Faber, 1988), p. 196.

3.   Compiled from references in the following episodes: 'The Man and the Hour', 'The Armoured Might of Lance Corporal Jones', 'The Two and a Half Feathers', 'Battle of the Giants', 'When Did You Last See Your Money?', 'The Face on the Poster' and 'Never Too Old'. (See also Perry and Croft, *Dad's Army*, p. 69.)

4.   Compiled from references in the following episodes: 'The Man and the Hour', 'Branded', 'The Test', 'All Is Safely Gathered In' and 'Is There Honey Still For Tea?' (See also Perry and Croft, *Dad's Army*, p. 89.)

5.   Clive Dunn, *Permission to Speak*, p. 198.

6.   Clive Dunn, speaking in part 1 of the documentary *Laughter In the House*, first broadcast on BBC1, 24 March 1999.

7.   Clive Dunn, quoted by Hart, *Dad's Army*, p. 28.

8.   Dunn, *Permission to Speak*, p. 198.

9.   Dunn, speaking in the *Omnibus* documentary, *Perry and Croft – The Sit-Coms*, first broadcast on BBC1, 18 April 1995.

10.   Dunn, *Permission to Speak*, p. 199.

11.   'Asleep in the Deep', first broadcast on BBC1, 6 October 1972.

12.   'Branded', first broadcast on BBC1, 20 November 1969.

13.   'Absent Friends', first broadcast on BBC1, 30 October 1970.

THE COMPANY

1.   Ian Lavender, interview with the author, 29 May 2000.

Chapter X

1.   Maj. John Langdon-Davies, *Home Guard Training Manual*, 6th edn (London: John Murray and Pilot Press, 1942), p. 23.

2.   Harold Snoad, *Directing Situation Comedy* (Borehamwood: BBC Television Training, 1988), p. 27.

3.   Recalled by Ian Lavender, interview with the author, 29 May 2000.

4.   Arthur Lowe, quoted by Stephen Lowe, *Arthur Lowe*, p. 143.

5. *Ibid.*, p. 105.

6. Arthur Lowe, quoted by Jimmy Perry, interview with the author, 21 June 2001.

7. Arthur Lowe, quoted by Stephen Lowe, *Arthur Lowe*, p. 144.

8. Ian Lavender, interview with the author, 29 May 2000.

9. *Ibid.*

10. David Croft, interview with the author, 23 May 2000.

11. Snoad took over from Sydney Lotterby as the producer-director of *Ever Decreasing Circles* for Series 3 (1986), 4 (1987) and an 80-minute Christmas special (1989). He produced and directed all five series of *Keeping Up Appearances* (1990–95).

12. Harold Snoad, correspondence with the author, 1 March 2000.

13. Harold Snoad, quoted by Pertwee, *Dad's Army: The Making of a Television Legend*, pp. 102 and 104.

14. *Ibid.*, p. 98.

15. *Ibid.*, p. 100.

16. In 1971, Arnold Ridley was 75, John Laurie 74, John Le Mesurier 59, Edward Sinclair 57, Arthur Lowe 56, Clive Dunn 51, Bill Pertwee 45, James Beck 42, Frank Williams 40 and Ian Lavender 25.

17. Pertwee, *Dad's Army*, p. 56.

18. Ian Lavender, interview with the author, 29 May 2000.

19. *Ibid.*

20. David Croft, interview with the author, 23 May 2000.

21. Clive Dunn, speaking in *The Arthur Lowe Story*, first broadcast on BBC Radio 2 on 28 December 1993.

22. Pertwee, *Dad's Army*, p. 102, and *A Funny Way to Make a Living*, p. 256.

Chapter XI

1. *Dad's Army*, 'Ring Dem Bells', first broadcast on BBC1, 5 September 1975.

2. David Mamet, *Some Freaks* (London: Faber, 1990), p. 134.

3. David Croft, interview with the author, 23 May 2000.

4. Norman Cohen, quoted by Iain F. McAsh, 'On manoeuvres with *Dad's Army*', *ABC Film Review*, January 1971, p. 9.

5. Ian Lavender, interview with the author, 29 May 2000.

6. Information gathered from conversations with David Croft, Jimmy Perry, Ian Lavender, Bill Pertwee and Frank Williams.

7. Ian Lavender, interview with the author, 29 May 2000.

8. See my *Cary Grant: A Class Apart* (London: Fourth Estate, 1996), pp. 109–16.

9. David Croft, interview with the author, 23 May 2000.

10. Jimmy Perry, interview with the author, 27 August 2000.

11. Dunn, *Permission to Speak*, p. 207.

12. John Le Mesurier, *A Jobbing Actor*, p. 129.

13. Bill Pertwee, interview with the author, 27 May 2000.

14. Ian Lavender, interview with the author, 29 May 2000.

15. *Ibid.*

16. Bean, *Who Do You Think You Are Kidding!*, p. 188.

17. See John Le Mesurier, *A Jobbing Actor*, p. 130. (The reason for Lowe's 'Kitty' nickname has yet to be revealed.)

18. *Ibid.*, p. 130.

19. Arthur Lowe, quoted by Pertwee, *Dad's Army*, p. 143.

20. See Stephen Lowe, *Arthur Lowe*, p. 115.

21. John Le Mesurier, *A Jobbing Actor*, p. 130.

22. Information gathered from conversations with the cast and crew.

23. *Dad's Army: The Movie* (Norcon/Columbia, 1971), screenplay by Jimmy Perry and David Croft.

24. Ian Lavender, interview with the author, 29 May 2000.

25. Bill Pertwee, interview with the author, 27 May 2000.

26. David Croft, interview with the author, 23 May 2000.

27. Jimmy Perry, interview with the author, 27 August 2000.

28. Dunn, *Permission to Speak*, pp. 207–8.

29. John Le Mesurier, *A Jobbing Actor*, p. 130.

30. *Ibid.*, p. 129.

31. Ian Lavender, interview with the author, 29 May 2000.

32. Dick Richards, *Daily Mirror*, 15 March 1971, p. 5.

33. Ian Christie, *Daily Express*, 15 March 1971, p. 12.

34. Derek Malcolm, *Guardian*, 19 March 1971, p. 12.

35. Alexander Walker, *London Evening Standard*, 17 March 1971, p. 16.

36. Sylvia Millar, *Monthly Film Bulletin*, April 1971, p. 70.

37. *Variety*, 24 March 1971, p. 19.

38. See Pertwee, *Dad's Army*, p. 143.

39. Source: BBC Daily Viewing Barometer, 5 May 1979. (The exact figure was 13,050,000).

40. David Croft, interview with the author, 23 May 2000.

Chapter XII

1. Max Beerbohm, 'The older and better music hall', in *Around Theatres* (London: Rupert Hart-Davis, 1953), p. 300.

2. George Mainwaring, 'The Godiva Affair' (original script), by Jimmy Perry and David Croft, in *Dad's Army*, p. 52.

3. Quoted by Pertwee, *Dad's Army*, p. 151.

4. Dunn, *Permission to Speak*, p. 208.

5. Richard Stone, *You Should Have Been In Last Night* (Sussex: The Book Guild, 2000), p. 117.

6. Hamish Roughead's television credits included episodes of *Doctor Finlay's Casebook* and *The Borderers*.

7. John Bardon appeared as 'Harold Forster' in one episode of *Dad's Army* ('Ring Dem Bells', first broadcast on BBC1, 5 September 1975), but he went on to play 'Jim Branning' in the BBC1 soap opera *EastEnders*.

8. Ian Lavender, interview with the author, 29 May 2000.

9. Jeffrey Holland went on to be a regular member of Croft and Perry's comic ensemble, appearing, for example, as 'Spike' in *Hi-de-Hi!* (BBC1, 1980–88) and 'James Twelvetrees' in *You Rang, M'Lord?* (BBC1, 1988–93).

10. Roger Redfarn, quoted by Webber, *Dad's Army: A Celebration*, p. 178.

11. John Le Mesurier, quoted by Bill Pertwee, *Dad's Army*, p. 38.

12. *Ibid.*, p. 153.

13. Bill Pertwee, interview with the author, 23 May 2000.

14. Pertwee, *Dad's Army*, p. 154.

15. Dunn, *Permission to Speak*, p. 208.

16. Stone, *You Should Have Been In Last Night*, p. 117.

17. *Ibid.*

18. Dunn, *Permission to Speak*, p. 209.

19. Stone, *You Should Have Been In Last Night*, p. 117.

20. John Le Mesurier, *A Jobbing Actor*, p. 139.

21. Stone, *You Should Have Been In Last Night*, p. 118.

22. Captain Mainwaring, quoted by Pertwee, *Dad's Army*, p. 167.

23. John Elsom, *The Listener*, 9 October 1975, p. 481.

24. Harold Hobson, *Sunday Times* (review section), 5 October 1975, p. 37.

25. B. A. Young, *Financial Times*, 3 October 1975, p. 3.

26. Ian Lavender, interview with the author, 29 May 2000.

27. The Royal Variety Performance took place on Monday, 10 November 1975; the recording was broadcast on ITV on Sunday, 16 November.

28. *Dad's Army – Original Cast Recording* was released on Warner Bros (K561196) in 1976.

29. *What Is Going To Become Of Us All?* was released on Warner Bros (K54080) in 1976. (See John Le Mesurier's account in *A Jobbing Actor*, pp. 140–1.)

30. Norman MacLeod, formerly the lead singer with the Canadian group The Maple Leaf Four, was one of the company's principal vocalists. The single 'Hooligans!'/'Get Out and Get Under the Moon' was released on EMI in 1975.

31. Arthur Lowe, quoted by Pertwee, *Dad's Army*, p. 158.

32. Arnold Ridley, quoted by Ted Hart, *Dad's Army*, p. 33.

33. Frank Williams, interview with the author, 4 October 2000.

34. Bean, *Who Do You Think You Are Kidding!*, p. 220.

35. *Ibid.*, p. 241.

36. Ian Lavender, interview with the author, 29 May 2000.

37. Pertwee, *Dad's Army*, p. 162.

38. John Le Mesurier, *A Jobbing Actor*, p. 142.

39. The letter of invitation, from Neville Chamberlain (the sixteen-year-old grandson of the Prime Minister), is reproduced in Stephen Lowe's *Arthur Lowe*, pp. 150–1.

40. Dunn, *Permission to Speak*, p. 208.

THE CLASSIC

1. Penelope Gilliatt, *To Wit* (London: Weidenfeld, 1990), p. 293.

Chapter XIII

1. James Thurber, *Collecting Himself*, ed. Michael Rosen (London: Hamish Hamilton, 1989), p. 218.

2. Wheldon, *The Achievement of Television*, p. 12.

3. Quoted by Jimmy Perry in Hart (ed.), *Dad's Army*, p. 4. (See also Dunn, *Permission to Speak*, p. 217.)

Notes to Chapter XIII

4. Bill Cotton, *The BBC as an Entertainer* (London: BBC, 1977), p. 49.

5. The radio version of *Dad's Army* consisted of previously broadcast television scripts adapted by Harold Snoad and Michael Knowles. The first series of 26 episodes was recorded during June and July 1973 and broadcast on BBC Radio 2 from 28 January to 18 June 1974. A Christmas special went out on 25 December 1974, followed by a second series of 20 episodes between 11 February to 24 June 1975, and a third series of 26 episodes between 16 March and 7 September 1976.

6. Dunn, *Permission to Speak*, p. 202.

7. *Romany Jones* – created by Ronald Wolfe and Ronald Chesney – featured two gypsy couples who lived on a rundown caravan site (Beck played Bert Jones, Jo Rowbottom played his wife, Arthur Mullard was Wally Briggs and Queenie Watts was his wife). The pilot was broadcast by Thames on 15 February 1972, followed, on London Weekend Television, by Series 1 (25 May–6 July 1973) and Series 2 (14 September–21 October 1973). The show continued for two more series after Beck's death, with two new characters taking the place of the Joneses. Most critics regarded the programme as one of the worst situation-comedies ever broadcast on British television.

8. *Bunclarke With An 'E'* was commissioned by the BBC in 1972 and a pilot was recorded early in 1973. Beck's death caused both the pilot and the project to be shelved, and, it seems, no tape of the half-hour performance remains. (See Stephen Lowe, *Arthur Lowe*, pp. 131–2.)

9. Bill Pertwee, interview with the author, 27 May 2000.

10. Ian Lavender, interview with the author, 29 May 2000.

11. Quoted in the *Sun*, 20 July 1973, p. 7.

12. 'The Recruit', recorded 22 July 1973; first broadcast on BBC1, 12 December 1973.

13. Death certificate, dated 7 August 1973.

14. *Daily Mail*, 7 August 1973, p. 11.

15. Clive Dunn, speaking in *Don't Panic! The Dad's Army Story*, first broadcast on BBC1, 28 May 2000.

16. David Croft, interview with the author, 23 May 2000.

17. BBC WAC: Audience Research Report (VR/73/628, 22 November 1973) on *Dad's Army*, 'The Deadly Attachment'. The Reaction Index was 64.

18. 'The Deadly Attachment' was watched by an estimated 12,928,000 people; the average audience for episodes during the fifth series had been 16.3 million (source: BBC Daily Viewing Barometers).

19. The edition of *Crossroads* that went out on 31 October 1973 attracted an audience of 6,413,500 (source: BBC Daily Viewing Barometer, 31 October 1973).

20. According to the BBC's Daily Viewing Barometer for 12 December 1973, *This Is Your Life* was watched by 12,827,000 people.

21. David Croft, interview with the author, 23 May 2000. (*World In Action* was ITV's principal current affairs programme.)

22. BBC Daily Viewing Barometer, 31 October 1973.

23. BBC WAC: Audience Research Report (VR/73/628, 22 November 1973).

24. Peter Black, *Daily Mail*, 1 November 1973, p. 25.

25. Shaun Usher, *Daily Mail*, 28 November 1973, p. 35.

26. Source: BBC Daily Viewing Barometers, 31 October–12 December 1973.

27. Jimmy Perry, interview with the author, 27 August 2000.

28. *Ibid.*

29. Ian Lavender, interview with the author, 29 May 2000.

30. *Ibid.*

31. The trailers were broadcast at various times during the days leading up to the first episode. The exhibition at the Imperial War Museum ran from 17 October 1974 to 29 June 1975.

32. BBC Daily Viewing Barometer, 15 November 1974.

33. Source: BBC Daily Viewing Barometers, 15 November–23 December 1974.

34. David Croft, interview with the author, 23 May 2000.

35. Jimmy Perry, interview with the author, 27 August 2000.

36. Dunn, *Permission to Speak*, p. 202.

37. Confirmed by Jimmy Perry, interview with the author, 27 August 2000.

38. John Laurie, quoted by Dunn, *Permission to Speak*, p. 201.

39. David Croft, interview with the author, 23 May 2000.

40. Arthur Lowe, quoted by Pertwee, *Dad's Army*, p. 26.

41. Ian Lavender, interview with the author, 29 May 2000.

42. BBC WAC: Audience Research Report (VR/75/513, 29 September 1975) on *Dad's Army*, 'Ring Dem Bells'. The estimated audience was 11,312,000, and the Reaction Index was 72.

43. BBC Daily Viewing Barometer, 10 October 1975.

44. Source: BBC Daily Viewing Barometers, 5 September–10 October 1975.

45. BBC WAC: Audience Research Report (VR/75/581, 16 November 1975), on *Dad's Army*, 'The Face on the Poster'.

46. 'My Brother and I', first broadcast on BBC1, 26 December 1975.

47. Ian Lavender, interview with the author, 29 May 2000.

48. Peter Black, *The Biggest Aspidistra in the World* (London: BBC, 1972), p. 225.

49. Ian Lavender, interview with the author, 29 May 2000.

50. Arthur Lowe, quoted by Pertwee, *Dad's Army*, p. 104.

51. John Laurie, quoted by Dunn, *Permission to Speak*, p. 211.

52. Arthur Lowe, in the Foreword to Perry and Croft's *Dad's Army*, p. 7.

53. *All in the Family* ran from 1971 to 1992 on CBS; it reached number one in the ratings during its first season, and stayed there for five years.

54. *Sanford and Son* ran from 1972 to 1977 on NBC; it reached number two in the ratings during its first season.

55. *Love Thy Neighbor* lasted from June to September 1973 on ABC.

56. Information from Jimmy Perry, interview with the author, 27 August 2000.

57. Arthur Julian had appeared as an actor in a number of movies (such as *How To Stuff a Wild Bikini*, 1965) and televised situation-comedies (such as *Bewitched*), but he was best known, and respected, for his writing, which included scripts for *M*A*S*H* and *Hogan's Heroes*.

58. Although the term 'Home Guard' had been used by various groups at various times in US history, the nearest American equivalent to Britain's wartime Home Guard was the State Guard, a subset of the National Guard, organised for home defence during the First and Second World Wars.

59. *The Rear Guard* (Herman Rush Associates in association with Wolper Productions), written by Arthur Julian, broadcast in the US by ABC on 10 August 1976. (The script is reproduced in Webber's *The Complete A–Z of Dad's Army*, pp. 252–5.)

60. *Ibid.*

61. David Croft, interview with the author, 27 August 2000.

62. *Ibid.*

63.   Cotton, *The BBC as an Entertainer*, p. 49.

64.   'The Love of Three Oranges', first broadcast by BBC1 on 26 December 1976, was watched by an estimated audience of 13,685,500.

65.   Huw Wheldon, quoted by Bill Pertwee, interview with the author, 27 May 2000.

66.   *It Ain't Half Hot Mum* – inspired by Jimmy Perry's memories of the time he spent in the Royal Artillery Concert Party in Deolali, India, and David Croft's spell as a military entertainments officer in the same area, ran on BBC1 for eight series, between January 1974 and September 1981. (See Perry's memoir in *Radio Times*, 22–8 October 1977, pp. 4–5.)

67.   *Are You Being Served?* ran on BBC1 for ten series between March 1973 and April 1985. A 'sequel', *Grace and Favour*, ran on BBC1 for two series between January 1992 and February 1993.

68.   There was, for example, a movie version of *Are You Being Served?* (which was released in 1977), and a very unconventional – and, as it turned out, injudicious – sci-fi situation-comedy, written by Croft and Lloyd, called *Come Back Mrs Noah* (the pilot of which was broadcast on 13 December 1977; one series followed in July 1978).

Chapter XIV

1.   William Hazlitt, 'On the Fear of Death', in *Table Talk* (London: J. M. Dent & Sons, 1959), p. 323.

2.   Jimmy Perry, interview with the author, 27 August 2000.

3.   Episode 1 of Series 1 was set in May 1940. Episode 2 of Series 6 was set near the start of 1942 (with the arrival of the first wave of US servicemen in Britain).

4.   Joan Le Mesurier, *Lady Don't Fall Backwards*, p. 184.

5.   *Ibid.*

6.   *Ibid.*, p. 185.

7.   John Le Mesurier, *A Jobbing Actor*, p. 144.

8.   David Croft, interview with the author, 23 May 2000.

9.   Arthur Lowe, quoted by Stephen Lowe, *Arthur Lowe*, p. 147.

10.   David Croft, interview with the author, 23 May 2000.

11.   Jimmy Perry, interview with the author, 27 August 2000.

12.   Croft's previous production assistant, Harold Snoad, had become a producer-director in his own right. Bob Spiers, whose first association with *Dad's Army* was as an assistant floor manager on the 1971 special 'Battle of the Giants', took over as production assistant from Series 6.

13.   Accounts vary as to when, and how firmly, the decision was actually expressed. Clive Dunn remembered the cast being told at the Bell Hotel in Thetford during June 1975 (see *Permission to Speak*, p. 212); Bill Pertwee, on the other hand, told me that the cast was consulted about the future of the show at the same location in the summer of 1977 (interview with the author, 27 May 2000); while Ian Lavender did not recall being told that the show would definitely never return until early September 1977, following the death of Edward Sinclair (interview with the author, 29 May 2000). What is clear, however, is that Croft and Perry had certainly informed the cast at some point between June and September 1977 that they were not planning another series in the foreseeable future (interviews with the author, 23 May and 27 August 2000).

14.   Arthur Lowe, quoted in the *Daily Mirror*, 1 October 1977, p. 15.

15.   John Le Mesurier, *A Jobbing Actor*, p. 145.

16.   Sinclair, who had been in indifferent health for some time, died, from a heart attack, while visiting relatives in Cheddar (see *Guardian*, 1 September 1977, p. 2).

17. Ian Lavender, interview with the author, 29 May 2000.

18. *Daily Mirror*, 1 October 1977, p. 15.

19. Peter Tinniswood, *Radio Times*, 1–7 October 1977, p. 17.

20. 'Wake Up Walmington', first broadcast on BBC1, 2 October 1977.

21. 'The Making of Private Pike', first broadcast on BBC1, 9 October 1977.

22. Ian Lavender, interview with the author, 29 May 2000.

23. Source: BBC Daily Viewing Barometers, 2 October–13 November 1977.

24. Joan Le Mesurier, *Lady Don't Fall Backwards*, p. 185.

25. Dennis Potter, *Sunday Times*, review section, 16 October 1977, p. 37.

26. Ian Lavender, interview with the author, 29 May 2000.

27. David Croft, interview with the author, 23 May 2000.

28. 'Never Too Old', first broadcast by BBC1 on 13 November 1977.

29. BBC Daily Viewing Barometer, 13 November 1977.

30. BBC WAC: Audience Research Report (VR/77/626, 21 December 1977), on *Dad's Army*, 'Never Too Old'. The Reaction Index was 77.

31. Peter Fiddick, *Guardian*, 14 November 1977, p. 10.

32. Bill Pertwee, interview with the author, 27 May 2000.

33. The *Daily Mirror* organised the event (see pp. 16–17 of its 14 November 1977 edition).

34. Dunn, *Permission to Speak*, p. 213.

35. John Le Mesurier, *A Jobbing Actor*, p. 145.

36. Dunn, *Permission to Speak*, p. 213.

37. David Croft, interview with the author, 23 May 2000.

38. Arthur Lowe, quoted by Dunn, *Permission to Speak*, p. 213.

39. Arthur Lowe, quoted in the *Daily Mirror*, 14 November 1977, p. 16.

40. John Le Mesurier, quoted *ibid*.

41. Clive Dunn, quoted *ibid*.

42. Ian Lavender, quoted *ibid*., p. 17.

43. Recalled by Clive Dunn, *Permission to Speak*, p. 213.

44. *Ibid*.

45. John Le Mesurier, *A Jobbing Actor*, p. 145.

46. *The Morecambe & Wise Show* was broadcast by BBC1 on 25 December 1977.

Chapter XV

1. R. G. Collingwood, *An Autobiography* (Oxford: Clarendon Press, 1978), p. 98.

2. Michael Mills, quoted by Jimmy Perry, interview with the author, 27 August 2000.

3. David Croft had produced summer shows for a holiday camp during the 1950s; Jimmy Perry, in the same decade, had worked as a Butlin's Redcoat. *Hi-de-Hi!* was set in the late 1950s, and featured the fictional Maplin's holiday camp, run by Jeffrey Fairbrother (Simon Cadell) and his troupe of 'Yellowcoats'. The show ran for eight successful series on BBC1 between February 1981 and January 1988.

4. John Laurie, quoted by Stephen Lowe, *Arthur Lowe*, p. 115.

5. See Stephen Lowe, *Arthur Lowe*, pp. 154–6, for an explanation of this policy.

6. Lindsay Anderson, speaking in *The Arthur Lowe Story*, BBC Radio 2, 28 December 1993. *Britannia Hospital* was released in 1983; Lowe's other movies during this period

included the remake of *The Lady Vanishes* (1979) and *Sweet William* (1982). He turned down an offer from Warren Beatty to appear in *Heaven Can Wait* because there was no role for his wife, Joan Cooper.

7. *Bless Me, Father*, written by Peter de Rosa, ran on ITV for three series from September 1978 to August 1981; *Potter*, written by Roy Clarke, ran on BBC1 for two series from March 1979 to April 1980 (a third series, made after Lowe's death, saw Robin Bailey take over the role); and *A. J. Wentworth, B.A.*, adapted by Basil Boothroyd from H. F. Ellis' *Punch* short stories, was screened posthumously on ITV between 12 July and 23 August 1982.

8. Arthur Lowe, quoted in *Daily Mirror*, 14 November 1977, p. 16.

9. Letter from John Le Mesurier to Arthur Lowe, date unknown, quoted by Stephen Lowe, *Arthur Lowe*, p. 183.

10. Quoted by Joan Le Mesurier, *Lady Don't Fall Backwards*, p. 174.

11. *Ibid.*, p. 186.

12. *Ibid.*

13. Le Mesurier appeared as 'Hugo Buxton' in Series 3, Episode 2 of *Hi-de-Hi!*, first broadcast by BBC1 on 7 November 1982.

14. Joan Le Mesurier, *Lady Don't Fall Backwards*, p. 186.

15. Bill Pertwee's books include a history of seaside entertainment, *Promenade and Pierrots* (Devon: Westbridge, 1979), *By Royal Command* (Newton Abbot: David & Charles, 1981) and *Dad's Army: The Making of a Television Legend*.

16. John Laurie, quoted by Hart, *Dad's Army*, p. 31.

17. Laurie's contribution to *The Old Boy Network* was broadcast by BBC2 on 21 September 1979.

18. See *Daily Mirror*, 14 November 1977, p. 17.

19. Arthur Ridley, quoted by Hart, *Dad's Army*, p. 33.

20. There were several occasions when two or more former members of the *Dad's Army* cast contributed to the same projects: Bill Pertwee and Arthur Lowe, for example, toured together during 1978 in the play *Caught Napping*, and both John Le Mesurier and Clive Dunn had cameo roles in *The Fiendish Plot of Dr Fu Manchu*, but *It Sticks Out Half a Mile* was the only bona fide *Dad's Army*-related reunion.

21. See Snoad's summary in Pertwee, *Dad's Army*, p. 176.

22. See Stephen Lowe, *Arthur Lowe*, p. 164.

23. The pilot was produced by Jonathan James Moore on 19 July 1981.

24. Lowe was appearing at the venue in a play called *Home At Seven*.

25. *Daily Mirror*, 16 April 1982, p. 2.

26. Clive Dunn, quoted in *Guardian*, 16 April 1982, p. 3.

27. Joan Cooper, quoted by Pertwee, *Dad's Army*, p. 176.

28. Episode 1 – the pilot – was broadcast on BBC Radio 2 on Sunday, 13 November 1983, at 1.30 p.m.; the series continued, with one seven month break, until October 1984. After John Le Mesurier's death, a television pilot, starring Michael Elphick and Richard Wilson, called *Walking the Planks*, was broadcast by BBC1 on 28 August 1985; when BBCTV passed on the series, Yorkshire TV bought the idea, retitled *High and Dry* and now starring Bernard Cribbins and Richard Wilson, and broadcast one series at the start of 1987.

29. See Joan Le Mesurier, *Lady Don't Fall Backwards*, p. 189.

30. *The Times*, 16 November 1983, p. 14.

31. John Le Mesurier, quoted by Joan Le Mesurier in her Epilogue to John Le Mesurier's *A Jobbing Actor*, p. 152.

Notes to Chapter XV

32. Derek Taylor, quoted by Joan Le Mesurier, *Lady Don't Fall Backwards*, p. 192.

33. *Ibid.*, p. 191.

34. Ian Lavender, interview with the author, 29 May 2000.

35. Arthur Lowe, quoted by Pertwee, *Dad's Army*, p. 24.

36. Ian Lavender, interview with the author, 29 May 2000.

37. Jimmy Perry, interview with the author, 22 November 2000.

38. Dunn, *Permission to Speak*, p. 240.

39. *You Rang, M'Lord?* was set in the late 1910s/early 1920s inside the Meldrum residence: 'upstairs' characters included Lord George Meldrum (Donald Hewlett) and his lascivious brother, Teddy (Michael Knowles); 'downstairs' characters included the 'head of the household', James Twelvetrees (Jeffrey Holland) and the butler, Alf Stokes (Paul Shane); Bill Pertwee played PC Wilson, and Frank Williams appeared as the bishop. The hour-long pilot episode was broadcast by BBC1 on 29 December 1988, and four series followed between January 1990 and April 1993.

40. David Croft, interview with the author, 23 May 2000.

41. A 1978 rerun of the ninth series was watched by a weekly audience that rose from 6,942,600 to 9,604,800 over the course of six episodes (source: BBC Daily Viewing Barometers, 11 September–16 October 1978).

42. 'A Man of Action', for example, was repeated on 28 November 1989 and was seen by 11,200,000 people. Six more repeats in this run also attracted over ten million viewers each (BBC Daily Viewing Barometers, 7 November–19 December 1989).

43. Most episodes now exist on video. The first (NTSC format) DVD compilations were released in Canada as a three-disc box set by BBC Worldwide/BFS Video in 2000.

44. An earlier attempt, in 1989, was unsuccessful. The Croft and Perry-endorsed *Dad's Army* Appreciation Society was set up in 1993 by Tadge Muldoon, who ran a skip-hire business in Keighly (see the 'Peterborough' column in the *Daily Telegraph*, 19 August 1993, p. 24, and Pertwee's *Dad's Army*, p. 200). In 1995, following Muldoon's death, Bill Wheeler took over the running of the society (the current contact address is: 8 Sinodun Road, Wallingford, OXON, OX10 8AA; e-mail dadsarmy@cwcom.net; website www.dadsarmy.cwc.net). A New Zealand branch was formed in March 1995 (the current contact address is: DAAS NZ, c/o Dave Homewood, 69a Vogel Street, Cambridge, New Zealand; e-mail dave__daasnz@hotmail.com; website www.whispersfromwalmington.com/daasnz/).

45. Aside from terrestrial broadcasters, BBC Prime screens the show to a wide range of countries, including, since 1998, Croatia.

46. Frank Williams, interview with the author, 4 October 2000.

47. See my 'Don't bury your treasures', *Financial Times*, 28 June 2000, p. 22.

48. On 27 January 2001, for example, a *Dad's Army* repeat went out on BBC1 at 6.45 p.m. and attracted an audience of 6,633,000 viewers (source: BBC Daily Viewing Barometer).

49. See *Guardian*, 6 September 2000, p. 3.

50. Jimmy Perry, interview with the author, 22 November 2000.

51. See the *Eastern Daily Press*, 15 May 2000, p. 9.

52. Frank Williams, interview with the author, 4 October 2000.

53. Clive Dunn, quoted in Perry and Croft, *Dad's Army: The Lost Episodes*, p. 8.

Notes to Epilogue

EPILOGUE

1. Wheldon, *The Achievement of Television*, p. 18.
2. Henry James, 'The middle years' (1893), in *The Figure in the Carpet and Other Stories* (Harmondsworth: Penguin, 1986), p. 258.
3. Recalled by Ian Lavender, interview with the author, 29 May 2000.
4. Wheldon, *The Achievement of Television*, p. 14.
5. See Perry and Croft, *Dad's Army: The Lost Episodes*, p. 115.
6. Tom Sloan, *Television Light Entertainment*.

Bibliography

Dad's Army

Ableman, Paul, *Dad's Army: The Defence of a Front Line English Village* (London: BBC, 1989).

Bean, Colin, *Who Do You Think You Are Kidding!* (London: Minerva, 1998).

Croft, David and Jimmy Perry, *Dad's Army* (London: Sphere, 1975).

Dad's Army: The Lost Episodes (London: Virgin, 1998).

Dunn, Clive, *Permission to Speak* (London: Century, 1986).

Hart, Ted (ed.), *Dad's Army* (London: Peter Way, 1972).

Le Mesurier, John, *A Jobbing Actor* (London: Elm Tree, 1984).

Longmate, Norman, *The Real Dad's Army* (London: Arrow, 1974).

Lowe, Stephen, *Arthur Lowe: Dad's Memory* (London: Virgin, 1997).

Pertwee, Bill, *Dad's Army: The Making of a Television Legend* (London: Pavilion, 1998).

Richards, Jeffrey, 'Dad's Army and the politics of nostalgia', in *Films and British National Identity* (Manchester: Manchester University Press, 1977).

Webber, Richard, *Dad's Army: A Celebration* (London: Virgin, 1999).

The Complete A–Z of Dad's Army (London: Orion, 2000).

General

Adorno, Theodor W., 'How to look at television', *Quarterly of Film, Radio, and Television*, vol. 3 (Spring 1954), pp. 213–35.

Askey, Arthur, *Before Your Very Eyes* (London: Woburn Press, 1975).

Bagehot, Walter, *The Best of Bagehot*, ed. Ruth Dudley Edwards (London: Hamish Hamilton, 1993).

The English Constitution (London: Fontana, 1993).

Balcon, Michael, *Michael Balcon Presents . . . A Lifetime of Films* (London: Hutchinson, 1969).

Barker, Ernest (ed.), *The Character of England* (Oxford: Clarendon Press, 1950).

Barr, Charles (ed.), *All Our Yesterdays* (London: BFI, 1986).

Beckett, Ian, *The Amateur Military Tradition, 1558–1945* (Manchester: Manchester University Press, 1991).

Beerbohm, Max, *Around Theatres* (London: Rupert Hart-Davis, 1953).

Beloff, Max, 'Broadcasting and twentieth-century civilization', *BBC Quarterly*, vol. 7, no. 1 (Spring 1952), pp. 18–24.

Bennett, Arnold, *The Old Wives' Tale* (Harmondsworth: Penguin, 1983).

Black, Peter, *The Biggest Aspidistra in the World* (London: BBC, 1972).

The Mirror in the Corner (London: Hutchinson, 1972).

'Can one person criticise the full range of television?' *Journal of the Society of Film and Television Arts*, vol. 2, no. 7 (1973), pp. 4–5.

Briggs, Asa, *The History of Broadcasting in the United Kingdom* (Oxford: Oxford University Press, 1961–79):

Vol. 1: *The Birth of Broadcasting*, 1961.

Vol. 2: *The Golden Age of Wireless*, 1965.

Vol. 3: *The War of Words*, 1970.

Bibliography

Vol. 4: *Sound and Vision*, 1979.

    The BBC: The First Fifty Years (Oxford: Oxford University Press, 1985).

Brophy, John, *Britain's Home Guard: A Character Study* (London: George G. Harrap & Co., 1945).

Bryant, Arthur, *The Lion and The Unicorn* (London: Collins, 1969).

Burke, Edmund, *Reflections on the Revolution in France* (Oxford: Oxford University Press, 1993).

    Pre-Revolutionary Writings, ed. Ian Harris (Cambridge: Cambridge University Press, 1996).

Busby, Roy, *British Music Hall: An Illustrated Who's Who from 1850 to the Present Day* (London: Paul Elek, 1976).

Cardiff, David, 'Mass middlebrow laughter: the origins of BBC comedy', *Media, Culture and Society*, vol. 10, no. 1 (January 1988), pp. 41–60.

Christie, Ian (ed.), *Powell, Pressburger and Others* (London: BFI, 1978).

Churchill, Winston, *The Second World War*, Vol. 3: *The Grand Alliance* (London: Cassell, 1950).

    The Speeches of Winston Churchill, ed. David Cannadine (Harmondsworth: Penguin, 1990).

Cotton, Bill, *The BBC as an Entertainer* (London: BBC, 1977).

    Double Bill (London: Fourth Estate, 2000).

Craig, Mike, *Look Back With Laughter*, Vols 1 and 2 (Manchester: Mike Craig Enterprises, 1996).

Crossman, Richard, *The Diaries of a Cabinet Minister*, Vol. 2 (London: Hamish Hamilton, 1982).

Crowther, Bruce and Mike Pinfold, *Bring Me Laughter: Four Decades of TV Comedy* (London: Columbus, 1987).

Curran, Charles, *Broadcasting and Society* (London: BBC1, 1971).

    In the Public Interest (London: BBC, 1971).

    A Seamless Robe: Broadcasting – Philosophy and Practice (London: Collins, 1979).

Curran, James and Vincent Porter, *British Cinema History* (London: Weidenfeld, 1978).

Deedes, W. F., 'With pikes and pitchforks, they waited for Hitler', *Sunday Telegraph*, 16 July 2000, p. 22.

Eden, Anthony, *Freedom and Order: Selected Speeches 1939–1945* (London: Faber, 1947).

    The Reckoning (London: Cassell, 1965).

Emerson, Ralph Waldo, *English Traits* (Cambridge, Mass.: The Riverside Press, 1903).

    Ralph Waldo Emerson, ed. Richard Poirier (Oxford: Oxford University Press, 1990).

    Essays and Poems (London: J. M. Dent, 1995).

    Representative Men (Cambridge, Mass.: Belknap Press, 1996).

Fitzgerald, F. Scott, *The Rich Boy and Other Stories* (London: Phoenix, 1998).

Freeman, Mickey and Sholom Rubinstein, *Bilko: Behind the Lines with Phil Silvers* (London: Virgin, 2000).

Frith, Simon, 'The pleasures of the hearth: the making of BBC light entertainment', in Tony Bennett *et al.* (eds), *Popular Culture and Social Relations* (Milton Keynes: Open University Press, 1983).

Gambaccini, Paul and Rod Taylor, *Television's Greatest Hits* (London: Network Books, 1993).

Gilbert, Martin, *Finest Hour: Winston S. Churchill*, Vol. 6 (London: Heinemann, 1983).

Gilliatt, Penelope, *To Wit: In Celebration of Comedy* (London: Weidenfeld, 1990).

Goethe, Johann Wolfgang, *Faust* (London: Penguin, 1949).

Grade, Lew, *Still Dancing* (London: Collins, 1987).

Graves, Charles, *The Home Guard of Britain* (London: Hutchinson, 1943).

Greene, Hugh Carleton, *The BBC as a Public Service* (London: BBC, 1960).

    The Conscience of the Programme Director (London: BBC, 1965).

    The Third Floor: A View of Broadcasting in the Sixties (London: Bodley Head, 1969).

Grossmith, George and Weedon, *The Diary of a Nobody* (London: The Folio Society, 1969).

Guinness, Alec, *Blessings in Disguise* (London: Hamish Hamilton, 1985).

Bibliography

Hancock, Freddie and David Nathan, *Hancock* (London: Ariel Books, 1986).

Harrison, Rex, *Rex: An Autobiography* (London: Macmillan, 1974).

Hazlitt, William, *Table Talk* (London: J. M. Dent & Sons, 1959).

Hewison, Robert, *Culture and Consensus: England, Art and Politics since 1940* (London: Methuen, 1995).

Hoggart, Richard, *The Way We Live Now* (London: Chatto, 1995).

Honri, Peter, *Working the Halls* (London: Futura, 1974).

Horrie, Chris and Steve Clark, *Fuzzy Monsters: Fear and Loathing at the BBC* (London: Mandarin, 1994).

Hudd, Roy, *Roy Hudd's Book of Music-Hall, Variety and Showbiz Anecdotes* (London: Robson Books, 1993).

 Roy Hudd's Cavalcade of Variety Acts: A Who Was Who of Light Entertainment 1945–60 (London: Robson, 1997).

Hughes, John Craven, *The Greasepaint War* (London: New English Library, 1976).

Jeffries, Stuart, *Mrs Slocombe's Pussy* (London: Flamingo, 2000).

James, Clive, *Clive James on Television* (London: Picador, 1991).

James, Henry, *The Figure in the Carpet and Other Stories* (Harmondsworth: Penguin, 1986).

Langdon-Davies, John, *Home Guard Training Manual*, 6th edn (London: John Murray and Pilot Press, 1942).

Laurie, John (ed.), *My Favourite Stories of Scotland* (London: Lutterworth Press, 1978).

Le Mesurier, Joan, *Lady Don't Fall Backwards* (London: Sidgwick, 1988).

Lewis, Peter, *A People's War* (London: Methuen, 1986).

Lewisohn, Mark, *Radio Times Guide to TV Comedy* (London: BBC, 1998).

Longmate, Norman, *How We Lived Then: A History of Everyday Life During the Second World War* (London: The Anchor Press, 1971).

McCann, Graham, *Cary Grant: A Class Apart* (London: Fourth Estate, 1996).

 'Why the best sitcoms must be a class act', *London Evening Standard*, 21 May 1997, p. 9.

 'An offer we *can* refuse', *London Evening Standard*, 2 December 1998, p. 68.

 Morecambe & Wise (London: Fourth Estate, 1998).

 'Sit back and wait for the comedy', *Financial Times*, 24 November 1999, p. 22.

 'Don't bury your treasures', *Financial Times*, 28 June 2000, p. 22.

McDonnell, James, *Public Service Broadcasting: A Reader* (London: Routledge, 1991).

McFarlane, Brian, *An Autobiography of British Cinema* (London: Methuen, 1997).

MacKenzie, S. P., 'Citizens in arms: the Home Guard and the internal security of the United Kingdom, 1940–41', *Intelligence and National Security*, vol. 6, no. 3 (July 1991), pp. 548–72.

Mamet, David, *Some Freaks* (London: Faber, 1990).

Mellor, G. J., *The Northern Music Hall* (Newcastle upon Tyne: Frank Graham, 1970).

 They Made Us Laugh (Littleborough: George Kelsell, 1982).

Miall, Leonard, *Inside the BBC* (London: Weidenfeld, 1994).

Milne, Alasdair, *DG: The Memoirs of a British Broadcaster* (London: Hodder, 1988).

Monkhouse, Bob, *Crying With Laughter* (London: Arrow, 1994).

Morrison, Herbert, *An Autobiography* (London: Odhams, 1960).

Mosley, Leonard, *Backs to the Wall: London Under Fire 1939–45* (London: Weidenfeld, 1971).

Muir, Frank, *Comedy in Television* (London: BBC, 1966).

Murphy, Robert (ed.), *The British Cinema Book* (London: BFI, 1997).

Napier, Valantyne, *Glossary of Terms Used in Variety, Vaudeville, Revue and Pantomime* (Westbury: The Badger Press, 1996).

Nathan, David, *The Laughtermakers* (London: Peter Owen, 1971).

Orwell, George, *The Collected Essays, Journalism and Letters*, Vol. 2 (London: Penguin, 1970).

 The Penguin Essays of George Orwell (Harmondsworth: Penguin, 1984).

Paine, Thomas, *The Rights of Man* (Harmondsworth: Penguin, 1985).

Perry, George, *The Great British Picture Show* (London: Hart-Davis, MacGibbon, 1974).

Pertwee, Bill, *Promenades and Pierrots* (Devon: Westbridge, 1979).

 By Royal Command (Newton Abbot: David & Charles, 1981).

Bibliography

A Funny Way to Make a Living! (London: Sunburst, 1996).

Philips, Brian, *Stand By Studio!* (Borehamwood: BBC Television Training, 1987).

Plomley, Roy, *Desert Island Lists* (London: Hutchinson, 1984).

Pownall, Henry, *Chief of Staff: The Diaries of Lieutenant-General Sir Henry Pownall*, Vol. 2, ed. Brian Bond (London: Leo Cooper, 1974).

Priestley, J. B., *English Humour* (London: Longmans, Green & Co., 1929).

Postscripts, (London: Heinemann, 1940).

The English Comic Characters (New York: Phaeton Press, 1972).

Richards, Jeffrey, *Visions of Yesteryear* (London: Routledge, 1973).

Films and British National Identity (Manchester: Manchester University Press, 1997).

Santayana, George, *Soliloquies in England* (New York: Charles Scribner's & Sons, 1922).

Seinfeld, Jerry, *SeinOff* (London: Boxtree, 1999).

Seymour-Ure, Colin and Jim Schoff, *David Low* (London: Secker, 1985).

Silvers, Phil, *The Man Who Was Bilko* (London: W. H. Allen, 1974).

Silvey, Roger, *Who's Listening?: The Story of BBC Audience Research* (London: Allen & Unwin, 1974).

Sloan, Tom, *Television Light Entertainment* (London: BBC, 1969).

Smith, Anthony, *British Broadcasting* (Newton Abbot: David & Charles, 1974).

Smith, Keith, 'Viewings: which, to whom, and for what?' *Journal of the Society of Film and Television*, vol. 12, no. 7 (1973), pp. 10–12.

Smith, Ronald L., *Who's Who in Comedy* (New York: Facts On File, 1992).

Snoad, Harold, *Directing Situation Comedy* (Borehamwood: BBC Television Training, 1988).

Stone, Richard, *You Should Have Been In Last Night* (Sussex: The Book Guild, 2000).

Street, A. G., *From Dusk Till Dawn* (London: Blandford Press, 1945).

Summerfield, Penny and Corinna Peniston-Bird, 'Women in the firing line: the Home Guard and the defence of gender boundaries in Britain in the Second World War', *Women's History Review*, vol. 9, no. 2 (2000), pp. 231–55.

Thurber, James, *Collecting Himself*, ed. Michael Rosen (London: Hamish Hamilton, 1989).

Took, Barry, *Laughter in the Air* (London: Robson/BBC, 1976).

'Whatever Happened to TV Comedy?', *The Listener*, 5 January 1984, pp. 7–8 and 12 January 1984, pp. 8–9.

Tracey, Michael, *A Variety of Lives* (London: Bodley Head, 1983).

Trethowan, Ian, *Split Screen* (London: Hamish Hamilton, 1984).

Waldron, Vince, *Classic Sitcoms*, 2nd edn (Los Angeles: Silman-James Press, 1997).

Wheeler-Bennett, J. W., *King George VI: His Life and Reign* (London: Macmillan, 1958).

Wheldon, Huw, *British Traditions in a World-Wide Medium* (London: BBC, 1973).

The Achievement of Television (London: BBC, 1975).

The British Experience in Television (London: BBC, 1976).

Whitehouse, Mary, *A Most Dangerous Woman?* (London: Lion, 1982).

Williams, Kenneth, *The Kenneth Williams Diaries*, ed. Russell Davies (London: Harper-Collins, 1993).

Wilmut, Roger, *Tony Hancock: Artiste* (London: Methuen, 1978).

Kindly Leave the Stage: The Story of Variety, 1918–1960 (London: Methuen, 1985).

Wintringham, Tom, 'The Home Guard can fight', *Picture Post*, 21 September 1940, pp. 9–17.

Wittgenstein, Ludwig, *Culture and Value*, ed. G. H. von Wright with Heikki Nyman (Oxford: Basil Blackwell, 1980).

Wyndham Goldie, Grace, *Facing the Nation: Broadcasting and Politics 1936–1976* (London: Bodley Head, 1977).

Yelton, D. K., 'British public opinion, the Home Guard, and the defence of Great Britain, 1940–1944', *Journal of Military History*, no. 58 (1994), pp. 461–80.

Index

Index